POP ISLAM

POP ISLAM

Seeing American Muslims
in Popular Media

—✺—

ROSEMARY PENNINGTON

INDIANA UNIVERSITY PRESS

This book is a publication of

Indiana University Press
Office of Scholarly Publishing
Herman B Wells Library 350
1320 East 10th Street
Bloomington, Indiana 47405 USA

iupress.org

© 2024 by Rosemary Pennington

All rights reserved
No part of this book may be reproduced or utilized in any form or by any means, electronic or mechanical, including photocopying and recording, or by any information storage and retrieval system, without permission in writing from the publisher. The paper used in this publication meets the minimum requirements of the American National Standard for Information Sciences—Permanence of Paper for Printed Library Materials, ANSI Z39.48–1992.

Manufactured in the United States of America

First printing 2024

Cataloging information is available from the Library of Congress.

978-0-253-06936-8 (hdbk.)
978-0-253-06937-5 (pbk.)
978-0-253-06938-2 (web PDF)

For Tedio Kadar Pennington

CONTENTS

Acknowledgments   ix

Introduction: America's Imagined Muslims   *1*

1. *Ms. Marvel* and the "Embiggening" of Muslims in America   *27*

2. The Scripted Lives of TV Muslims   *53*

3. Big Screen, Small Stage: Negotiating Identity through Comedy   *79*

4. Identity and Religion in Reality TV   *104*

5. A Glossy Islam: Muslim Lives in Fashion Magazines   *128*

Conclusion: The Complications of Visibility   *157*

Bibliography   *173*

Index   *193*

ACKNOWLEDGMENTS

THIS IS A BOOK THAT I never thought I would finish. It arose out of a conversation I had with my then editor at Indiana University Press, Jennika Baines. We were talking about a project I was just wrapping up with the press when I told her about something I was starting on that I thought would be an article. She looked at me over her coffee and said, "Rosemary, that's a book." You want an editor to care about your work and to understand it, and Jennika was an amazing shepherd of my projects. But there were definitely moments when I rued that afternoon coffee in the basement of King Library at Indiana University.

The problem with writing a book about popular culture is that it is constantly changing. As I was wrapping up work on the revisions to *Pop Islam*, the Disney+ series *Ms. Marvel* began streaming. My husband, Tim Bolda, asked me if I needed to watch that before I sent the book off, and I told him, "No, someone else will have to write something about that," which was a strange thing to say given that Kamala Khan's Ms. Marvel was the genesis of this project. Tim, knowing my interest in Muslim representation in media, brought the first issue of G. Willow Wilson's *Ms. Marvel* home one afternoon. I fell in love with Wilson's plucky heroine, but I also realized that moment was going to lead me here—to finishing a project focused on American Muslim representation in things like comic books, reality TV shows, and prime-time dramas. That comic book unlocked a larger project I'd been wanting to work on for a long time, and it feels bittersweet to be at its end.

I am at its end in large part because of the faith Jennika Baines, and the other staff at Indiana University Press, has had in my work. When you find an editor who understands who you are and what you are trying to say, hold on to them

ACKNOWLEDGMENTS

tightly. Sophia Herbert helped me after Jennika left the press, and I'm thankful for her guidance. Bethany Mowry has stepped in to guide me to the end; I am grateful for her care as I've wrapped this up. I am also grateful for the anonymous readers who reviewed early versions of this manuscript—their thoughtful and insightful comments are much appreciated. I'd also like to thank the copyeditor who helped polish this book in its final form.

I am lucky to be connected to a large and ever-growing network of scholars who make my work better. They include Nabil Echchaibi, Krissy Peterson, and Andrea Stanton—all of whom I have had conversations with at conferences that helped me as I worked on *Pop Islam*. So, thank you for listening. I am also appreciative of the interest Rob Rozenhal, Sahar Khamis, and Hussein Rashid have shown in my research. Thank you, too, Hilary Kahn, Rafia Zakaria, and Shireen Ahmed for being early collaborators and supporters.

The work on *Pop Islam* began at Miami University, and I will forever be grateful that Richard Campbell did not discount me as a candidate for my job after I threw some shade, by way of rival Ohio University, Miami's way during our first conversation. My colleagues in the Department of Media, Journalism, and Film have made it easy to live life as a teacher-scholar. I am particularly thankful for Joe Sampson's willingness to listen to me vent and Jim Tobin's thoughtful advice. The leadership of the department—Bruce Drushel, Mack Hagood, Ron Becker, Hongmei Li, and Kerry Hegarty—have helped shape an environment where media and communication research can thrive at Miami, as did former journalism area coordinator Patti Newberry. The support College of Arts and Science dean Chris Makaroff and senior associate dean Renée Baernstein have provided for my research has been invaluable to my ability to finish the work. I am also indebted to Miami University Humanities Center director Timothy Melley and assistant director Pepper Stetler for opportunities to workshop this project as well as to two groups of Altman scholars and fellows who have helped shape aspects of this work. A grant from the Committee on Faculty Research facilitated work on one of the chapters in this volume, and I am appreciative that resource exists at Miami. And a big thanks goes to the Mongeese for just being stellar human beings.

One final note of thanks for colleagues at Miami University. Sitting in my office is a pile of at least twenty books that do not belong to me; they are the property of the Miami University Libraries. I have renewed these books three years in a row now (I think; maybe it's just two). Libraries are amazing resources in a community. Public libraries provide spaces for everyone to gather together while making materials available to people regardless of circumstance. University libraries are marvels. Repositories of knowledge. Keepers of archives.

ACKNOWLEDGMENTS

Champions of material culture. The staff at the Miami University Libraries are incredible, and I am so grateful to have their intelligence, and all their books, at my fingertips.

Of course, research networks exist far beyond where one sits at any one time. My graduate studies at Indiana University connected me to people who not only helped me steer my ship when it went astray but also pulled me onto the door when things seemed to be sinking, unlike Rose in *Titanic*. Thank you, Chris Ogar, Lisa Hatley Major, and David Weaver, for encouraging a scared master's student when she felt less than capable. Your faith led me here. Thank you, Jason Martin, Gerry Lanosga, Lindita Camaj, Ammina Kothari, Manaf Bashir, and Jessica Gall Myrick, for being amazing fellow travelers. Jessica von Ahsen Birthisel, Spring Serenity Duvall, Lori Henson, and Stacie Meihaus Jankowski are the sorts of cheerleaders we should all be so lucky to have in our lives—thanks for being my shining stars.

I have found my undergraduate students to be shining stars of another sort. Two of them, Sabrina Herman and Nellie Givens, contributed labor to this book that made my life easier and the chapters they worked on better. So thank you both. I finished this book as I taught a workshop on media and identity at Miami University's campus in Differdange, Luxembourg, during the summer of 2022. Teaching overseas was sort of terrifying, but I had with me eleven of the best students you could hope for. They were good sports as I asked them to write skits, perform scenes from a play, and write their own Eurovision songs. The joy they brought me made completing this book possible. So thank you, Caroline Braud, Gabbi Byrd, Adam Debevec, Shelby Dolley, Jack Ernstberger, Reece Gormley, Deanna Hay, Raegan Hilbrandt, Sarah Lowe, Callie Meyer, and Edward Orzech, for putting up with my shenanigans. I am only a little sorry for our twenty-two thousand steps in Metz.

This book was a labor of love, and in a way, aren't we all? I should first apologize to my family for ruining media we consume sometimes with my spontaneous rants—so, sorry. But I also want to thank my brother Leon Pennington for always being in my corner and my brother Josh Pennington for all those dumb arguments we got into as kids. Lenore and Lainey, thank you for making my bad days better. To my mother, Rhonda Pennington, I owe a debt of gratitude I can never repay. Thank you for being kind to me when I could not be kind to myself.

My daughter, when she was very small, once asked me why I had to study so much. I hope it's obvious by now, Sofia Bolda, but thank you for all your patience with a distracted mother. My husband, Tim Bolda, already got a name-check in this thing, but I should probably thank him again, just to be polite.

ACKNOWLEDGMENTS

Finally—I promise this is the end—I have to say something about my dad. Tedio Kadar Pennington died in 2017, but his spirit lives on in his children, in his grandchildren, and in this book I never thought I'd finish. My dad immigrated to the United States when he was two. It was his stories of discrimination that set me on the path I trod—first as a journalist and later as an academic—but it was also his stories that helped me see outside the borders of the small town I grew up in. Thank you, Dad, for the kung fu movies, the comic books, and the Edith Piaf and for just listening and letting me grow. I miss you every day.

POP ISLAM

INTRODUCTION

America's Imagined Muslims

STANDING UNDER HOT STAGE LIGHTS, a golden background seeming to glow behind him, comedian Ramy Youssef stepped up to the microphone and said, "I would like to thank my god. Allahu Akbar. Thank you, God. This is thanks to God and Hulu." What aired on Hulu was his breakout series, *Ramy*, and what he was thanking God for was the Golden Globe he held in his hand, awarded to him for winning Best Actor in a Comedy Series. Youssef was not the first Muslim American to win a Golden Globe, but his quiet uttering of "Allahu Akbar" was new. The phrase—meaning simply "God is great"—is often heard in the background of news stories about wars in Muslim countries or in films about the so-called war on terror. Rarely in American popular media is it portrayed as what it is—a simple offering of thanks to God. Rarely is someone like Youssef portrayed as what he is—an American with an interesting family history.

Ramy tells the story of one Egyptian American millennial's quest to figure out what he wants from life and to find his place in the world. It's the story of how a child of immigrants works to reconcile himself to the tension between what his community expects of him and what he wants for himself. It's also the story of how an American Muslim navigates life in a country that doesn't always see him as fully belonging there, that sees him as a problem to be solved. The show has been a critical darling, with Hulu signing on for three seasons so far. Standing in his maroon tuxedo and white sneakers backstage after winning the Golden Globe, Youssef said of the show's success, "Symbolically, hopefully it allows more people to make stories . . . so there's not just one show for one group." *Ramy* is just one example of the kind of media examined in this book—media that make American Muslim experiences accessible to broad audiences. However, the Muslim representation featured on Youssef's show and in other popular media has left some wondering what is lost in the creation of accessible representation.

Youssef's win came in 2020, after a rise in Islamophobia and anti-Muslim sentiment partly fueled by the political rhetoric of former president Donald Trump. While campaigning for the US presidency in 2016, Trump had at times leaned on the specter of the Muslim "threat" as he worked to convince voters that he would keep Americans safe. It was a specter with a long history in American politics and American media—its appearance and persistence in media contributing to a framing of Muslims, even those born in the United States, as not fully American.

Media shape the boundaries of the communities we imagine we belong to, shaping imaginary geographies that are brought to life by the stories told of who we are.[1] For years, the story told of Islam was that it existed outside the West; Muslims were imagined as people who practiced a strange religion that belonged anywhere but in the United States or western Europe. This happened because in order to maintain a definition of *us*, societies often seek enemies elsewhere or enemies that *appear* to be from elsewhere. To know who you are, you must understand who you are not. Building on misunderstandings and misrepresentations that date back centuries, Islam has frequently been imagined as *the* enemy other, with Muslims often understood as *the* threat to be overcome. It was this historic understanding of the faith and its believers that Trump tapped into while campaigning for the presidency. One of Trump's first major acts as president was to sign an executive order banning travel from seven Muslim-majority nations. As airports across the country filled with protesters expressing support for American Muslims and for international Muslim travelers, some American news outlets debated whether such a ban was necessary. Some pundits and reporters even wondered whether a Muslim travel ban might be a good thing, raising concerns about Islamic extremism on early-morning talk shows and evening newscasts.

The American news media have a long history of portraying Islam and Muslims as threats to freedom and liberty. Often, the only time Americans encounter Muslims is in such news reporting, although that is beginning to change. Comic books such as *Ms. Marvel* and television programs such as *American Crime* have featured Muslim characters who challenge the idea that Muslims are always a threat or that they are always the enemy. Such representations are the focus of this book. *Pop Islam: Seeing American Muslims in Popular Media* explores the changing nature of Muslim representation in American popular media, considering how it may make Muslim lives not only more visible but also more accessible to a public that has been conditioned to see Muslims as a threat. Popular culture is an area of study that has not always been associated with Islam or Muslim life, as Islam has been imagined to exist in an antithetical state to popular culture—a frozen faith, unable to engage with the dynamic way popular culture shifts over time.[2] Media are one avenue to communicate popular culture, making it a fertile space for exploration. The representation of Islam and Muslim life in popular media has been explored in a global context, notably in Anna Piela's edited collection *Islam and Popular Culture*.[3] This book, *Pop Islam*, focuses on the representation of Islam and Muslims in American popular media as it considers the nuance and diversity of experience that may be lost in the name of accessible representation. It argues that even as American Muslims become more visible in popular media, even as they begin creating space for themselves in everything from magazines to prime-time television to stand-up comedy specials, this move toward accessibility can reinforce fixed ideas of who Muslims are and what Islam is. It is a book about the ways popular media and popular culture can be used to challenge stereotypes while still considering the ways such media might reinforce stereotypes. It asks, Is there a way to be visible, to be accessible, in media that allows for complication and nuance? Historically, that's been hard to find.

The representation of Islam and Muslims in non-Muslim texts has often framed them as something strange, enemy, or exotic. Sophia Rose Arjana has shown how the concept of monstrosity also shaped the ways Muslims were imagined in such texts. She writes, "Muslims are the monsters of the present, phantasms that result from an imaginary Islam that has been shaped over many centuries"[4]—an Islam that was imagined as poised to devour the Christian world, with the Prophet Muhammad believed to be an almost Antichrist-like figure, if not the Antichrist himself, and Muslims imagined as literal beasts who would consume Europe and ravage Europeans.[5] At the very least, Muslims were imagined to be idolaters whose presence in Christian lands polluted them. This understanding extended to the area considered the Holy Land.[6] In the case of Jerusalem, an important city for Jews, Muslims, and Christians alike, the presence of Muslims there was seen as an affront to God. Suzanne Akbari notes that just Muhammad's footprint at the Dome of the Rock in Jerusalem was viewed as an assault on the Christian world: "The stone itself was an idol, a material object that directs the worshiper toward the fleshly world of creation rather than the heavenly realm of spirit. It is not a sign marking the orientation of the divine, but rather a pollution of the sacred space."[7]

The people who suggested Muslims were a monstrous threat to the Christian world or a polluting force generally had little to no experience with Muslims

4 POP ISLAM

and so spread myths that were often completely imagined.[8] The Orient was considered both "beautiful and dangerous" because the culture of the region was seen as adaptable, "open to assimilation and that which must be utterly rejected."[9] This highlights a deep discomfort with the idea of mixing—races, religions, or cultures—that overlooks the reality that "cultures survive through mixing."[10] All cultures are mixtures, the ever-emerging result of contestations over affiliations, definitions, and narratives, none of which remain stable for very long.[11] In what was considered the Orient, this hybridity, or something like it, was on full display.[12] However, Tomaž Mastnak suggests that prior to the First Crusade, the "threat" of Islam was not seen as a particularly remarkable one; while it was perhaps seductive and a threat to the purity of a Christian Europe, it was just one threat among many facing Europe and the European church.[13] It was the conquest of Spain that Mastnak marks as the moment when Muslims began to be seen as a *special* kind of threat, one that might lead to the erasure or the mutation of Europe's Christian identity.[14] It is this, coupled with the lead-up to the First Crusade, that Mastnak thinks helped produce a rhetoric in which Muslims began to be imagined as members of one singular, monolithic culture.[15] In order to produce a singular, cohesive Christian identity during a time of instability in Europe, a singular, cohesive enemy had to be imagined.[16] This reality began shaping the way Islam and Muslims appeared in Western media.

Perhaps, the most famous of early examples of Muslim representation in a Western text comes in the guise of Othello, the Moor at the heart of Shakespeare's tragedy of the same name. Othello is a military hero who has defended Venice from invading Turks, an African who has married the beautiful daughter of one of the city's prominent families. It is jealousy on the part of someone Othello thought of as a friend that leads to the death of Desdemona, Othello's wife, as well as the Moor himself. Iago, the friend, works to convince the Venetians that Othello is not their hero, that he is a threat to the city. He is a monster whom, Iago suggests, Venice cannot trust—a monster not only because of the color of his skin but also because of the beliefs of his religion.[17]

It is implied in the text that Othello is likely a Muslim convert to Christianity, though the Bard never makes this clear. What is clear is that Iago incites the Venetians' fear of the Muslim other, particularly potent as Venice was often at odds with its Muslim Ottoman neighbors, and Europe's general anxiety about dark-skinned Africans to turn Venice against its Moorish hero.[18] Shakespeare's villain exploits the general anxiety in the city over the threat of the Muslim and the dark-skinned other to sharpen the contrast between "us" and "them" in relation to Desdemona and Othello. Fear and violence reduce both to tragic

Fig. 0.1 The story of Othello has inspired artists and writers since the play first premiered in the early 1600s. This image was produced by French artist Théodore Chassériau. According to the Met, the image shows the character Lodovico pointing "to the tragic results of Iago's jealous manipulation—the death of the guiltless Desdemona, Emilia slain by Iago for revealing the truth, and Othello dying, after stabbing himself in despair." (Courtesy the Met and the Harris Brisbane Dick Fund, 1932)

figures. The irony is that Shakespeare's play exposes the shortsightedness and danger of perpetuating such superficial fear; it highlights the ways our understanding of difference is influenced and formed by the narratives we tell of who it is we believe we are and just how destructive it can sometimes be.

It is not simply differences in behavior or cultural practices that give rise to our notions of who is *other* and who is *us*—Umberto Eco has suggested that just the existence of difference, the visibility of such difference, is enough to mark some as enemy and some as friend.[19] Cultural theorist Stuart Hall has pointed out that "difference . . . persists—in and alongside continuity."[20] We need someone against whom to measure ourselves, against whom to define ourselves. At the same time, there has been a move to try to erase difference in order to avoid the fear and discomfort such difference produces in ourselves;[21]

particularly, the move to embrace a more multicultural understanding of Western societies has worked to erase difference even as it claims to embrace it.[22] Ethnic food or world music is embraced or ethnic neighborhoods are celebrated—such as the Kreuzberg area of Berlin or the Adams Morgan neighborhood in Washington, DC—but only insofar as they do not challenge mainstream, hegemonic understandings of what it means to be German or American. Kitschy or consumable differences are acceptable, but differences that actually challenge us to reconsider our definitions of self are not. All of this is a reflection of a Eurocentric view of the world, supported by various state actors, which has centered Christianity at its heart alongside Western understandings of culture and knowledge production.[23] In doing this, Eurocentrism has obscured all the ways those nations that were eventually imagined on the periphery of Europe flourished, changed, and developed over time.[24] These so-called periphery nations—many of which were home to Muslim-majority populations—were imagined as somehow stuck in time and that stuckness rendered them monstrous to modernity.[25] Media that reinforce these Eurocentric narratives have helped produce an understanding of what is good and bad in a culture designed to be more exclusive than inclusive—an understanding that is meant to maintain borders, not break them down. When it comes to Muslim representation, a Eurocentric view of the world has also shaped popular understandings of who qualifies as a good Muslim and who qualifies as a bad Muslim.

Scholars and activists alike have lamented this dichotomization of Muslim representation, which has produced the idea of bad Muslims and good Muslims, moderate Islam and radical Islam. In discussing the linkage between the development of Islamophobia and imperialism, Deepa Kumar has pointed out that relations between the East and the West were not always marked by hostility and tension; they *were* marked by difference, but there were moments of engagement and appreciation.[26] Specifically, she points to Muslim Spain as an example of this engagement. Like Mastnak, Kumar suggests that it was as other pagan threats to Christian Europe converted and were folded into the Catholic flock that Muslims began to be singled out as a particularly pernicious threat. However, with the rise of nationalism and the eventual breakdown of a Christian Europe controlled by one creed, the Muslim threat became less urgent. It wouldn't be until the Ottomans rose to power, Kumar suggests, that Muslims would once again be seen as *the* threat to Christian Europe.[27]

Western understandings of Islam and of Muslim life were shaped by the European colonial project as much as by encounters during the Middle Ages. When Napoleon decided to stretch his empire to North Africa, the artists and

Fig. 0.2 Victorian artist Edwin Longsden Long was known for his rich images of an exotic and imagined Near East. In this painting, *Love's Labour Lost*, Long depicts a domestic scene from an Egyptian household. Though Long did travel to Egypt in 1974, the Dahesh Museum of Art notes that "like many Orientalist painters, Long rarely drew from memory, choosing instead to rely upon descriptions in books, photographs, or objects in the collection of, for example, the British Museum." (Courtesy Wikimedia Commons)

scientists he left behind in Egypt spent decades exploring and studying the region, sending back to the continent tales of ancient, mystical cultures swathed in silk and sand.[28] Their renderings of a seductive place, not dissimilar to the idea of the seductive Orient of the Middle Ages, help repopularize the idea of the Orient as a place ruled by passion, heat, and sex. As in the Middle Ages, the nations of the Near and Middle East were imagined as monstrous, but instead of being monstrous because they were largely unknown, this new monstrosity was bred from imperial familiarity. The Orient was monstrous because it was known, because it was *seen*. Fueled by the work of French and British Orientalists and their academic and artistic descendants, the Orient was imagined as a monstrously uncivilized place that needed the guiding hand of rational, cooler, Western powers in order to become fully modern.[29] The Muslims who were made visible in such an Orientalist framing were portrayed as unmodern individuals who could not control their passions. The Europeans who would immigrate to the United States would take with them an understanding of Islam very much shaped by this history.

The idea of the Muslim threat became particularly potent in the United States as one of the country's earliest conflicts was a war with the Barbary pirates who patrolled the waters of North Africa. The pirates demanded tribute from ships sailing through their territory in the Mediterranean; those who did not pay in money paid in captives taken by the pirates. The United States refused to pay tribute and so went to war, the rhetoric of which Peter Gottschalk noted involved "religiously stereotyping the pirates was a way to rally Americans and denigrate the enemy."[30] Images of the Barbary threat relied on stereotypes such as the "Arab headdress and large, crooked noses"[31] in order for viewers to understand not only the present threat but also the historic one these Muslim pirates presented to the young nation. Of course, this focus on Muslims living someplace else obscured the reality that Muslims have been part of the fabric of the United States since its earliest beginnings. It was Muslim geographers who drew the maps that guided explorers to the Western Hemisphere,[32] and it was partly on the backs of enslaved Muslims that the nation was built.[33]

Though Jonathan Curiel traces the ways Muslim slaves practiced their religion, making that identity visible,[34] Ed Curtis suggests that the Islam of enslaved persons was often mistaken for being African indigenous religion and so some slaves' identities as Muslims went unrecognized.[35] This may have provided enslaved Muslims some safety, as Allan Austin points out that enslaved Muslims were often literate in Arabic,[36] the language of the Qur'an. Slaves who were literate were slaves who could organize and possibly rebel against their bondage, as they did in Brazil in 1835 and aboard the *Amistad* in 1839,[37] with Arabic providing an avenue for slaves to organize in a way that was illegible to their non-Arabic literate slave masters.[38] Such a rebellion would destroy the burgeoning economy of the United States, which relied on slave labor to thrive. Although, Allen notes, slaveholders sometimes would place literate Muslim African slaves into positions of authority over other enslaved persons, and in one case, such an individual became a plantation manager.[39] Some abolitionists would point to the existence of such literate and, therefore, "civilized" Muslim slaves as evidence of the need to eradicate the institution of slavery altogether.[40]

Some of the earliest narratives about the American Muslim experience came in the form of slave stories, which often chronicled an individual's pre-slavery life as well as their experience in bondage and, sometimes, their escape to freedom.[41] Perhaps the most famous Muslim slave narrative is that of Omar ibn Said, whose Arabic autobiography chronicled his journey from free West African to enslaved African American. Akel Kahera has noted that while

Fig. 0.3a & Fig. 0.3b Omar ibn Said belonged to the Fula ethnic group whose homelands stretch across parts of Western and Central Africa. The scholar spent much of his life into early adulthood studying such subjects as math, business, and theology. Captured and sold into slavery in 1807, ibn Said wrote fourteen manuscripts in Arabic, including his famous autobiography. Ibn Said remained enslaved until his death in 1864. (Courtesy Beinecke Rare Book and Manuscript Library, Yale University, and the Library of Congress)

imprisoned and before he could speak English, Said used ashes from a fire to write Qur'anic scripture on the walls of his jail cell to protest his incarceration and enslavement.[42] This use of the Qur'an to protest the institution of slavery also shows up later in this autobiography, "boldly exposing the unlawfulness of such practices at a spiritual level."[43] However, Muslim slave narratives such as those of Said rarely became widely read. Allen Austin notes that in the mid-1800s "nearly everything in print about Africans became condescending or negative. A few African Muslim individuals were noticed shortly around our Civil War, before a kind of suppression of information about such people that lasted into the 1980s."[44]

At the same time that Muslim Africans were brought to what would become the United States as slaves, American politicians were educating themselves about Islam, with a number of early American thinkers looking to the Qur'an or other Islamic texts for alternate approaches to law.[45] As the Founding Fathers began to form an idea of the liberties available to white American men, they debated the importance of providing space for all religions in the new nation—including Islam.[46] Though seen as a strange and possibly dangerous religion, it was also recognized as one that existed in the Americas and one that should be protected.

As this tension between the idea of Islam as a danger and Islam as a thing to be protected played out in politics and economics, Islam slowly began to creep into American culture. The prayers and songs of enslaved Muslims would help shape the foundation of American blues music.[47] Vestiges of Islam live on in the music of the Gullah culture in the American South as well as in other types of music in the South and Caribbean. The reports and illustrations of the early European Orientalists also began making their way to the United States, influencing American architects to include Oriental details in their designs.[48] Islam in the political guise was a danger; Islam in the popular imagination became wrapped up with spectacle, mysticism, and the fantastic, even influencing some of the acts in P. T. Barnum's theatricals.[49] The idea of what Islam is and who Muslims are was fashioned in the American imagination by history, politics, and popular narratives that often did not connect with the real, lived experiences of American Muslims. That imaginary Islam was also shaped by American foreign policy and global geopolitics as the United States grew in power.

An early diplomatic mission of the United States was to work with Christian European countries in outreach to Muslim countries with the goal of converting their populations to the Christian faith.[50] This was spurred by the continued belief that Muslim countries were uncivilized and would benefit from Western intervention. This belief fueled interventionist American foreign

Fig. 0.4 Fueled by a growing interest in "Eastern" cultures, showmen such as P. T. Barnum began including so-called Oriental elements in their productions. These elements were shaped by the reports sent west by scientists, artists, soldiers, and others who participated in the colonization of the Near East. As suggested by this advertisement for "Wild Moors," these elements often communicated that residents of the Near East were uncivilized savages. (Courtesy National Museum of American History, https://americanhistory.si.edu/collections/search/object/nmah_659508)

policy choices in eastern Europe, the Middle East, and the Philippines and continued well into the twentieth century, as US ally Israel fought conflicts with various Arab nations and as the United States diplomatically and physically clashed with Iran and Iraq.[51] In the case of the coverage of American conflicts with Iran, Edward Said noted that the coverage was generally filled with "cliches, caricatures, ignorance, unqualified ethnocentrism, and inaccuracy."[52] Editorial cartoons are one media space where particularly potent anti-Muslim and anti-Islam representations appeared in the United States, helping perpetuate Islamophobia in the country.[53] All of this fueled media representations that continued to portray Muslims as foreign threats to American freedom and identity. After the September 11 attacks, this legacy of representation created a situation for every Muslim in America so that "unless proved to be 'good,' every Muslim was presumed to be 'bad.' All Muslims were now under the obligation to prove their credentials by joining in a war against 'bad Muslims.'"[54] Muslims are "presumed guilty" whenever something terror related takes place,[55] with their very status as American citizens often called into question.[56]

As news media and political rhetoric focused on the supposed threat posed by foreign Muslims, the story of the Black American Muslim experience was often lost from sight. Islam had served as a site of resistance and safety for some Black Americans during the country's founding and its early years. Richard Brent Turner argues that history of resistance in early American Islam would influence future iterations: "Pan-Africanism and Black bitterness towards Christian racism were new seeds planted in the consciousness of nineteenth-century African Americans that in turn flowered into a new American Islam in the early twentieth century. This new American Islam in the African-American community was multicultural; and it developed a distinct missionary and internationalist political agenda."[57]

It was a multiculturalism that was not embraced by many other parts of American society at the time, nor was it entirely embraced by all fellow Muslims. In the late 1800s and early 1900s, an anti-Black feeling developed in some Muslim communities, one that mirrored the anti-Black attitudes that circulated as the United States worked to frame itself as a white, Christian nation.[58] In order to assimilate into American society, some Muslim immigrants to the United States "changed their names to Christian ones and passed as de-facto white non-Muslims."[59] Where some Black Muslims had found a site of resistance in Islam, some other Muslims or former Muslims resisted open association with the faith. Muslim missionaries to the United States had to contend with the complex construction of racial identity in the country as they worked to win converts to Islam.[60] In the early 1900s, many Black American Muslims were Sunni members of the Ahmadiyyah Movement of Islam or the Islamic Mission of America.[61] These Muslims, however, would not be who made Islam's connection to Black America visible to mainstream society, nor would it be the long history of Islam in the United States that did that. Instead, the Moorish Science Temple of America and the Nation of Islam (NoI) would be how many twentieth-century Americans learned of the Black Muslim experience.

The Moorish Science Temple was based in American cities and adopted a multicultural and pan-African agenda that positioned it as separate from not only white Christian America but also "Arab and Eastern European Muslims in America."[62] The organization's founder took inspiration from Indian philosophy as well as from the Black Freemason movement as he shaped a Black and American version of Islam. For some Black Americans, "Islam served as a means of breaking with dominant society," one based on in Christianity that "was seen as a means of legitimating the oppression and injustice experienced by Blacks."[63] This attempt to break with the dominant society meant that Black

Fig. 0.5 Members of the Moorish Science Temple of America assembled for its national gathering in October 1928. Founder Noble Drew Ali stands in the middle of the group dressed in white. On its website today, the group declares its members to be "Moslems" and their nationality to be "Moorish American." The group faced competition from the Nation of Islam when it was founded in 1930. (Courtesy Wikimedia Commons)

Muslim communities in the United States were often surveilled by American law enforcement over fears of how they might change mainstream America or connect to "foreign agitators" in some way.[64] The founder of the Moorish Science Temple, Noble Drew Ali, felt it was imperative that Black Americans' racial and religious identity be linked with their national identity if they were to progress as citizens of the United States.[65] Ed Curtis notes that by the end of the 1920s, the competition between "Shi'a, Sunni, Ahmadi, and Moorish Muslim institutions" in the United States was an "indication that Islam had become a bona fide American religious tradition,"[66] one marked by a diversity of experiences. Interest in the Islam practiced by the Moorish Science Temple and the NoI was fueled both by an increasing interest in Africa and by an increasing interest in Black nationalism.[67] They were also tied together by Wallace D.

Fard, who would become better known as Wallace Fard Muhammad and who would found the NoI.

There were rumors that before founding the NoI, Muhammad had been a member of the Moorish Science Temple, and the politics of both groups was often wrapped up with Black nationalism.[68] Black nationalism influenced by Islam arose in a post–Civil War United States that was not quite sure what it meant to be a nation made up of diverse races and religions and that continued to treat people of color as lesser citizens long after they were freed from their chains.[69] In the case of the NoI, Black identity was imagined as being in opposition to white identity,[70] as "Fard preached a message that resonated with some African Americans, that they were good, and that the White people oppressing them were evil."[71] Fard was a complicated figure who the NoI claimed was born to a Black father and a white mother in Mecca and who the FBI claimed was a white man born in either Oregon or New Zealand.[72] He worked to counter mainstream white Christian understandings of the creation of mankind with the idea that the first humans were actually Black and that white people were inferior copies of those first humans.[73] Both the Moorish Science Temple and the NoI sought to help Black Americans shape a new identity. In the case of the NoI, this would be done by "ascribing to them a new national identity founded on select Islamic beliefs and practices."[74] The NoI preached the need for a complete separation of Black and white communities, with white people thought to be out to corrupt and destroy African American communities.[75] This ideology was frightening to much of mainstream America, but as much as the NoI sometimes scared people, it also "taught young Black men to love themselves."[76]

Muslim women have often been framed in political and media narratives as victims of Islam and of Muslim men, but for some Black American women, Islam offered up a potential space to resist the oppression they experienced in their everyday lives. Sylvia Chan-Malik notes that Islam has provided some women a "safe harbor" from which to resist both white supremacy and the violence of patriarchy.[77] Aminah McCloud suggests that choosing what identity to foreground—race, religion, or nationality—is a complicated choice for Black Americans given the history of racial violence in the United States: "American Muslims who are black are at crossroads in concretizing their identity as American Muslims as they decide what is being enabled by one name or another. If American comes first in the identity, then that is one kind of labeling which evokes a particular nationalist seating that betrays their spiritual choice as formulated around protest of racism and discrimination."[78]

Rarely has the complexity of this experience been made visible in American media. News media, in particular, have focused on the more sensational or radical expressions of the Black American Muslim experience. Charismatic members and leaders of the NoI—individuals such as Malcolm X, Louis Farrakhan, and even boxing champ Muhammad Ali—have driven public understandings of Black Muslim communities, working to obscure the diversity of experience within those communities.[79] In public discourse, the focus has begun to move away from radical Black Muslim thought, although it's not necessarily less fraught. In her book on what she calls "Muslim cool," Su'ad Abdul Khabeer has shown how the Black Muslim experience is increasingly defined by an idea of coolness,[80] one that can be problematic when it appears in media as it can serve to objectify Black bodies. This objectification is another avenue for the framing of Muslims as others in the country in which they live, a framing that permeates American popular media.

The otherness of Muslims has been featured in films, in books, and in prime-time TV dramas. One example of this is FOX's series 24. In it, super-agent Jack Bauer saves the United States from repeated terrorist threats—one season features Muslim terrorists working inside the United States. The first season of the rebooted 24, 24: Legacy, carried on this tradition with a storyline centered on Islamic terrorists working, once again, inside the United States. Showtime's award-winning program Homeland, an American adaptation of an Israeli drama, is centered on the threat radical Islam poses to the United States and, by extension, to the larger Western world. Deepa Kumar has suggested that the result of this is the transformation of terrorism into a televisual spectacle designed to be consumed, one that relies on the audience buying into the idea that Muslims are, in fact, bad "dudes"—to use Trumpian parlance.[81]

When Muslims in popular media aren't terrorists, they are often wrapped up with ideas of consumerism and consumption. Evelyn Alsultany has shown how the program Shahs of Sunset—in which only some of the characters are Muslim, though all are members of the Iranian diaspora—works to normalize the identities of its characters by showing them consuming vast quantities of goods.[82] If Muslims become coded as a threat in other texts because they are "foreign" and therefore do not assimilate,[83] then they become coded as "American" by their ability and desire to assimilate into a capitalist economy. The idea of the Muslim threat also lessens when Muslims become transformed into consumable objects of some kind.[84] For instance, in the music video for the Katy Perry song "Dark Horse" men who appear to be from North Africa or

Fig. 0.6 In the music video for her song "Dark Horse," pop star Katy Perry frames herself as a sort of Cleopatra figure. Her fantastical version of ancient Egypt trades on Orientalist tropes about what the Near East is and what people of the Near East are like. Over the course of the song, Perry enacts a version of empowered feminism that relies on the consumption of men seemingly from Eastern cultures in order to be realized.

the Middle East are tamed and consumed by Perry in the guise of a neon bright Cleopatra.[85] The threat these men pose to her power as a female monarch is destroyed by her consumption of them. No longer are they men to be feared; instead, they are mocked and discarded.

Interestingly, while Muslim characters have not always been framed in positive ways in popular media, Islam and Orientalist ideas of who Muslims are have certainly influenced a number of important popular texts. Frank Herbert's book *Dune*, and its film adaptations, borrow names, mythology, and even a conflict over a resource (Dune's spice is often equated with Middle Eastern oil) from popular understandings of Islam and Muslims.[86] The beliefs and ideas floating around George Lucas's *Star Wars* universe are partly inspired by Sufism, long seen as the mystical aspect of Islam.[87] Rebecca Hankins and

INTRODUCTION

Joyce Thornton suggest that "Arab- or Muslim-inspired backdrops are easy to incorporate into western science fiction because there is less knowledge of the religion on the part of the public, and so authors' creative imaginations can 'run wild.'"[83] This lack of knowledge juxtaposed against a historic Orientalist representation of Islam and Muslims means the fantastic worlds conjured up by sci-fi writers who are influenced by Islam retain a kind of glancing familiarity for the audience. The strange and the fantastic are somehow made to feel *less* strange because of their Islamic inspiration.

The narrative that emerges in the American imagination from this cornucopia of negative and Orientalist representations of Muslims is this: They are imagined as a monolithic, backward group prone to violence. They are oppressors who prey on the weak and monsters who persecute those who do not believe as they do. They are unthinking people who act as a block and never question authority. They are unenlightened, unmodern—the antithesis of what it means to be Western, what it means to be American—or Muslims are portrayed as a conduit to a mystical understanding of the universe that perpetuates their framing as others, just as *useful* others instead of scary ones. However, there is some evidence that things may be beginning to change.

In 2013, Marvel Comics announced their *Ms. Marvel* label was going to be relaunched with an American Muslim teenager taking over the mantle of Ms. Marvel. Though Muslim characters have appeared in the pages of American comic books in the past, this was the first time a Muslim superhero would get their own title. The gamble paid off. Ms. Marvel was such a success that she's begun showing up in other Marvel properties and is starring in her own show on the streaming network Disney+. Streaming service Hulu has also had luck with a program featuring a Muslim main character as its series *Ramy* has become a critical darling. In both texts—*Ms. Marvel* and *Ramy*—the characters are shown to want to find a way to be both American and Muslim, to not have to sacrifice one in service to the other. In a way, the depiction of the religion in these two texts helped make Islam accessible to a public that has been told the religion is one to be feared, a public that has been conditioned to believe there is something abnormal in the religion and its believers. After centuries of being shown Muslims who were scary others or who, when not scary, were the exception to that rule, American audiences were shown complicated Muslim characters living lives not all that different from their own. Islam's depiction in media such as *Ms. Marvel* and *Ramy* is helping the religion creep ever closer toward inclusion in the definition of what it means to be American. This book considers the stakes of that inclusion. It traces the imaginaries found in recent popular media in order to understand how they help make particular Muslim identities visible and accessible to a broad public. Umberto Eco wrote that "trying to understand other people means destroying the stereotype without denying or ignoring the otherness."[89] As Muslims become more visible in popular media, as stereotypes are destroyed or challenged, what aspects of Muslim experience are being highlighted, whose perspectives are made accessible, and why?

This discussion thus far has focused on the various ways Muslims have historically been seen by those in the West, highlighting how Muslim identities are seen as inaccessible, unknowable, and indecipherable to those outside what's considered the Muslim world. Though the language around accessibility is often wrapped up in discussions of disability, in addition to meaning "providing access," the term *accessible* can also mean "capable of being used or seen" as well as "capable of being understood and appreciated." It is those last two meanings, being able to be "seen" and being able to be "understood," with which *Pop Islam* is concerned. These are, after all, what Pierre Bourdieu suggests lie at the heart of struggles over identity:

> [They are] struggles over the monopoly of the power to make people see and believe, to get them to know and recognize, to impose the legitimate definition of the divisions of the social world and, thereby, to *make and unmake groups*. What is at stake here is the power of imposing a vision of the social world through principles of division which, when they are imposed on a whole group, establish meaning and a consensus about meaning, and in particular about the identity and unity of the group, which creates the reality of the unity and the identity of the group.[90]

The power to make and unmake groups, the power to be seen, also lies at the heart of debates and conversations about media representation. Media can shape how we understand our world and who belongs in it. Media can make some identities, some experiences, more accessible to audiences than others. French philosopher Michel Foucault has written of the ways in which language and discourse have been used to make some experiences visible while being used to police others. It is Foucault's ideas about visibility that help frame the argument of this book.

In *Discipline and Punish*, Foucault argued that "visibility is a trap."[91] His argument hinges on the idea that by becoming visible, making themselves seen, people then open themselves up to surveillance and judgment. Basing his discussion of visibility on Jeremy Bentham's concept of the panopticon—an entity that is all seeing, but one in which those in power, those who see, are invisible—Foucault notes that those who are observed are trapped in spaces "like so many cages, so many small theatres, in which each actor is perfectly alone, perfectly individualized and constantly visible."[92] The social power exerted by the mere existence of observers serves to divide and conquer; individuals concerned with their own performances of visibility become focused on their own experiences to the detriment of collective identities to which they may belong. Foucault suggests that in such a system an individual "must never know whether he is being looked at any one moment; but he must be sure that he may always be so."[93] The knowledge that someone can, and may, see you exerts a kind of control over how you may behave.

At the same time, individuals want to be understood; they want to be seen. In seeking to make visible what they feel to be an *authentic* version of themselves, individuals can become trapped in a public performance of that visibility—that visibility, that accessibility, can reproduce a kind of artifice. Becoming visible can be empowering while also trapping those seen into behaving in society approved ways. One is granted visibility if one does not rock the boat, or if one forces visibility, there still exists the possibility of being seen but of not being *heard*. An argument can be made that Muslims in the West have been seen for centuries, the problem is that the version that's been made visible has been produced *of* them and *for* them, not *by* them. But even when given the power and the ability to create what they feel are truer representations of themselves, Muslims can find themselves trapped, forced into that binary of good Muslim / bad Muslim.

Visibility and the traps it lays for us are at the core of arguments made by both Evelyn Alsultany and Nabil Echchaibi. In her book *Arabs and Muslims in Media: Race and Representation after 9/11*, Alsultany details the ways popular media have reified the idea of the scary Muslim/Arab other through their continued portrayal as terrorists or corrupt figures.[94] However, even when media try to carve out more positive representations, they fall into the stereotype trap; Alsultany noted, "These seemingly positive representations of Arabs and Muslims have helped form a new kind of racism."[95] It is one that seems to embrace multiculturalism on its surface while it "produces the logics and affects necessary to legitimize racist policies and practices" and helps produce sanitized and safe forms of American Muslim identity.[96]

Alsultany's argument is similar to Echchaibi's conceptualization of what he calls "the double burden of representation": "[This] sees Muslims compelled to defend their faith and their fellow believers but only from a narrow media agenda that leaves little room for any discursive flexibility. The equation of Islam and violence/extremism is inescapable, and Muslim intervention is made possible mostly from within the confines of this equation, to

20   POP ISLAM

guard against sweeping generalizations and still prove their loyalty to the United States."[97]

Within such a framework, positive appearances are responses to stereotype, and because of that, the stereotype—not actual, diverse, lived experiences—remains foregrounded. Responding to negative stories about Muslims and working to challenge stereotypes can reinforce them while trapping Muslims in a good Muslim / bad Muslim binary.[98] By attempting to counter stereotypes, Muslim activists and, perhaps by extension, media producers can find themselves still trapped by those very same stereotypes. As they work to unmake the negative imaginings of Muslims that exist in American popular culture, they may remake them instead. Becoming accessible can mean, at times, reifying staid ideas of what it means to be Muslim even as that accessibility is meant to challenge them.

If visibility is a trap, then the project of this book is, in part, to explore what traps Muslims may be forced into in American popular media and whether there is a way for them to escape those traps. This exploration begins in chapter 1 with a discussion of one of the more contextualized recent representations of Muslims—that found within the pages of the *Ms. Marvel* comic book series. It uses Kamala Khan, Marvel's enormously popular Muslim Ms. Marvel, as a lens through which to consider what well-rounded representation could look like. It suggests that while Kamala may help "embiggen" our understanding of the Muslim American experience, that "embiggening" may very well be dependent on her identity, not only as an American Muslim but specifically as an American Muslim *teenage girl*. As Sophia Rose Arjana has argued so beautifully in her book on Muslim monsters, Muslim women have generally not been seen as a violent threat to the West. Kamala's complicated framing in the comic book may partly be due to the fact that Muslim women have often been seen as less of a threat to what it means to be Western, what it means to be American, than Muslim men. The gendered aspect of this representation is picked up in chapter 2 as it explores the framing of Muslim characters in scripted television programming.

Muslims who appear in scripted TV shows tend to do so in one of two guises: As a terrorist planning to take American lives or as a possible terrorist who decides, at the last minute, he does not want to kill innocent people. Programs such as *24*, *Homeland*, and even the rebooted *X-Files* have featured such characterizations. But there are other Muslim characters appearing on American TV screens who do not fit inside the "Muslim as threat" framework. Programs such as *Quantico*, *Lost*, *American Crime*, and *The Night Of* have featured Muslim characters who were not framed as threats or whose challenge of

INTRODUCTION 21

such a frame was written into their characterization on the program. Chapter 2 explores the more positive representations found in such programs as it considers who is allowed to be visibly and unproblematically Muslim and who is seen to struggle with that identity.

The Muslim identities of a number of comedians and entertainers have been foregrounded, and then sometimes marginalized, as they found mainstream success with movies such as *The Big Sick* or TV shows such as *Master of None*. Chapter 3 examines how issues of belonging, identity, and Islamophobia are approached by comedic Muslim entertainers such as Hasan Minhaj. This chapter focuses on scripted comedy series and stand-up specials to understand how Muslims use jokes, gags, and other types of comedic writing to challenge stereotype and bigotry as well as tease apart how those same jokes may reinforce negative stereotypes of Muslims.

The issue of reality and what representations are "real" is the focus of chapter 4. A number of high-profile reality TV programs—such as *Master Chef, Project Runway*, and *the Great British Baking Show* (yes, British, but it found wide popularity when rebroadcast on PBS in the United States)—have featured Muslim contestants the last several years. This chapter explores the narratives the programs weave of who these individuals are and how they fit into American and British culture. It considers what contestants are allowed to say on camera about their Muslim identities as well as what is said *about* them.

What is said about Muslim identities and experiences is the focus of chapter 5 as it explores Muslim representation in fashion magazines. Outlets such as *Teen Vogue* are increasingly featuring the photos and writing of young Muslim women discussing their lives. Picking up on the themes connected to gender that weave through earlier chapters, chapter 5 asks whose experiences are allowed to be made visible, are allowed to be made consumable, on the pages of publications like *Teen Vogue* and why?

The Muslim representations examined in this book are not only visible; they are hypervisible. They are received by audiences who do not simply consume them; the representations are often picked up and discussed in social media spaces as Muslims and non-Muslims alike consider how authentic they are and consider how American they are. This book closes with a discussion of how this hypervisibility in popular media can make Muslims accessible to a broader public, one that has been conditioned to fear Muslims, while also considering the nuance and complexity that may be lost in the name of accessibility. Popular media texts are designed to have broad appeal—their success, their very survival, depends on masses of individuals being willing to pay to receive those texts and the messages relayed in them. Though popular media is often overlooked as trivial fluff, in reality, shows like *Lost*, comic books like *Ms. Marvel*, or comedians like Hasan Minhaj reach a far wider audience than media that are considered more serious, such as newspapers or foreign films. To truly understand where American narratives of who Muslims are come from, we must engage with popular media while also considering who is allowed to be seen there and why.

NOTES

1. Benedict Anderson, *Imagined Communities: Reflections on the Origins and Spread of Nationalism*, 1986, rev. ed. (London: Verso, 2006); Shani Orgad, *Media Representation and the Global Imagination* (Cambridge: Polity, 2012); Edward Said, *Orientalism* (New York: Vintage Books, 1979).

2. Karin van Nieuwkerk, Mark Levin, and Martin Stokes, "Introduction," in *Islam and Popular Culture*, ed. Karin van Nieurwkerk, Mark Levine, and Martin Stokes (Austin: University of Texas Press, 2016), 1–20.

3. Anna Piela, *Islam and Popular Culture* (New York: Routledge, 2017).

4. Sophia Rose Arjana, *Muslims in the Western Imagination* (New York: Oxford University Press, 2015), 3.

5. Ibid.

6. Suzanne Conklin Akbari, *Idols in the East: European Representations of Islam and the Orient, 1100–1450* (Ithaca, NY: Cornell University Press, 2009).

7. Ibid., 247.

8. Ibid.; Arjana, *Muslims in the Western Imagination.*

9. Akbari, *Idols in the East*, 5.

10. Myra Georgiou, *Diaspora, Identity, and the Media: Diasporic Nationalities and Mediated Spatialities* (Cresskill, NJ: Hampton Press, 2006), 3.

11. Stuart Hall, "Culture, Identity, and Diaspora," in *Identity, Community, Culture, & Difference*, ed. Jonathon Rutherford (London: Lawrence & Wishart, 1990), 392–403; Marwan Kraidy, *Hybridity; Or, the Cultural Logic of Globalization* (Philadelphia: Temple University Press, 2005).

12. Akbari, *Idols in the East.*

13. Tomaz Mastnak, "Western Hostility toward Muslims: A History of the Present," in *Islamophobia/Islamophilia: Beyond the Politics of Enemy and Friend*, ed. Andrew Shryock (Bloomington: Indiana University Press, 2010), 29–52.

14. Ibid.

15. Ibid.

16. Arjana, *Muslims in the Western Imagination.*

17. Ibid.

INTRODUCTION

18. Ibid.

19. Umberto Eco, *Inventing the Enemy and Other Occasional Writings* (New York: Houghton Mifflin Harcourt, 2012).

20. Hall, "Culture, Identity, and Diaspora," 227.

21. Arjun Appadurai, *Fear of Small Numbers: An Essay on the Geography of Anger* (Durham, NC: Duke University Press, 2006).

22. Evelyn Alsultany, *Arabs and Muslims in the Media: Race and Representation after 9/11* (New York: New York University Press, 2012).

23. Vassilis Lambropoulous, *The Rise of Eurocentrism: Anatomy of Interpretation* (Princeton, NJ: Princeton University Press, 1993).

24. Samir Amin, *Eurocentrism*, 2nd ed. (New York: Monthly Review, 2010).

25. Dipesh Chakravarty, *Provincializing Europe: Postcolonial Thought and Historical Difference*, new ed. (Princeton, NJ: Princeton University Press, 2008).

26. Deepa Kumar, *Islamophobia and the Politics of Empire* (Chicago: Haymarket Books, 2012).

27. Ibid.

28. Scott Trafton, *Egypt Land: Race and Nineteenth-Century American Egyptomania* (Durham, NC: Duke University Press, 2004).

29. Said, *Orientalism*.

30. Peter Gottschalk, *American Heretics: Catholics, Jews, Muslims, and the History of Religious Intolerance* (New York: St. Martin's, 2013), 175.

31. Ibid., 176.

32. Jonathon Curiel, *Al' America: Travels through America's Arab and Islamic Roots* (New York: New Press, 2008).

33. Sylviane A. Diouf, *Servants of Allah: African Muslims Enslaved in America* (New York: New York University Press, 2013); John Esposito, *What Everyone Needs to Know about Islam* (New York: Oxford University Press, 2002); Junaid Rana, "The Story of Islamophobia," *Souls* 9, no. 2 (2007): 148–61.

34. Curiel, *Al' America*.

35. Edward Curtis, "The Black Muslim Scare of the Twentieth Century: The History of State Islamophobia and Its Post-9/11 Variations," in *Islamophobia in American: The Anatomy of Intolerance*, ed. Carl W. Ernst (New York: Palgrave Macmillan, 2009), 75–106.

36. Allan D. Austin, *African American Muslims in Antebellum America: Transatlantic Stories and Spiritual Struggles* (New York: Routledge, 1997).

37. Richard Brent Turner, *Islam in the African-American Experience* (Bloomington: Indiana University Press, 2003).

38. Diouf, *Servants of Allah*.

39. Austin, *African American Muslims*.

40. Kambiz GhaneaBassiri, *A History of Islam in America* (Cambridge: Cambridge University Press, 2010).

41. Allan Austin discusses several slave narratives in his 1997 book *African American Muslims*.

42. Akel Kahera, "God's Dominion: Omar Ibn Said use of Arabic Literacy as Opposition to Slavery," *South Carolina Review*, 2014.

43. Ibid., 133.

44. Austin, *African American Muslims*, 13.

45. Kevin J. Hayes, "How Thomas Jefferson Read the Qur'an," *Early American Literature* 39, no. 2 (2004): 247–61.

46. James H. Hutton, "The Founding Fathers and Islam: Library Papers Show Early Tolerance for Faith," *Library Congress Information Bulletin* 61, no. 5 (2002), https://www.loc.gov/loc/lcib/0205/tolerance.html.

47. Diouf, *Servants of Allah*; Curiel, *Al' America*.

48. Curiel, *Al' America*; Trafton, *Egypt Land*.

49. Curiel, *Al' America*.

50. Karine V. Walther, *Sacred Interests: The United States and the Islamic World, 1821–1921* (Chapel Hill: University of North Carolina Press, 2015).

51. Ibid.; Melani McAlister, *Epic Encounters: Culture, Media & U.S. Interests in the Middle East since 1945*, updated ed. (Berkeley: University of California Press, 2005).

52. Edward Said, *Covering Islam: How the Media and the Experts Determine How We See the Rest of the World* (New York: Vintage Books, 1997).

53. Peter Gottschalk and Gabriel Greenberg, *Islamophobia: Making Muslims the Enemy* (Lanham, MD: Rowman & Littlefield, 2008).

54. Mahmood Mamdani, *Good Muslim, Bad Muslim: America, the Cold War, and the Roots of Terror* (New York: Three Leaves Press, 2004).

55. Todd H. Green, *Presumed Guilty: Why We Shouldn't Ask Muslims to Condemn Terrorism* (Minneapolis: Fortress Press, 2018).

56. Asma T. Uddin, *When Islam Is Not a Religion: Inside America's Fight for Religious Freedom* (New York: Pegasus Books, 2019).

57. Turner, *Islam in the African-American Experience*, 449.

58. GhaneaBassiri, *History of Islam in America*.

59. Jonathon Curiel, *Islam in America* (London: I.B. Tauris, 2015), 17.

60. GhaneaBassiri, *History of Islam in America*.

61. Aminah Beverly McCloud, "African American Islam: A Reflection," *Religion Compass* 4, no. 9 (2010): 538–50.

62. Turner, *Islam in the African-American Experience*.

63. Gilles Kepel, *Allah in the West: Islamic Movements in America and Europe* (Stanford, CA: Stanford University Press, 1997).

64. Curtis, "Black Muslim Scare of the Twentieth Century."

65. GhaneaBassiri, *History of Islam in America*, 219.

66. Ibid., 89.

INTRODUCTION 25

67. Amir Hussain, *Muslims and the Making of America* (Waco, TX: Baylor University Press, 2016); GhaneaBassiri, *History of Islam in America*.

68. McCloud, "African American Islam."

69. Kepel, *Allah in the West*; GhaneaBassiri, *History of Islam in America*.

70. Charles Eric Lincoln, *The Black Muslims in America* (Boston: Beacon Press, 1961).

71. Hussain, *Muslims and the Making of America*, 33.

72. GhaneaBassiri, *History of Islam in America*.

73. The NoI's creation myth is discussed in a footnote in chapter 3 of Edward E. Curtis and Danielle Sigler's 2009 book, *The New Black Gods: Arthur Huff Fauset the Study of African American Religions* (Bloomington: Indiana University Press).

74. GhaneaBassiri, *History of Islam in America*, 224.

75. Ibid.

76. Hussain, *Muslims and the Making of America*, 35.

77. Sylvia Chan-Malik, *Being Muslim: A Cultural History of Women of Color in American Islam* (New York: New York University Press, 2018).

78. McCloud, "African American Islam," 544.

79. GhaneaBassiri, *History of Islam in America*.

80. Su'ad Abdul Khabeer, *Muslim Cool: Race, Religion, and Hip Hop in the United States* (New York: New York University Press, 2016), 225.

81. Kumar, *Islamophobia and the Politics of Empire*.

82. Evelyn Alsultany, "The Cultural Politics of Islam in U.S. Reality Television," *Communication, Culture and Critique* 9, no. 4 (2016): 595–613.

83. Nathan Lean, *The Islamophobia Industry: How the Right Manufactures Fear of Muslims* (London: Pluto Press, 2012).

84. Arjana, *Muslims in the Western Imagination*; Rosemary Pennington, "Dissolving the Other: Orientalism, Consumption and Katy Perry's Insatiable Dark Horse," *Journal of Communication Inquiry* 40, no. 2 (2016): 111–27; Said, *Orientalism*.

85. Pennington, "Dissolving the Other."

86. Rebecca Hankins and Joyce Thornton, "The Influence of Muslims and Islam in Science Fiction, Fantasy, and Comics," in *Muslims and American Popular Culture*, vol. 1, *Entertainment and Digital Culture*, ed. Iraj Omidvar and Anne Richards (Santa Barbara, CA: Praeger, 2014), 323–48.

87. Sophia Rose Arjana, *Buying Buddha, Selling Rumi: Orientalism and the Mystical Marketplace* (London: Oneworld, 2020).

88. Hankins and Thornton, " Influence of Muslims and Islam in Science Fiction, Fantasy, and Comics," 330.

89. Eco, *Inventing the Enemy*, 18.

90. Pierre Bourdieu, *Language and Symbolic Power* (Cambridge, MA: Polity, 1991), 221.

91. Michel Foucault, *Discipline and Punish: The Birth of the Modern Prison*, 2nd ed. (New York: Vintage Books, 1995), 200.

92. Ibid.

93. Ibid., 201.

94. Alsultany, *Arabs and Muslims in the Media*.

95. Ibid., 16.

96. Ibid.

97. Nabil Echchaibi, "Unveiling Obsessions: Muslims and the Trap of Representation," in *On Islam: Muslims and the Media*, ed. Rosemary Pennington and Hilary Kahn (Bloomington: Indiana University Press, 2018), 62.

98. Alsultany, *Arabs and Muslims in the Media*.

ONE

—⁘—

MS. MARVEL AND THE "EMBIGGENING" OF MUSLIMS IN AMERICA

KAMALA KHAN IS AN AMERICAN teenager, and like so many others, she fights with her parents, she struggles to fit in at school, and she attempts to navigate the pitfalls of teen love with as much grace as she can muster. She is vain and humble. She is American and Muslim. Of all the identity struggles Kamala is faced with, it is her religious identity that brings her the most attention and at times frames her experience as she fights for what's right.

Kamala Khan is an American Muslim superhero.

In November 2013, Marvel Comics announced that it was relaunching its *Ms. Marvel* series with a new woman in the role. The character originated in the late '70s when air force officer Carol Danvers, who first appeared as the love interest of a male Captain Marvel in 1968,[1] gained superpowers after receiving an infusion of alien DNA during an explosion. Danvers's blond, curvy, all-American good looks and brash persona made her a popular character with comic book readers. Introduced during the Silver Age of comics and envisioned as Marvel's feminist superhero,[2] Ms. Marvel headlined her own series before eventually joining the superhero teams of the Avengers and X-Men. Ms. Marvel's powers gave her superstrength, the ability to fly, and the ability to absorb and redirect energy, making her one of the most powerful heroes in the Marvel universe. But her stories also showcased her human vulnerability, depicting her attempts to cope with the reality of having been raised in abusive household or a battle with alcoholism that almost led to her expulsion from the Avengers at one point. In 2012, Marvel announced at WonderCon that Danvers would no longer serve as Ms. Marvel, unveiling an image of Danvers in a blue-and-red costume emblazoned with a bright yellow star and explaining that she would be taking on the mantle of Captain Marvel.

After Danvers took over the role of Captain Marvel, Ms. Marvel's boots were left empty. Not long after announcing Danvers's departure from the role, Marvel shocked many by announcing that the next Ms. Marvel would be Muslim; instead of the buxom and blond Carol Danvers, small and dark Kamala Khan would don Ms. Marvel's lightning bolt. Kamala is an American Muslim whose parents came from Pakistan, whose brother seems to be a religious fundamentalist, and whose life is often circumscribed by the expectations of others—Muslim and non-Muslim alike. Navigating all this proves at times to be just as difficult for Kamala as fighting bad guys. Being seen and recognized for who she is, is something Kamala struggles with before becoming a superhero, and it only becomes more complicated once she accepts the responsibilities inherent to a superhero's life. This chapter explores how the issues of visibility and accessibility are woven into the first run of this new *Ms. Marvel* series.

The American relationship with comic books is complicated. Because they often deal with controversial subject matter or include sexual innuendo, comic books in the mid-twentieth century were often censored; they were seen as being "capable of perverting the morals of American youth."[3] Comic books were imagined as having no lasting social value. Superhero stories still are often seen as trivial types of media designed to entertain more than anything else. While that is partially true—and one could argue for the importance of entertainment in our lives—sometimes obscured by the bright colors and fantastical situations found in the frames of comic books are stories that carry deep social weight. Jon Hogan suggests "the superhero comic book is part of popular culture because it can help us better understand what traits we value and why we value them."[4] They can help make visible things we often take for granted while also providing places where critiques of dominant culture can be produced and disseminated and where political beliefs and ideologies can be reinforced. Such was the case with Marvel's *Civil War* series and the Patriot Act.

In the aftermath of the September 11 attacks, the US government began implementing measures it said were designed to keep the country safe. As part of this, Congress wrote and passed the Patriot Act, a bill giving law enforcement wide latitude in the collection of data that it said might stop the next big terrorist attack. While the country was still largely swept up in patriotic fervor, there were some who were concerned over the act's "perceived threat to civil liberties,"[5] as it granted agencies such as the CIA, FBI, and NSA unprecedented surveillance powers. The debate over whether the government should have such reach was taken up in Marvel's *Civil War* series, although not explicitly.

The heart of the story arc was the fight between various superheroes over whether or not they should support the "Superhero Registration Act" that would require superheroes to register their real names with the government so that it could keep tabs on people with superpowers in the United States. The act created a divide in the Marvel universe, as a group of superheroes led by Iron Man/Tony Stark supported registering and a group led by Captain America was against it. Throughout the series, the characters debate what it means to be free and what liberties are worth giving up in order to keep people safe. In the end, Captain America turns himself in after a series of conflicts, deciding that "opposing the act is doing more harm than good and, what is more, is deflecting from the real task of fighting evil."[6] The suggestion is that some freedoms are worth giving up in order to secure the greater good—the story arc, though controversial, was seen as supporting the Patriot Act.

The aftermath of September 11 framed the narrative of DC Comic's *Human Target* series as well. The memory of the trauma experienced by New Yorkers was foregrounded as the main character, Christopher Chance, attempted to come to terms with what he saw and felt that day. J. Gavin Paul argues that as readers see the main character's memory of that experience unfold, they become engaged with the story and activate their own memories of the trauma and violence they witnessed.[7] He suggests that the gutters existing between comic book story panels allow the reader to fill the empty spaces of the narrative with their own experiences and interpretations. Readers engage with the text in a way that is deeply personal and can, at times, be deeply meaningful, as "comic book art appeals to people because, visually, a cartoon drawing is a nondescript place to be filled with the reader's empathy."[8] Comic books are symbolic environments where the interplay of the textual and the visual not only constructs the narrative of the story itself but also provides space for readers to insert their own feelings and understandings of the world into the narrative.

Comic books, and their literary sibling graphic novels, have created moments of engagement with events such as the Holocaust, the Bosnian War, and the Iranian Revolution, detailing the trauma experienced by those living through those conflicts and tragedies while helping readers process the events themselves. Ariela Freedman writes that "because comics employ both word and image, they can try to bridge the internal and external representation of pain; they can tell pain and show it."[9] In the case of the *Maus* graphic novels, which recount the story of the Holocaust with mice in the place of Jews and cats in the place of Nazis, Michael Staub suggests that they retell the story of Holocaust in a way "that is much more accessible to a general audience than many other accounts, because it is particularly effective at inviting emotional involvement."[10] He suggests that Art Spiegelman's presentation of his family's story of the Holocaust as a kind of illustrated oral history helped readers

Fig. 1.1 *X-Men* was a popular Saturday morning cartoon on FOX during the 1990s. Many of the show's storylines revolved around the mutants' struggles to fit into a society that othered them as well as their fight against politicians who want to erase them.

connect with the tale in a way they may not have with a more serious text. The art of *Maus* made the story of the Holocaust accessible to readers who had largely approached it through the distant gaze of black-and-white documentary photos and film.[11]

The words, images, and empty spaces of comic books allow readers to ponder trauma and pain and consider sorrow and loss on their own terms as well as in relation to the experience of others and sometimes in relation to the othering of individuals or groups who are not like them.

Among the most famous comic series dealing with issues of othering and marginalization is Marvel's *X-Men*. An unlikely and often scrappy band of superheroes, the X-Men consist of individuals living with various genetic mutations. For some, this means they can manipulate the elements; for others, they gain inhuman speed or strength, and still others are able to psychically connect to other beings. While many of these mutants look like any other human being, their mutations—or gifts, as X-Men leader Charles Xavier refers to them—mark them as different, as other, and nonmutants often see them as freaks. Many of the major storylines of the series (and its spin-offs) revolve around the marginalization of the X-Men; at one point, political leaders OK the development and use of huge robots called Sentinels designed with the sole purpose of hunting mutants down.[12] Because the mutants are different, they are seen as a threat to the rest of society and, therefore, must be tightly controlled and in some storylines eradicated. Launched in 1963, the X-Men family of stories were seen as a fantastical mirroring of larger societal conversations about race, ethnicity, and sexuality.[13] However, Marvel's high-profile superhero team is far from the only instance of this type of mirroring. Arguably, the most popular superhero—Superman—was a pushback against hate and bigotry.

The creation of Jewish American artists Jerry Siegel and Joe Shuster, and first published in 1938, Superman launched the superhero comic genre,[14] ushering in what has been called the Golden Age of American comics.[15] Superman was created on the eve of World War II, when American comics were increasingly tackling the rise of the Axis powers in Europe and overtly producing antifascist storylines.[16] Superman's stories often found the hero fighting villains who wanted to take away the rights of others, with the concepts of truth and justice sitting squarely at the center of these stories.[17] Because of Superman's defense of the rights of all and because of his focus on justice, he has sometimes been connected to the story of Jesus Christ, seen as a kind of pop culture Jesus figure.[18] However, given the Jewish identity of his creators, Superman has been often embraced as a Jewish superhero whose Jewish identity was at times obscured in order to appeal to a broad reading public.[19]

Superman was fast, strong, virile—the embodiment of a kind of American masculinity that has come to dominate what we understand men to be; the antisemitism that followed Jewish communities wherever they went meant that Jewish men were not often seen to fit into this understanding of masculinity.[20] Writing of the artists and writers who created Superman and a number of other comic book heroes, Harry Brod notes, "The Jewish men who created supermen were men who were themselves seen as not measuring up to the standards of what real men were supposed to be."[21] In the superheroes they created, these men were able to wrap up a Jewish understanding of the world in a casing of brawny, hegemonic American masculinity. With such a focus on the bodies of these superheroes, their objectification seems almost unavoidable.

Karen McGrath points out that in order to make the strength and vigor of superheroes visually apparent, the "characters' bodies become objectified."[22] This objectification is particularly problematic for female characters as it is often tied to their overt sexualization on the pages (if not always in the stories themselves). As mentioned earlier, the original Ms. Marvel was a buxom blond who epitomized American beauty standards in the same way Superman served as the embodiment of American male masculinity. Ms. Marvel's various costumes were drawn in order to show off long legs and full breasts even as she saved the earth and the universe from a variety of cosmic threats. She's hardly the only female comic book character whose body has been fetishized by artists and audiences. For instance, though she is an Amazon warrior, depictions of Wonder Woman have often emphasized her long legs or large breasts over her strength, with images of her in distress seemingly designed to titillate the viewer.[23] In her analysis of twenty years of depictions of women in comic books, Carolyn Cocca found that almost every issue of the comic books she examined contained hypersexualized portrayals of female characters meant to show off their "t and a."[24] And in 2014, the same year the company would garner glowing critical praise for its relaunching of the Ms. Marvel title with a Muslim hero and for introducing comic book readers to a female Thor and a Black Captain America,[25] Marvel came under fire for a variant cover of Spider-Woman produced by controversial Italian artist Milo Manara.[26] The cover featured the superhero bent over in such a way that all the curves of her body were on display, appearing more prepared to engage in sexual intercourse than any sort of crime-fighting activity. Writer Rob Bricken of the online outlet io9 wrote of Spider-Woman's depiction on the cover: "She looks like she's wearing body-paint, and that's a big no-no for an industry still trying to remember that women exist and may perhaps read comics and also don't want to feel completely gross when they do so."[27] For a comic book company that was attempting to convince its audience and the broader public that it was leaving stereotyped understandings of heroes and bodies behind, it was an ugly, enormous misstep. Manara had been commissioned to produce variant covers for other Marvel series, but his other covers were scuttled after the Spider-Woman controversy.[28]

The bodies of characters of color also become sites where stereotypes can become reified. Anna Beatrice Scott found that representations of the bodies of Black superheroes in comic books often portrayed them as impossibly powerful. While this is standard for the superhero genre, it also fed into white supremacist understandings of Black bodies as belonging to "mythological beasts with epic powers and tragic presaged endings."[29] Outside comic books, these powerful bodies are imagined as a threat to white America. Even as they attempt to challenge stereotypes, comic book representations of minorities can also serve to reinforce them, as Derek Parker Royal notes, "Comics are a heavily coded medium that rely on stereotyping as a way to concentrate narrative effectiveness."[30] The case of the Muslim superhero is no different.

Fig. 1.2 Dust first appeared in the *New X-Men* comic book series, later appearing in other media, such as the *Wolverine and the X-Men* cartoon. Dust, whose name is Sooraya, is a Sunni Muslim woman whose power is to turn into what looks like sand. Though her faith is an important aspect of her identity, Dust's wearing of the niqab was seen by some as an echo of Orientalist stereotypes.

The identities Muslim and Arab are often conflated, with the monolithic public understanding of Muslims framing them as almost exclusively Arab. While this is a shortsighted understanding, the fact that these identities have been so tightly wound up together in the popular imagination means that examining the way Arabs are portrayed in media can help us understand portrayals of Muslims as well. In his examination of the representation of Arabs in comic books, Jack Shaheen found that rarely were Arabs portrayed as heroes; instead, they showed up in the stories as commoners, as neutral figures who did not take sides, or as villains.[31] There were no Arabs saving the world, but there were Arabs trying to end it.

When Muslims have been given the superhero treatment in American comic books, their representation has often been problematic as well. In 2002, a new member of the X-Men was unveiled: Dust. A young woman from Afghanistan who was rescued from slavers, Sooraya Qadir gained the name Dust when it

Fig. 1.3 The Burka Avenger is from a fictional town in northern Pakistan. The superhero was created to advocate for the importance of girls' education. A schoolteacher by day, the Burka Avenger fights those who would attempt to shut down girls' schools. The show was originally broadcast for four seasons in Urdu Pakistan and has been dubbed into a number of languages, including Arabic, Pashto, and Turkish.

was discovered that her mutant abilities allowed her to transform her body into literal dust particles.[32] For centuries what has been framed as the Orient has often been portrayed as a place of blowing sands, a place full of dust in the wind. Sooraya is the embodiment of that stereotype even though Afghanistan is a mountainous nation that bears little physical relationship to Arabia, where the association of Muslims with sand comes from via Orientalism. Dust's characterization trades in stereotype in another way as well, as she wears a long black burka. The burka and its sister garment, the niqab, have long been imagined as disempowering and oppressive pieces of clothing. In fact, during the run-up to the US war in Afghanistan, women in sky-blue burkas appeared in news media about the possible conflict as victims of the Taliban in need of saving by Western forces.[33] Marvel's "empowered" Muslim woman was, in part, a brightly reimagined Orientalist trope.

Like Dust, Pakistan's Burka Avenger wears a burka as part of her superhero persona; unlike Dust, Miss Jiya was purposefully designed to counter the stereotype of the passive, oppressed Muslim woman. A schoolteacher by day, the Burka Avenger works to protect young Pakistani girls and to ensure that they have access to education. Fighting with pens and pencils, the avenger keeps her

MS. MARVEL AND THE "EMBIGGENING" OF MUSLIMS IN AMERICA   35

Fig. 1.4 *Ms. Marvel* was the best-selling series for Marvel Comics in the year of its launch. The issues on display in this comic bookstore in the Cincinnati, Ohio, area show the wide variety of issues the series explores, including issues of identity, Islamophobia, and romance. Kamala Khan's version of Ms. Marvel proved to be so popular that she began appearing in other Marvel properties and starred in her own streaming show for Disney+ in 2022. (Photo by author)

distance from the men she fights, never actually striking them, which, Miranda Brar argues, helps "demonstrate her symbolic value, indicating that women's participation in the nationalist movement is permissible and recognized only from within the cultural religious fabric of the Muslim nation."[34] The Burka Avenger is a Muslim superhero designed to reflect what are seen as the values of one Muslim nation. Sophia Rose Arjana has pointed out that a number of *Muslimah* superheroes have appeared in popular culture who serve a similar purpose—their existence serving as a counterpoint to the idea of the perpetually oppressed Muslim woman lacking agency to decide the course of her life.[35]

While Kamala Khan is not the first Muslim to don superhero garb, she is the first American Muslim to headline her own comic book series. And, perhaps more importantly, her series was written by G. Willow Wilson, an American Muslim, and edited by another, Sana Amanat. Wilson had written essays, graphic novels, and comics before writing *Ms. Marvel*, although she was perhaps best known at the time of the comic book's launch for her debut novel *Alif the Unseen*. Nicholas Pumphrey suggests that the Muslim identity of both Wilson and Amanat helped propel the success of the new Ms. Marvel, as "it is their insider perspective that is attractive to a new diverse readership and shifts the dominate portrayal of Muslims that was previously authorized, leading to Ms. Marvel being a new American superhero."[36] Wilson announced in 2018 that she would be leaving *Ms. Marvel* when the original series ended as she took over author duties for DC's 2019 run of *Wonder Woman*.[37] In an open letter published on Marvel's website, Wilson wrote that she was overwhelmed by the response of fans to her version of Ms. Marvel. "Kamala is not just what you read on the page or watch on TV," Wilson wrote, "she is this community. And she has made all of us better human beings."[38] After noting that she had written sixty issues of *Ms. Marvel* in her five years on the book, Wilson closed her letter saying, "In a couple of months, I will step down as the writer of Ms. Marvel. But I will be a fan of her for life."[39] Many of the readers of Wilson's *Ms. Marvel*, Muslim and non-Muslim alike, also became fans for life because they found something familiar and universal in Kamala Khan's struggle to reconcile the various aspects of her identity.

When we first meet Kamala Khan, she is sitting at a computer in her bedroom, wearing a fuzzy winter hat, as she squeals with delight that her *Avengers* fan fiction is growing in popularity on a fan site. The thin and somewhat gangly young woman is dressed in blue jeans as she sits hunched over her computer in a messy bedroom, looking like any other American teenager. And like many other American teenagers, she is scolded by her mother when she is not quick enough to disengage from her technology in order to eat dinner with her family. Kamala huffs and puffs as she has to stop what she's doing to do what her mother asks of her. It was a rather quiet and almost ordinary way to introduce a superhero to her audience, but it was effective in immediately making Kamala seem safe and familiar.

Critics responded well to Kamala's quiet and unassuming arrival, saying she was a relatable teen character who would have wide appeal. They also praised the humanity and humor of Marvel's new Muslim hero, one critic writing, "Kamala is conflicted and quirky. She's a bit of a rebel. She wants freedom and choices and bacon. She's you. She's us."[40] However, Miriam Kent suggests that some of the gushing may have glossed over how many of Kamala's struggles as an American teen were framed by her religious identity.[41] There was some concern that Kamala might be trapped by what Nabil Echchaibi calls the "double burden of representation"—the idea that by pushing for fuller representation, or challenging negative representation, Muslims are often trapped in the good Muslim / bad Muslim binary.[42] Often, the good Muslim is the one who is not overtly religious while the bad Muslim is seen to be devout, often overly so. However, Kamala seems to avoid this particular trap of representation. There are moments in the series when Kamala is seen to struggle both with aspects of Islam and with her parents' seemingly conservative approach to raising her. However, never Islam nor Kamala's loved ones are framed as something strange or weird or bad. In fact, as Kamala continues to develop as a superhero, her faith and her family become sources of strength and inspiration. An early moment in the comic's run illustrates the way Kamala navigated her faith in relation to her identity and her family.

Not long after Kamala gains her superpowers, which include the ability to "embiggen" or "disembiggen"—her phrases for growing larger or smaller—her parents become suspicious of her behavior. At his wits' end, her father finally demands she meet with their local sheikh, hoping the authority figure might be able to get Kamala to shape up. Kamala, as many a teen before her, grumblingly agrees to go, fully expecting to receive a lecture on being a good Muslim daughter and woman. (The visit comes after Kamala loudly questions the separation of men and women in the mosque.) However, Sheikh Abdullah is not interested in lecturing the young woman; instead, he engages her in a conversation about what's driving the behavior that is concerning her parents. "Your father says you have been sneaking out and acting strangely," Sheikh Abdullah says to Kamala after they sit down together in the Islamic Masjid of Jersey City. "Can we just get to the part where I say I'm sorry and skip the rest?" Kamala asks. "No we cannot. Because if something is wrong, I need to know about it," he replies.[43] What follows is kind and empathetic conversation between Kamala and the sheikh as he tries to give her what guidance he can based on what little information she will tell him.

The exchange is important for two reasons. First, it shows Kamala as a young Muslim woman who is not questioning her faith but instead is trying to find a way to live it that is authentic to herself while still respecting her parents and their traditions and expectations. Second, the discussion with Sheikh Abdullah is also important because of how he was portrayed in the panels. Historically, imams, sheikhs, and other Muslim religious leaders have been portrayed as overbearing, paternalistic, oppressive, and often violent.[44] Instead of being the religious fanatic that Muslim religious leaders are often portrayed as in media, Sheikh Abdullah is framed as a teacher and a guide during his exchange with Kamala. When he asks about her sneaking out of her home, Kamala explains, "I don't mean to disobey Abu and Ammi. It's just that sometimes I have to in order to do the right thing." To which the sheikh replies, "Well, if you're not very

38 POP ISLAM

good at it—helping people, that is—perhaps you need a teacher."[45] Kamala is shocked that instead of telling her not to disobey her parents, Sheikh Abdullah is telling her to find someone to help her get better at it because he knows a lecture to "avoid Satan and boys" would do no good: "I am asking you for something more difficult. If you insist on pursuing this thing you will not tell me about, do it with the qualities befitting an upright young woman: Courage, strength, honesty, compassion and self-respect."[46]

Kamala leaves her meeting with Sheikh Abdullah seemingly a bit more at ease with herself and not long after runs into a guide and teacher of another kind.

A longtime staple of Marvel Comics, the mutant Wolverine has been featured in numerous *X-Men* titles as well as books of his own. He's a tiny ball of rage of a man who, with his unbreakable metal skeleton and incendiary anger, epitomizes the scrappiest prizefighter version of masculinity imaginable. Wolverine, though shrouding himself in the cloak of a loner, is also often the first mutant to welcome recruits, particularly young ones, into the X-Men fold. He's also the first superhero Kamala encounters after adopting the Ms. Marvel persona. She runs into him as she is tracking her first nemesis through the sewers of Jersey City, and her reaction is one any fan might have—utter and gushing delight. "I can't believe it. I'm gonna pass out," she says after attempting to attack Wolverine before realizing who he is.

The inclusion of Wolverine so early in *Ms. Marvel*'s first arc of stories suggests that Marvel understands the importance of this hypermasculine character's embracing of the other—it suggests to readers that they, too, should trust this person. In the case of *Ms. Marvel*, the person happens to be a Muslim Pakistani American teenager, not the most trusted of demographics. By the end of the second issue Wolverine appears in, the mutant seems not only amused by Kamala but to also respect her. He ends his time with Kamala by calling up a friend, alerting her to Kamala's existence, and seemingly asking the friend to watch out for the teenager. "Kamala is one of us," he seems to be saying to both his friend and the reader—she is someone we can trust.

Kamala's interlude with Wolverine also serves to introduce the villain of this particular story: a clone of Thomas Edison, also called Thomas Edison, who is a hybrid man-cockatiel. Kamala works to save her friends and her community from this villain and other threats as she also works to understand what it means to be a superhero. Kamala grows, as both an individual and a hero, during the first run of *Ms. Marvel*. Kamala Khan's experience is a deeply human one, with her story often revolving around the important relationships in her life. There is the one with her parents, who want their daughter to be thoughtful about the choices she makes and to heed the advice of her elders. There is the sibling relationship framed by love and frustration as she spars with her more religiously conservative brother, Aamir, over her own devotion to Islam and her behavior outside the home. Her friend Nakia is constantly concerned that Kamala's occasional impetuous nature will get her in trouble, and Kamala's childhood buddy Bruno struggles to reconcile his feelings for her with the reality of their family situations—he's of Italian Catholic background while Kamala, as already made clear, is Muslim.

One thing the academic research on the children of immigrants has shown is that they often feel stuck—caught between the expectations of their parents' culture and the expectations of the culture in which they grow up, which can make it hard to know where they fit.[47] Kamala's transformation into Ms. Marvel is facilitated by that very tension. In the first issue, Kamala and her friends are invited to a party down by the river, with a blond teen boy saying to Kamala and Nakia, "You guys should come too. If, uh, you're allowed to do that kind of stuff."[48] As one might expect, when Kamala asks permission to go to the party, she is refused, which results in an enormous family blowup and Kamala being sent to her room. There's not a bedroom built that can keep a teenager from chasing her own desires, and Kamala sneaks out of her house and makes her way to the river. As Kamala prepares to climb down a tree outside her window and make her getaway, she mutters to herself, "Everybody else gets to be normal. Why can't I?"[49] This angst over not being normal is one many a teenager has experienced, but one that is only heightened by Kamala's identity as a Muslim, as the child of immigrants, and as a young woman of color. Down by the river, she runs into Zoe, a blond teen girl who seems set up to be Kamala's main antagonist, who asks if she's going to get in trouble if her parents find out that she's there. It's a question Bruno also asks when they run into one another, which leads to Kamala storming off from the party. It's after the argument with Bruno that a strange mist descends over the gathering, a mist that will bestow on Kamala her powers.

The transformation is a crisis moment for Kamala. Shocked by the rapid changes of her body—at one point, she assumes the physical form of blond Carol Danvers's Ms. Marvel—Kamala's actions in the aftermath of the misting are more instinctual than reasoned. Kamala, in the form of the blond Ms. Marvel, saves Zoe from drowning after she's knocked into the river and is photographed and recorded doing so. As she rushes from the river and heads toward home, Kamala grabs a coat from a homeless man who shouts at her, "Chilly out! Maybe you oughtta think about puttin' on some pants!"[50] When Kamala begins to make her way home, it dawns on her that something life-changing has happened, something that may have the potential to mark forever her difference and distance from her family. It's that family who confronts her in her bedroom when she returns from her outing, her father saying, "I'm disappointed in you, beta. Very disappointed."[51] Kamala attempts to tell first her brother and then her parents what has happened to her that night but stops when she realizes how ridiculous the story must sound. Kamala becomes the type of superhero she has spent her life idolizing because she decided to disobey her family, and now she is triply marked—an outsider because of her religion and skin color, a nerd because of her obsession with comic books, and now a superhero who must hide her supernature from those she loves.

The struggle Kamala faces in trying to navigate family along with her own needs and desires is poignantly highlighted about midway through *Ms. Marvel*'s first run when the son of family friends, Kamran, shows up in her home. He is handsome, thoughtful, and seemingly also chaffing at family expectations and Kamala develops a crush on Kamran as her friend Bruno jealously simmers on the sidelines. In Kamran, Kamala sees a compatriot who "gets" her, who understands her struggles to do what her family thinks is right and what she feels is right, who understands how much she just wants to live a "normal" life and not be marked by difference—be it racial, religious, or super. Kamran and Kamala grow close during the story arc, only to have Kamran eventually turn on Kamala. He throws into her face all the things she worries about; this becomes especially poignant when Kamran, working for a group with murky motives, kidnaps Aamir because they suspect he may have superpowers like Kamala. "You think some little part of Aamir isn't angry?" Kamran taunts Kamala. "Looking like he does, believing what he does . . . you think he doesn't wish he could live in a world where he gets to make the rules?"[52]

As Sophia Rose Arjana points out, up to this point in the narrative, "Aamir and Kamala represent the dichotomy between the 'traditional' and 'progressive' Muslim."[53] Kamran is suggesting that because he feels marginalized because he's a conservative Muslim and because he has experienced racism, Aamir would be more than willing to embrace any superpowers he might have in order to shake things up in Jersey City. Kamran is raising the specter of the violent Muslim man in his exchange with Kamala. But as Arjana also points out, the division between "traditional" and "progressive" is a false one. It is as Kamala rescues Aamir that the falsity of that division is made clear.

When Kamala, working with Captain Marvel, finds Aamir, he is shrouded in a mist similar to the one that presaged Kamala's transformation into Ms. Marvel. Kamran and the group he works for are trying to activate whatever powers lie latent in Aamir. As Aamir comes to be shrouded in strange green light, Kamran explains that he can help Aamir connect to a new community, a new family of sorts, so that Aamir can embrace his destiny. "I've already got a family," Aamir says, "And you are going to stay away from them—from all of us. Especially Kamala."[54] When Kamran expresses his disbelief that Aamir could possibly be happy with his life, "You're a ... you're ..." "I'm a what?" Aamir asks. "A religious freak? An MSA nerd? A Salafi? Yeah. I'm all of those things. And I'm not ashamed of any of them. And if you think that means you can take advantage of my sister—that I'll blame her for whatever happened between you, while you sashay off into the sunset 'cause you're a guy and nothing is ever your fault—well, my brother, you would be incorrect."[55]

Watching the exchange, Kamala is surprised by what she hears: "He—he doesn't hate me. Sometimes I used to think he did." Aamir's exchange with Kamran highlights all the stereotypes associated with conservative, religious Muslim men while also suggesting how shortsighted and ill informed they actually are. It throws into relief the good Muslim / bad Muslim binary Evelyn Alsultany suggests media representations often fall into (when not wholly focusing on portrayals of bad Muslims).[56] Aamir's monologue and his relationship with his seemingly more progressive sister complicates that binary. When he and Kamala finally make their way back to their parents, Kamala nurses Aamir's injuries as he says he will turn to this religion his religion to find his way forward, saying to his sister, "Allah never burdens a soul beyond its capacity."[57]

By the end of the narrative arc involving Kamran, Kamala has come to realize that the sacrifices incumbent to a superhero's life might be more than she can bear, might be beyond her capacity to manage alone. Can she be a good friend and Ms. Marvel? Can she be the daughter she wants to be and still fight for what's right? Can she be Muslim and super? This struggle leads Kamala to eventually admit to her mother that she is Ms. Marvel. Instead of the angry reaction she had been expecting, her mother simply says, "Oh, beta ... I know,"[58] suggesting, perhaps, that Kamala may not have to fight for the good of her community alone, that she could choose to allow others to support her.

The concept of choice is a major theme throughout the first run of *Ms. Marvel*. Kamala is often forced to choose between obedience and what she feels is morally right, between family and duty, between love and justice. These are choices that many of us face; they are familiar choices to us as readers. Our father may not have sent us to the sheikh when we were behaving poorly, but certainly many of us have had to deal with a scolding and angry parent. Many of us have had to choose, at some point, between doing what we *feel* is right and doing what our parents think is right. As Kamala is learning what it means to be a superhero, she often finds herself considering how duty, compassion, and heroism intersect. A few of the most powerful panels in the first run of

Ms. Marvel focus on Kamala's contemplation of this intersection. One series of panels comes after Kamala has embiggened a few times to take on bad guys but in doing so has had to again disobey her parents. After sneaking in late one night, she is discovered eating in the kitchen by her parents. Her mother yells at her and then leaves the room, but her father stays behind to talk with her. He asks Kamala what's wrong, she says she's fine, and he says he wants to believe her. He then explains the meaning of her name.

> "Do you know why we named you Kamala?" he asks.
>
> "No. It's a weird name. Everybody else gets to be Yasmine and Layla and stuff," she responds.
>
> "It's a special name," he says. "Kamal means 'perfection' in Arabic. Your mother had a very difficult time when she was pregnant with Aamir. After he was born, the doctors told us we couldn't have any more children. We were devastated. Then, five years later, you came along. Our little miracle. I held you in my hands at the hospital—a tiny, screaming, pinkish-brown baby—and thought you were the most perfect thing I had ever seen. That's why we gave you your name. You don't have to be someone else to impress anybody. You are perfect just the way you are."[59]

By the end of the chat, Kamala's father has pulled her into his arms, as though with that hug, he could prove to her just how perfect she is to him.

The conversation is the catalyst that ultimately forces Kamala to embrace her new superhero nature. To this point, she had been trying to do things the way Captain Marvel or other comic book heroes she adored might; after her conversation in the kitchen with her father, she ponders his admonition that she is perfect just the way she is. Seemingly a day later, after working with Bruno to figure out the limitations of her ability to embiggen, Kamala decides to alter the blue burkini she had been wearing when venturing out at night as Ms. Marvel. It is as she begins the process of adding what will become her iconic yellow lightning bolt that Kamala finally understands what good means for her. "Good is not a thing you are," she says. "It's a thing you do."[60]

It is a powerful moment because, historically in media, good has not been a thing that Muslims are allowed to do but has been a thing done to them—in the guise of the civilizing mission of Western imperial expansion or in the liberation offered by Western forms of feminism. Muslims are not often portrayed as individuals who choose to do good, and when they are, their goodness is often portrayed as somehow inferior, as was the case with Malala Yousafzai. In the summer of 2019, Yousafzai was photographed with Quebec's education minister. The two met to discuss education and international development.

The minister is a supporter of Quebec's ban on the wearing of hijab by public schoolteachers in the province and people on social media called him out on the hypocrisy of his supporting the Quebec headscarf ban and posing with a hijab-wearing Yousafzai.[61] The minister responded to this criticism by saying that, of course, were Yousafzai to teach in a Quebec school she'd have to do so without her headscarf.[62] The good that Malala Yousafzai has done as a youth and education activist, good that garnered her a Nobel Peace Prize in 2014, was seemingly not good *enough* because of her headscarf.

Throughout *Ms. Marvel*, we see Kamala Khan struggling to make the choice, for herself, of what is good against the background of her faith and her cultural heritage. This struggle arises not only in connection to her calling as a hero for Jersey City but also in her interactions with others in her day-to-day life as an American teenager. She is seen sniffing haram bacon in the convenience store her friend Bruno runs, telling her friends how much she'd love to taste it but ultimately walking away from temptation. When facing the Birdman's henchmen of rabid teens, Kamala's first impulse is to try to save or rehabilitate them, not hurt them. Her desire for justice means she continually chooses compassion over violence when she can. Kamala's continual dialogue about good being a choice and her continually choosing love over hate is a reminder to the reader that love *is* a valid choice, that to do good is to lead with love. It stands in stark contrast to the stereotyped idea that Muslims are inherently violent and are somehow supernaturally fueled by hate and anger.

Doing good is something Kamala commits to and follows through on even when the odds seem impossible. Throughout the series, Kamala finds herself in situations where she feels like she's failing, where she or someone she cares about is in danger of being hurt. Kamala's heroism arises not out of an ability to overcome suffering but in discovering that she can't—she won't—win every battle. This is made poignantly visible at the end of the first series' run. Kamala finds herself on top of her high school with Bruno, the two of them watching what seems to be the destruction of their hometown and possibly the end of the world. In the building below are all the people in their community they love and care about, people whom Kamala, with the help of Bruno and her other friends, has been able to get to safety. Alone together, Kamala and Bruno seem to realize the safety they've been able to provide their loved ones may only be temporary. Standing in the glow of the end of the world, Bruno tells Kamala he loves her. "It's not like I imagined it would be," Kamala narrates as she and Bruno are engulfed in a bright, white light, "The end of the world. It doesn't feel like nothing. Standing here with my best friend, it feels like everything. Everything and more."[63]

Good is a choice, Kamala is reminded again and again. Good is a choice that Kamala makes again and again. Good is a choice, one that may not always produce the outcome Kamala wants but that feels true to who she believes herself to be. It's a choice media have rarely shown American Muslims making.

After they rescue Aamir, and before she flies off to whatever battle awaits in New York, Captain Marvel hands Kamala a pendant that combines Kamala's lightning bolt and Captain Marvel's star. "I wanted you to have something you could hold. To remind you that you don't have to do all this alone," Captain Marvel tells her.[64] After the two share a hug, Captain Marvel warns Kamala of what's coming, reminds her that people are depending on Ms. Marvel, and finally tells Kamala she's proud of her as she flies away. Just as Wolverine suggested to the audience that Kamala was someone we could all trust, Captain Marvel is telling readers that the new Ms. Marvel is one of us.

Kamala's participation in the Avengers fandom and her writing of fan fiction places her inside the community the book is trying to reach. Kamala is both insider and outsider; her comic serves as a third space in which identity negotiation is made visible as she traverses her various roles and worlds and as she struggles to understand what it means to her to be Muslim, American, and super. Kamala is these things individually, but they are all so interwoven into her identity that it is hard to know where one ends and the other begins. Her identity is complex and complicated, which is something rarely seen in media representations of Muslims. The series never shies away from Kamala's religion. Her brother, Aamir, is studying in hopes of becoming an imam. In Sheikh Abdullah, Kamala finds an adult who will engage in an open, honest, respectful dialogue with her about Islam. Kamala's best friend from grade school, Nakia, wears hijab and both girls discuss their faith—in public and in masjid. Though Nakia sometimes chides Kamala for rushing into situations or for speaking before thinking, there is never an insinuation that one woman's experience of Islam is more correct or more devout than the other's. There is no attempt to hide Kamala's Muslim identity from anyone or to make her religious choices seem either exceptional or better than those of another.

Even her choice to create her supersuit out of the burkini her mother bought her signals her religious identity. Uncomfortable in the revealing superhero suit she first finds herself in when transforming, she crafts one that feels more her, that is a better reflection of who she feels she is. Kamala's choice of supersuit is a stark contrast with those seen on other female superheroes, including another teenage crime fighter. In her discussion of the representation of gender and race in Marvel's *Amazing Fantasy* and *Araña* comic books, Karen McGrath points out that the fifteen-year-old superhero of those stories, while seemingly aware of the objectification and sexualization of her body, still chooses a midriff-baring shirt and tight spandex pants for her costume. She's aware of her sexualization but cannot escape it.[65] Kamala can and does. Her clothing allows for ease of movement when she's embiggening and punching and kicking bad guys while also making her feel safe and at ease as she does so. The mask she wears over her eyes allows her to cover her face while the tunic and leggings allow her to cover her body so that the focus is on her, on her abilities and her strengths, not, to borrow phrasing from songwriter Ed Sheeran, on the shape of her. Her costume is both modest and practical.

The use of the colors red and blue in the costumes of superheroes is often designed to project a kind of patriotism and help American audiences connect to the fantastical person behind the cape and mask. Marvel's Captain America is the very embodiment of this, swathed in the colors and carrying a blazing white star on his shield for good measure. The epitome of the male superhero, Superman, wears blue and red in a nod to the new life he built in the United States after being exiled as an infant from his native planet. It is no small thing that Kamala chooses red and blue for the colors of her own Ms. Marvel uniform. They were the colors worn by the original Ms. Marvel, Carol Danvers, but they are also American colors. The red and blue, as opposed to the pink and black teased on the cover of the very first issue of Kamala's run as Ms. Marvel, suggest she is not only a Muslim superhero; she is an American one as well.

A single comic book series with a Muslim superhero will not change how Americans understand Muslims on its own. However, what it can do is enlarge—or embiggen, to use Kamala's term—the framework individuals have access to for understanding Islam and Muslim life. By transforming their superhero Ms. Marvel into an American Muslim teenager, Marvel seems to be suggesting that Muslims are trustworthy. Through her interactions with first Wolverine and then Captain Marvel, Kamala Khan is shown to be a rightful inheritor of the mantle of Ms. Marvel even if her religion in other media is often framed as anti-Western, anti-American, and the very opposite of super. Kamala's struggle with all facets of her identity—including the fantastic and the religious—is a familiar one, even if her religion is not.

Perhaps more important than Kamala simply appearing in the comic books is the fact that she is also a playable character in a number of different Marvel video games. Now, not only do Americans have the ability to read about her struggles to reconcile her faith with all the other parts of her identity, but they can also choose to *be* the Muslim Ms. Marvel. They can live her life, even if it's only within the parameters of a video-game world. But, still, the ability to be a

Fig. 1.5 After Kamala Khan's popularity soared, she began appearing in a number of other Marvel properties, including Marvel video games. In *Marvel's Avengers*, players can actually be Ms. Marvel, using her power to embiggen to take on villains in the game as well as reassemble the Avengers team.

Muslim character in a video game and to have that character not be a villain is a fairly massive change. Kamala has also appeared in the *Avengers: Secret Wars* cartoon, fighting with such heroes as Ant-Man, Vision, and her predecessor in the Ms. Marvel role, Captain Marvel. The Muslim Ms. Marvel is not being treated like a side story in a longer story arc, she's being folded into a number of different Marvel properties. With each appearance, with each story, she presents to readers, viewers, and players a Muslim identity that is framed by love and by doing good, not by jihad or terrorism.

In writing of the way diverse representation in media can at times feel empty, Kristin Warner notes that media producers (and sometimes audiences) will uncritically embrace a positive representation even if there's not much to it. She calls this idea "plastic representation"[66] because while the representation seems meaningful on its surface, if you dig deep, you find that it is hollow and lacks any real substance. Though Kamala stretches like soft plastic when she's in the midst of fighting for what's right, her appearance in the comic book series and other Marvel media properties is the opposite of plastic representation as her

Fig. 1.6 Kamala Khan's version of Ms. Marvel has become enormously popular with comic book fans from all backgrounds. Conventions and other events regularly see individuals cosplaying as the character. A group of cosplaying *Ms. Marvel* fans got to meet original writer G. Willow Wilson at 2016 San Diego Comic Con. (Photo courtesy of cosplayer Sonthebun)

Ms. Marvel is uniquely her own. Kamala's Ms. Marvel is a hero whose religion and immigrant background is an important aspect of her identity, not just window dressing. A trust test of whether Kamala's representation is plastic or not will depend on how her ethnic, religious, and racial identities are treated in media designed to continue Marvel's moneymaking success. Will she become trapped by the visibility such media provide or will Kamala's fans and critical praise allow her a more nimble and nuanced representation than Muslims have had in the past? Things look promising so far.

In June 2022, Marvel and Disney+ released to critical praise the TV miniseries *Ms. Marvel* based on the comic book series. The actress cast to play Kamala, Canadian Iman Vellani, is, like Kamala, the teenage daughter of Muslim immigrants from Pakistan. Though the show at times veered from the story in its source material, it was also celebrated for presenting an image on TV of a Muslim who was not a villain—a Muslim who continually chose to do good. The show also serves to set up the Marvel Studios film *The Marvels*, which will see Captain Marvel Carol Danvers and Ms. Marvel Kamala Khan team up on the big screen for the first time. Kamala's fans are already legion—the question

48   POP ISLAM

remains whether the TV show and movie will capitalize on what audiences loved about the character. And audiences do love her.

Though Kamala Khan was celebrated by many members of American Muslim communities, non-Muslims have also embraced the newest Ms. Marvel. Critics have been charmed by her obsessive love of comic book heroes and her plucky personality, while others have found reflections of themselves in Kamala's all-American teenage struggle to find her place in the world. Comic cons are filled with men, women, and children wearing Kamala's now-iconic blue tunic and red scarf with cosplayers coming in all shapes, sizes, and races. All of them trying to channel the spunky spirit of the Muslim Ms. Marvel. Kamala's story has not only embiggened American understandings of what it means to be Muslim; it is also working to embiggen understandings of what it means to be American.

A short coda: As this book goes into press, Marvel Comics has killed of Kamala Khan outside her title. The Muslim Ms. Marvel was stabbed in Spider-Man's book as she was protecting perennial Spider-Man love interest Mary Jane Parker.[67] Fans of the superheroine quickly took to social media when news of Ms. Marvel's death was made public, accusing Marvel Comics of "fridging" their popular character in order to prop up white Peter Parker.[68] Publications focused on popular media also took Marvel to task over their killing of Kamala, with one individual noting that, while Spider-Man's current writer suggested Ms. Marvel was a "pivotal" supporting character, she in fact really only shows up in time to sacrifice herself to save Mary Jane.[69] Killing off Kamala Khan outside her own series served to show that even a character who might help embiggen American understandings of the American experience wasn't immune from being treated as a disposable other in the end. After news of Kamala's death died down, Marvel announced she would be resurrected in a new series "Ms Marvel: New Mutant" which would see her join the storied X-Men franchise.[70] The series will be written by Imani Vellani, who played Kamala on the Disney+ show, and Sabir Pirzada, who was the show's writer. Reportedly part of the storyline will involve Kamala's family not knowing she's alive, leaving many fans wondering what other aspects of her life will have to be erased as she explores her new mutant identity.

NOTES

1. Andrew Wheeler, "Oh Captain My Captain: How Carol Danvers Became Marvel's Biggest Female Hero," *Comics Alliance*, November 10, 2014, http://comicsalliance.com/captain-marvel-carol-danvers-marvel-biggest-female-hero/.
2. Ibid.

3. Phoebe Gloeckner, "Comic Books: A Medium Deserving Another Look," *ETC: A Review of General Semantics* 46, no. 3 (1989): 246.

4. Jon Hogan, "The Comic Book as Symbolic Environment: The Case of Iron Man," *ETC: A Review of General Semantics* 66, no. 2 (2009): 199–214, quotation at 201.

5. Francisco Veloso and John Bateman, "The Multimodal Construction of Acceptability: Marvel's Civil War and the PATRIOT Act," *Critical Discourse Studies* 10, no. 4 (2013): 427–43, quotation at 428.

6. Ibid., 430.

7. J. Gavin Paul, "Ashes in the Gutter: 9/11 and the Serialization of Memory in DC Comics' Human Target," *American Periodicals* 17, no. 2 (2007): 208–27.

8. Hogan, "The Comic Book as Symbolic Environment," 199.

9. Ariela Freedman, "'Sorting through My Grief and Putting It into Boxes': Comics and Pain," in *Knowledge and Pain*, ed. Esther Cohen, Leona Toker, Manuela Consonni, and Otoniel E. Dror (Leiden, The Netherlands: Brill, 2012), 381–99.

10. Micheal E. Staub, "The Shoah Goes On and On: Remembrance and Representation in Art Spiegelman's *Maus*," *Melus* 20, no. 3 (1995): 33–46, quotation at 33.

11. Thomas Doherty, "Art Spiegelman's *Maus*: Graphic Art and the Holocaust," *American Literature* 68, no. 1 (1996): 69–84.

12. John Trushell, "American Dreams of Mutants: The X-Men-'Pulp' Fiction, Science Fiction, and Superheroes," *Journal of Popular Culture* 38, no. 1 (2004): 149–68.

13. Joseph Darowksi, *X-Men and the Mutant Metaphor: Race and Gender in the Comic Books* (Lanham, MD: Rowman & Littlefield, 2014).

14. Marco Amaudo, *The Myth of the Superhero* (Baltimore: Johns Hopkins University Press, 2013).

15. Martin Lund, *Re-constructing the Man of Steel: Superman 1938–1941, Jewish American History, and the Invention of Jewish-Comics Connection* (New York: Palgrave Macmillan, 2016).

16. Amaudo, *Myth of the Superhero*; Art Spiegelman, "Golden Age of Superheroes Were Shaped by the Rise of Fascism," *Guardian*, August 17, 2019, https://www.theguardian.com/books/2019/aug/17/art-spiege-man-golden-age-superheroes-were-shaped-by-the-rise-of-fascism.

17. Gary Engle, "What Makes Superman So Darned American?," in *Popular Culture: An Introductory Text*, ed. Jack Nachbar and Kevin Lause (Bowling Green, OH: Popular Press, 1992), 314–43.

18. Anton K. Kozlovic, "Superman as Christ-Figure: The American Pop Culture Movie Messiah," *Journal of Religion and Film* 6, no. 1 (2016): article 5; Sarah Kozloff, "Superman as Saviour: Christian Allegory in the Superman Movies," *Journal of Popular Film and Television* 9, no. 2 (1981): 78–82; Adam Barkman, "Superman: From Anti-Christ to Christ-Type," in *Superman and*

Philosophy: What Would the Man of Steel Do?, ed. Mark T. White (Malden, MA: Wiley Blackwell, 2013), 111–20.

19. Scholars have long connected Superman's identity and origin with that of the Jewish faith and identity of his creators. However, there has been some debate over how overt this connection was meant to be. Martin Lund in his 2016 book, *Re-constructing the Man of Steel*, argues that scholars have overgeneralized, and perhaps been too loose, in their finding of an overt Jewish-Superman connection. Though, in a review of Lund's book, Chris Reyns-Chikuma suggests that Lund's work lacks a "thickness" that would produce a more contextualized reading that might consider the ways Jewish American identity has been made more or less visible in relation to the ebb and flow of American identity politics. (For the review see: Chris Reyns-Chikuma, "Lund, Martin. Re-constructing the Man of Steel: Superman 1938–1941, Jewish American History, and the Invention of Jewish–Comics," *Belphégor: Littérature populaire et culture médiatique* 15, no. 2 [2017] https://journals.openedition.org/belphegor/947).

20. Harry Brod, *Superman Is Jewish? How Comic Book Superheroes Came to Serve Truth, Justice, and the Jewish-American Way* (New York: Free Press, 2012).

21. Ibid., xviii.

22. Karen McGrath, "Gender, Race, and Latina Identity: An Examination of Marvel Comics," *Atlantic Journal of Communication* 15, no. 4 (2007): 268–83, quotation at 272.

23. Edward Avaray-Natale, "An Analysis of Embodiment of Six Superheroes in DC Comics," *Social Thought and Research* 32 (2013): 71–106.

24. Carolyn Cocca, "The 'Broke Back Test': A Quantitative and Qualitative Analysis of Portrayals of Women in Mainstream Superhero Comics, 1993–2013," *Journal of Graphic Noves and Comics* 5, no. 4 (2014): 411–28.

25. Alex Abad-Santos, "Spider-Woman Isn't Good for Women When She Looks Like This," Vox, August 20, 2014, https://www.vox.com/xpress/2014 /8/20/6046577/marvel-spider-woman-cover-sexist.

26. Elain Dockterman, "Marvel Is Actually Going to Publish That Sexist Spider-Woman Cover," *Time*, November 19, 2014, https://time.com/3594514 /marvel-spider-woman-cover/.

27. Rob Bricken, "Check Out Spider-Woman #1, Starring Spider-Woman's Ass," *io9*, August 20, 2014, https://io9.gizmodo.com/check-out-spider-woman -1-starring-spider-womans-ass-1624535918.

28. Katie Rife, "Marvel Cancels Milo Manara Covers after Spider-Woman Butt Controversy," AV Club, September 23, 2014, https://news.avclub.com /marvel-cancels-milo-manara-covers-after-spider-woman-bu-1798272365.

29. Anna Beatrice Scott, "Superpower vs. Supernatural: Black Superheroes and the Quest for a Mutant Reality," *Journal of Visual Culture* 5, no. 3 (2006): 295–314, quotation on 312.

30. Derek Parker Royal, "Coloring America: Multi-Ethnic Engagements with Graphic Narrative," *Melus* 32, no. 3 (2007): 7–22, quotation on 7.

31. Jack Shaheen, "Arab Images in Comic Books," *Journal of Popular Culture* 28, no. 1 (1994): 123–33.

32. Nicholas Pumphrey, "Avenger, Mutant, or Allah: A Short Evolution of the Depiction of Muslims in Marvel Comics," *Muslim World* 1 (2015): 781–94.

33. Lila Abu-Lughod, "Do Muslim Women Really Need Saving? Anthropological Reflections on Cultural Relativism and Its Others," *American Anthropologist* 104, no. 3 (2002): 783–90.

34. Miranda Brar, "The Nation and Its Burka Avenger, the 'Other,' and Its Malala Yusafzai: The Creation of a Female Muslim Archetype as the Site for Pakistani Nationalism," *Prandium—The Journal of Historical Studies* 3, no. 1 (2014): 1–8, quotation at 5.

35. Sophia Rose Arjana, *Veiled Superheroes: Islam, Feminism, and Popular Culture* (Lanham, MD: Lexington Books, 2017).

36. Pumphrey, "Avenger, Mutant, or Allah," 793.

37. James Whitbrook, "Kamala Khan's Creator Is Stepping Away from Ms. Marvel," *io9*, December 14, 2018, https://io9.gizmodo.com/kamala-khans -creator-is-stepping-away-from-ms-marvel-1831104153.

38. Jamie Frevele, "Farewell to Ms. Marvel: An Open Letter from G. Willow Wilson," Marvel.com, December 14, 2018, https://www.marvel.com/articles /comics/farewell-to-ms-marvel-an-open-letter-from-g-willow-wilson.

39. Ibid.

40. Joshua Yehl, "Ms. Marvel #1 Review," IGN, February 5, 2014, https://www .ign.com/articles/2014/02/05/ms-marvel-1-review-2.

41. Miriam Kent, "Unveiling Marvels: Ms. Marvel and the Reception of the New Muslim Superheroine," *Feminist Media Studies* 15, no. 3 (2015): 522–27.

42. Nabil Echchaibi, "Unveiling Obsessions: Muslims and the Trap of Representation," in *On Islam: Muslims and the Media*, ed. R. Pennington and H. Kahn (Bloomington: Indiana University Press, 2018), 57–70.

43. G. Willow Wilson, *Ms. Marvel*, no. 006 (New York: Marvel, 2014).

44. Sophia Rose Arjana, *Muslims in the Western Imagination* (Oxford: Oxford University Press, 2015); Edward Said, *Orientalism* (New York: Vintage, 1979).

45. Wilson, *Ms. Marvel*, no. 006.

46. Ibid.

47. For a deeper understanding of this issue, see Jennifer Brinkerhoff, *Digital Diasporas: Identity and Transnational Engagement* (New York: Cambridge University Press, 2009); Myria Georgiou, *Diaspora, Identity, and Media: Diasporic Transnationalisms and Mediated Spacialities* (Cresskill, NJ: Hampton Press, 2006); David Morley and Kevin Robins, *Spaces of Identity: Global Media, Electronic Landscapes and Cultural Boundaries* (New York: Routledge, 1995);

Christine Ogan, *Communication and Identity in the Diaspora: Turkish Migrants in Amsterdam and Their Use of Media* (Lanham, MD: Lexington Books, 2001).

48. G. Willow Wilson, *Ms. Marvel*, no. 001 (New York: Marvel, 2014).

49. Ibid.

50. G. Willow Wilson, *Ms. Marvel*, no. 002 (New York: Marvel, 2014).

51. Ibid.

52. G. Willow Wilson, *Ms. Marvel*, no. 016 (New York: Marvel, 2014).

53. Arjana, *Veiled Superheroes*, 59.

54. G. Willow Wilson, *Ms. Marvel*, no. 018 (New York: Marvel, 2014).

55. Ibid.

56. Evelyn Alsultany, *Arabs and Muslims in Media: Race and Rrepresentation after 9/11* (New York: New York University Press, 2012).

57. Wilson, *Ms. Marvel*, no. 018.

58. Ibid.

59. G. Willow Wilson, *Ms. Marvel*, no. 005 (New York: Marvel, 2014).

60. Ibid.

61. Ashleigh Stewart, "'Shameful Hypocrisy': Canadian Education Minister Called Out after Posting Picture with Malala Yousafzai," *National AE*, July 7, 2019, https://www.thenational.ae/arts-culture/shameful-hypocrisy-canadian -education-minister-called-out-after-posting-picture-with-malala -yousafzai-1.883403.

62. Rowaida Abdelaziz, "Malala Would Have to Remove Her Headscarf to Teach in Quebec: Education Minister," HuffPost, July 9, 2019, https://www .huffpost.com/entry/malala-quebec-education-headscarf_n_5d238397e4b04c4 814183c83.

63. G. Willow Wilson, *Ms. Marvel*, no. 019 (New York: Marvel, 2014).

64. Ibid.

65. McGrath, "Gender, Race, and Latina Identity."

66. Kristin Warner, "In the Time of Plastic Representation," *Film Quarterly* 71, no. 2 (2017): 32–37.

67. Avi Gibson, "Even Marvel Knows Its Handling of Kamala Khan's Death Was Disrespectful," Screen Rant, July, 18, 2023, https://screenrant.com/ms -marvel-kamala-khan-death-disrespectful-mutant-mcu/.

68. Ibid.

69. Pierre Chanlieu, "Why the Death of Ms. Marvel Is a Major Insult to Fans," The Direct, May 29, 2023, https://thedirect.com/article/ms-marvel-death-fans.

70. Marvel.com, "Kamala Khan Joins the X-Men in 'Ms. Marvel: New Mutant,'" July 18, 2023, https://www.marvel.com/articles/comics/ms-marvel -the-new-mutant-variant-covers-kamala-khan-joins-x-men.

TWO

—w—

THE SCRIPTED LIVES OF
TV MUSLIMS

ABC'S DRAMA *LOST* IS PERHAPS one of the most important TV shows of
the early twenty-first century. Regularly ranked as one of the best American
dramas, the program features a group of plane crash survivors as they struggle
to find a way off the Pacific island where they awoke amid wreckage. Over the
course of six seasons, viewers watched as a core group of the survivors work to
get off the island and then come to terms with the lives they left behind there.
The show deals with issues both transcendental and mundane, leaving viewers
pondering this life as well as the next. Surgeon Jack Shepard serves as the flawed
and fragile leader of the main group of survivors, in love with another survivor
but unable to love himself. A different surgeon also serves as one of *Lost*'s main
characters and as one of the moral hearts of the show.

When Sayid Jarrah—whose last name can be translated from Arabic into
English as "surgeon"—first appears on the island he is accused, because of his
brown skin and accent, of having been responsible for the plane's crash. He is
engaged in a fistfight with fellow survivor Sawyer, a white man with a thick
southern accent. As they are separated, Sayid yells at Sawyer, "Tell everyone
what you told me! Tell them that I crashed the plane! Go on, tell them that
I made the plane crash!"[1] When asked what's going on, Sawyer and another
survivor explain that handcuffs were found near the crash site. Sawyer then
points at Sayid and says, "And this guy was sitting in the back row of business
class the whole flight. Never got up. Hands folded underneath the blanket. And
for some reason, just pointing this out, the guy sitting next to him didn't make
it."[2] Because of his skin color and his background, and because Sawyer claims
to have seen him pulled out of the boarding line for an extra security check,

Fig. 2.1 In the season 6 *LOST* episode "The Candidate," the survivors attempt to escape the island on a submarine. As they are diving, they discover that a bomb has been unknowingly carried aboard by one of them. In order to save the rest, Sayid scoops up the bomb and runs toward the other end of the submarine in order to give his friends a chance of surviving the explosion.

Sawyer assumes Sayid is the criminal who had been wearing the handcuffs. Sayid, by simply existing, is suspect.

Almost always dressed in undershirts that show off his muscly arms and shoulders, suggesting a powerful and masculine physicality, Sayid has a quiet and easygoing manner that is only disturbed when he is confronted with overt racist behavior, like that of Sawyer, or when he is pushed into violence by forces outside his control. His almost serene way of speaking and moving through the world obscure his violent past and stand in stark contrast with the potent moments of violence Sayid is sometimes pushed into. The specter of violence is something Sayid is seen to struggle with throughout his arc on the program—both on the island and off. He is an interesting, complicated character in a show full of them.

Sayid's first name is another interesting aspect of the character. Written as Sayid, it is sometimes used as an English version of the word *sayyid*. In Arabic the term *sayid* refers to an individual who is happy or blessed while the word *sayyid* indicates that an individual is a descendant of the Prophet Muhammad. Sayyids are considered nobility in many Muslim cultures, and in Iraq, where *Lost*'s Sayid comes from, even poor sayyids were set above other Muslims of a similar socioeconomic background.[3] Whether poor or wealthy, Sayid Jarrah's name suggests a noble heritage for the character, even if he behaved in sometimes ignoble ways while serving in Iraq's Republican Guard. His fellow survivors find out about Sayid's involvement in the organization when he offers to try to repair the wrecked plane's radio in an effort to try to get help. Sayid explains he learned how to use such devices while serving in military intelligence. When asked what branch of the military he served in, Sayid responds, "The Republican Guard" to which fellow castaway Hurley visibly blanches.[4]

Sayid's connection to Iraq's Republican Guard, an elite military group known for its use of violence and torture while operating under Saddam Hussein,[5] conjures up the ancient stereotype of the cruel and brutal Muslim man that Sawyer used to justify his attack on Sayid in the immediate aftermath of the crash. Historically, Muslim men have been seen as violent, irrational brutes who lack control over their worst impulses.[6] This narrative was perpetuated in discourses of domination and of imperialism with the help of various types of media—both popular and serious in nature. Sayid's admission of his involvement with the Republican Guard, and his admission of his use of torture while a member of it, sets his characterization within this historic "violent Muslim men" framework, even if his first name suggests something less violent and more spiritual. Sayid's flashbacks of his time in Iraq even show him torturing his love interest, Nadia, while in the guard. This framing of Muslim men as violent in political, cultural, and media discourses has perpetuated the idea that they are perpetually suspicious characters.[7]

Suspicion frames the first season of *Lost*, as the survivors of the plane crash work to find a way to live together on the island. There are debates over what types of punishments should be meted out for what crimes by what individuals. There are debates over what spiritual beliefs or philosophies should guide the community the survivors would have to build together. At one point, the group splits in two: one group wants to stay on the beach where they crashed in the hope that rescuers might find them; the other wants to go into the jungle on the island to look for food, potable water, and shelter. As Jack attempts to justify his decision to head into the jungle to Sayid, Sayid looks at him and asks, "Is there a reason you didn't consult us when you decided to form your own civilization?" It is a pointed question, one loaded with histories of imperialism and colonization as Sayid asks it.

Sayid's home country of Iraq lies in the Fertile Crescent, imagined as the "cradle of civilization"—although, during Europe's colonization of what would become Iraq and its neighboring countries, that history was erased as the colonizers promised to civilize and modernize the Middle East. Samuel Huntington's clash of civilizations theory—the idea that historic and unmalleable cultural differences would spawn wars between the East and West in the aftermath of the Cold War—fueled political rhetoric and informed American foreign policy when *Lost* premiered.[8] Sayid's question to Jack about his founding of a "civilization" seems to be, in a way, not only a critique of Jack's assumption of a leadership role among the survivors but also a critique of the ways white men have assumed they have the right and the ability to civilize others.

Civilized or not, Sayid is one of the few original survivors to make it all the way to the series' end. Along the way, he fights shadow monsters and human monsters, and he leaves the island only to return to it. Throughout all of it, he seems almost apathetic about his continued existence, seeming at times to be merely marking time rather than actually living. It is when other survivors are in danger that he breaks out of his ennui, looking for ways to help or to avenge them, often willing to sacrifice his own physical well-being or even his life for the sake of others. The violence perpetuated by this Muslim man is not the violence of a terrorist or a suicide bomber; it is the violence of an avenging angel or a pathos-fueled antihero. When Sayid's death wish is finally fulfilled, it is during an act of sacrifice as a group of survivors work to escape the island on a commandeered submarine. On the sub, the group finds a bomb that Sawyer accidentally sets off. Sawyer is the character who first questioned whether Sayid is a danger to the group, and it is Sawyer who sets him up to be, in this moment, its savior. As the bomb begins counting down, Sayid picks it up and runs to the other end of the submarine, embracing and running into the act of violence rather than being pushed into it. Sayid's death on *Lost* is heroic and is the inverse of the stereotyped representation of the Muslim suicide bomber frequently found in popular media. Rather than being a Muslim who kills himself in an attempt to kill and harm others, Sayid sacrifices himself in a bombing to save others. But even dying a hero's death, Sayid played second fiddle to *Lost*'s white male hero, dying so that Jack might be able to complete his work and move on.[9] Sayid even says to Jack as he picks up the bomb, "It is going to be you, Jack"[10]—implying that it is Jack who will find a way to save the remaining survivors. Sayid's identity as an Iraqi and as a Muslim are integral facets of his characterization; he was not a plastic representation of a Muslim, but in the end, he was an expendable one.

In his book, *Orientalism*, Edward Said shed light on the ways artistic and cultural Orientalism was used to prop up Europe's expansion into lands it considered "other"—often lands where Muslims lived.[11] The ideas produced by Orientalist writers, thinkers, and artists about the Orient, Said argued, framed it as an unmodern, seductive, and sometimes savage place that needed the intervention of Western thinking and Western modernity if it ever hoped to

THE SCRIPTED LIVES OF TV MUSLIMS   57

emerge from the sands of the past. The Orient was monstrous because it was
not Western—it was not modern. Upon first glance, Sayid Jarrah seems as
though he is cut whole cloth from Orientalist tropes. And yet, over the course
of the first few episodes of *Lost*'s first season, it becomes clear that Sayid is not
a Muslim monster; instead, he is a complicated, thoughtful, Muslim antihero
and monster *fighter*. Sayid never fails to warn other survivors that he could be a
threat—"My name is Sayid Jarrah and I am a torturer"[12] he says in one second-
season episode—but the violence Sayid commits on the island is generally to
protect the other survivors. Sayid is depicted as a Muslim man who is capable
of violence but who does not approach it in an irrational manner. Sayid was a hit
man (off the island) and a torturer who was himself tortured, he is complicated
in a way that few (if any) Muslim characters had been allowed to be before *Lost*,
complicated in a way few members of minority groups have been allowed to
be on American television. This chapter explores the representation of Muslim
characters in American prime-time TV dramas to understand the kinds of
Muslim experiences American audiences are exposed to.

Television has been imagined both as a place of wonders and as a waste of
time, but it is largely acknowledged as a medium that powerfully influences
the way we see the world. When it comes to the representation of minorities,
Sarah Nilsen and Sarah Turner note that "television, as the primary discursive
medium today, plays a central role in the articulation, construction, and con-
testation of racialized identities in the United States."[13] Scholars have explored
the representation of minorities in American television in a number of ways.
Some have examined their framing on TV newscasts, finding in the 1990s that
most often minorities were either undercovered or covered in prejudicial or
stigmatizing ways when they did appear in newscasts.[14] Though members of
minority groups do seem to appear in TV news with more frequency, their representation there remains problematic as various minority groups are framed
as threats to the social fabric of America or as problems to be managed.[15] Jeremiah Garretson suggests that the increase in the visibility of both women
and members of minority communities on American TV does seem to have
increased levels of tolerance for these individuals in viewers of programs featuring minority characters.[16] However, the casts of most American TV shows have
overwhelmingly been white,[17] and although the last several decades have seen
an increase in diversity on American television, that diversity has not always
translated into better representation. In a study of some of the most popular
TV shows airing between 1987 and 2009, Riva Tukachinsky and her coauthors
found that Native Americans, Asian Americans, and Latinos remained woe-
fully underrepresented and when members of minority groups did appear on

58   POP ISLAM

the screen, they tended to be portrayed stereotypically.[18] An important caveat is that the authors also found that even though stereotyped, minorities tended to be represented as "likable" or "moral" individuals in American prime time, which is an improvement over representations of the past. However, even those likable minorities have been thought to help perpetuate a kind of "enlightened racism" in which racist attitudes held by white audiences can seem to go unchecked because they happen to like a show with likable minority characters.[19] Watching and liking a program like *The Cosby Show* was seen as evidence that a white viewer wasn't racist and seemed to reinforce the idea that the experience of inequality was the result of individual actions, not systemic racism.[20] It's not all that different from the "I'm not racist, some of my best friends are Black" meme that has become particularly potent in a "postrace" America.[21]

In a study of the relationship between stereotyped TV portrayals and viewers' attitudes toward minority groups, Dana Mastro found a significant relationship between the negative framings of Latinos (the minority group Mastro focused on) and the attitudes of white viewers of those framings, suggesting the negative portrayals led to white viewers more intensely identifying Latinos as not belonging to the same social group.[22] When individuals from minority communities have appeared on prime-time TV, it has most often been in ways that reinforce differences between groups that may lead to a hardening of stereotypes.[23] Interestingly, one study found that TV shows somehow connected to the criminal justice system actually represented white people and members of minority groups in similar ways; however, the authors do note that "the relative scarcity of images, particularly with regard to Latinos, may impact stereotype formation in a more subversive manner."[24] They suggest that this "scarcity of images" may lead viewers to the idea that members of minority groups are "inconsequential."[25] It continues to reinforce the idea of a homogeneous America via the absence of characters of color.

One of the traps of visibility, as suggested by Michel Foucault, is the possibility that an individual (or perhaps a group) will perform in ways expected by society or dictated by society and not in ways that may reflect their own, authentic experiences.[26] Whose truth, then, should representations reflect? On TV, it might be a truth that is seen to be celebratory but that actually is as reductive as representations of the past, just in a different way. Rather than focus on the veracity of representations, Herman Gray has suggested that we consider the various ways such representations make us *feel* and why they make us feel that way.[27] What are the histories and legacies that prime us to think some representation are exaggerations and some are truthful? It's not enough simply to correct representations, Gray suggests, but we

THE SCRIPTED LIVES OF TV MUSLIMS 59

must interrogate the constellations that shape particular representations—interrogate what has led to their feeling of authenticity. Why are some minorities seen as "likable" while others are not? It's an important question to consider even as we acknowledge that seeing likable minorities on American television is an improvement over representations of the past, particularly in the case of Muslims.

Programs such as HBO's prison drama *Oz* have presented American Muslim experiences while continuing to highlight the ways in which Muslims are somehow set apart from mainstream American society (the Muslims who appear in *Oz* are all prisoners). Amir Hussain has suggested that "in dramas, Muslims are not recognized on American television as citizens of their own country, but are instead portrayed as dangerous immigrants with a religion that is both alien and wicked."[28] This echoes what some American Muslims felt in the aftermath of the September 11 terrorist attacks—that they would not be seen or treated as full citizens of the United States.[29] Islam in TV dramas has been a religion of violence, with little room for any other religious reality.[30] The Showtime series *Sleeper Cell* made this apparent in not only its subject matter (the investigation into a possible Muslim terrorist network in the United States) but also its marketing materials—Hussain noted that the comments of one of the show's stars as well as the remarks of an American general placed the program, and its understanding of Islam and Muslims, within a "clash of civilizations"–type framing.[31] This framing was perhaps made most visible for television audiences in Fox's hit drama 24.

The show 24 was focused on the efforts of Jack Bauer, a member of an elite counterterrorism unit, to save Americans from threats domestic and foreign. The first season saw Jack racing around Los Angeles in an attempt to stop the assassination of a presidential candidate which was meant to plunge the United States into war with an unnamed Middle Eastern country. (The season's main villains were individuals who were angry about a mission Bauer had participated in during the Kosovo war.) The fifth season of 24 leaned even harder into the specter of a Middle Eastern and Muslim threat as it featured Bauer once again traveling around Los Angeles in an attempt to stop what was presented as a Middle Eastern terrorist group from detonating a dirty nuclear bomb in the city. The season featured a terrorist cell that used the framework of family as a cover for its activities—ultimately, it is the love the mother has for her son, whom she does not wish to see killed for his father's cause, that ends up thwarting the cell's plans. Muslim women have generally fared better than Muslim men in terms of their representation on prime-time TV, less likely to be represented as violent threats, but just as likely to have their experiences homogenized so that the Muslim female experience is portrayed as something monolithic.[32] In the fifth season of 24, the only Muslim woman we see is trapped by her obedience to her husband and only disobeys when their son is in danger (put there by her husband's long-term machinations), fitting within the framework of the passive, obedient Muslim woman long perpetuated in media representations of Islam and Muslim life.

Rolf Hake has suggested that 24 at times attempted to counter the negative representations of Muslims found on the program with representations meant to confound that framing; however, the "good" Muslims were marked so by discourses of Americanness in which they were "represented in line with a white set of cultural practices and codes that are simulated and imitated."[33] Cultural differences were erased so that 24's good Muslims were marked as good because they mimicked the behaviors of white Americans, not because the producers decided to highlight less stereotypical framings of Islam or its believers. Amir Hussain has suggested that "when what matters is ratings, the controversial and the provocative are privileged over the thoughtful and the accurate."[34] TV producers want to ensure that people will watch their shows, so creating characters who will draw an audience, and not challenge that audience too much, are preferable to characters who might be complicated or who might complicate an audience's understanding of the world. Evelyn Alsultany has also pointed out that Jack Bauer's use on 24 of what have been called "enhanced interrogation techniques"[35] in order to track down terrorists helped normalize "the need for torture given the impending threat Arab/Muslim terrorists pose to U.S. national security."[36] That 24 aired while the United States waged the so-called war on terror in Muslim countries meant that positive depictions of Muslims couldn't be *too* positive and that the fear of Islamic terrorists at the time may have helped propel the show's popularity.[37] While this constant struggle over the framing of Muslims as villains or heroes on shows centered on terrorism and national security is not surprising, they are not the only programs where this has been, and continues to be, contested.

In the aftermath of September 11, Yvonne Tasker found that narratives centered on terrorism and terrorist threats migrated from more action-oriented programs to more staid crime procedurals such as NBC's *Law & Order* or CBS's *NCIS*.[38] With the narratives came storylines that made it seem normal to assume that Islam or Muslims were in some way a dangerous threat in need of further investigation. When such actions were challenged, Evelyn Alsultany points out that the challenge usually came via African Americans or Euro-Americans on the programs who "serve as mediating bridges to sympathy."[39] The programs failed in their attempts to humanize Muslims on American

Fig. 2.2 A promo for the second-to-last episode of season 10 of *The X-Files* shows the bombing of an art gallery called "Ziggurat." In the episode, the suicide bombing is orchestrated by two American Muslims but is really just a side story in an episode that features main character Mulder tripping on mushrooms. The show was criticized for leaning on anti-Muslim stereotypes for its use of the suicide bombing plot point.

television with these storylines because they sidelined the voices and experiences of Muslims in search of a multicultural morality tale.

Even the rebooted *X-Files* traded on this framing in its first season back. In an episode titled "Babylon"—a nod to the ancient civilization once located in Iraq—Agents Scully and Mulder are called in to investigate the bombing of an art gallery in Texas. (The gallery's name, Ziggurat, also seems to be a reference to the ancient pre-Islamic cultures of Mesopotamia.) The bombers are two young Muslim men, one of whom is seen praying just before the bombing and who seems to have second thoughts just before the bomb goes off. The gallery is targeted because it is featuring an exhibit containing a controversial image of the Prophet Muhammad. All of this—the episode's name, the art gallery's name, the controversial image of the prophet and the Muslim bombers' violent reaction to it—is driven by the historic framing of Muslims as irrational and of the Middle East as a violent, ancient, unmodern place. *The X-Files* has been known in the past for its trafficking in, and then subversion of, various types of stereotypes.[40] That was not the case with "Babylon"; instead, the program leaned hard into stereotypes about violent Muslim men and the supposed violent nature of Islam. The episode's writer, and program creator, Chris Carter

62 POP ISLAM

said he was attempting to challenge the Muslim terrorist stereotype in the episode, but many critics suggested he fell far short of that goal.[41] What was perhaps most shocking about *The X-Files'* misstep is that it took place at a time when TV producers do seem to be working to create more positive representations of Muslims.

Lost's Sayid appeared on American TV screens in 2004 and, though an imperfect representation of a Muslim man, seemed to suggest that TV producers were beginning to understand that they needed to create more nuanced and complicated Muslim characters. Sayid was a sort of promise of representations to come—which was never quite realized. However, in the late 2010s, several TV dramas premiered featuring arguably more positive, or perhaps more nuanced, ways of representing Muslim identity. One such representation was featured on HBO's *The Night Of*.

One of the oft-used narratives when telling stories of the young American Muslim (or European Muslim) experience is that of disconnection and disenchantment. Such narratives often feature a young, good-looking Muslim individual who is caught in a conflict between their more conservative immigrant parents' traditions and cultures and those of the country in which their family now lives. This conflict sits at the heart of the German comedy *Turkish for Beginners*, and it sits at the heart of *The Night Of*. Based on the BBC program *Criminal Justice*, *The Night Of* tells the story of a young American Muslim man, Nasir, in New York accused of murdering a white, non-Muslim woman after the two engage in an alcohol- and drug-fueled one-night stand.

When we first meet Nasir, we are introduced to an attractive and seemingly successful college student, a guy who seems like he wants to do right by his Muslim family but who also wants to live a life he finds fulfilling. When his father forbids him from attending a party in the city—a narrative driver also present in the first issue of *Ms. Marvel*—Nasir steals his father's cab. It is a decision with brutal consequences for Nasir, as it is the cab that allows him to meet Andrea, the young woman who is murdered in bed next to him. Over the course of the series, we learn that the naive young man whom Nasir, or Naz, seemed to be when the audience first meets him actually is a much more complicated individual, as he committed acts of violence while in school and sold drugs while enrolled in college. When asked by his lawyer about an incident that took place in grade school, Nasir says:

> I was in fifth grade when the towers came down. I didn't understand why I was getting beat up, why my little brother was, why my dad got jumped in his cab twice. Pakistani kids, North African kids, any type of Muslim, it was a

slaughterhouse. You tried to fight back, it only made it worse. I didn't have a fight with Steve Diaz, I just shoved him down those stairs. Why? Because I just did. I wish I could tell you something else, but I just did it. It was like pushing open a door. You just push it.[42]

As Naz tells his story, it becomes clear to the audience that this young man was pushed into this moment of violence by the bigotry and racism he experienced growing up. The Islamophobia he experienced and witnessed pushed him so far he finally pushed back. It also provides a window into understanding why he might have sought escape from such experiences—either by attending parties his parents disapproved of or by taking and selling drugs. Nasir seems to be a young man in need of an escape from racism, Islamophobia, and the conservative values of his parents. His is a familiar story to any young person who has experienced bigotry because of the color of their skin, because of the religion they belong to, or because of the accent they speak with. Naz is fearful of the police when first arrested after the young woman's death because he knows that, as a brown Muslim man, he's automatically assumed to be a threat and automatically assumed to be guilty of *something*. Even so, his religion is often obscured as *The Night Of* works to show how the experience of incarceration can turn people who are nonviolent into violent actors, forcing us to question our own complicity in the production of violence, extremism, or even radicalization in our communities.

While the story is centered on the experience of an American Muslim, Islam is barely visible as the show tackles issues of systemic racism in the justice system and the problems associated with eyewitness testimony. Leaving the audience to wonder whether this an American Muslim story or a story in which the American Muslims could be swapped out for any other group and the same points be made. If they could be swapped, is that a positive or negative development as far as Muslim representation goes? Is Naz simply an example of what Kristin Warner has called "plastic representation"?

Warner describes plastic representation as "a combination of synthetic elements put together and shaped to look like meaningful imagery, but which can only approximate depth and substance because ultimately it is hollow and cannot survive close scrutiny."[43] She uses this term to describe how a culture that pushes the idea that "representation matters"—implying that any positive representation is good representation—"uses the wonder that comes from seeing characters on screen who serve as visual identifiers for specific demographics in order to flatten the expectation to desire anything more."[44] Plastic representations lack depth and complexity as they present individuals

64   POP ISLAM

meant to make us feel good and meant to be easily consumed. They are not difficult representations or challenging ones, lacking the nuance or complexity that more fully realized characters might present to the audience. While Naz's characterization is certainly not meant to make us feel good as his story is not an uplifting one, at the same time marketers can point to the fact that he is not framed as a terrorist or extremist as a positive development in Muslim representation. We should feel good *because* Nasir's story could have been the story of almost any other American if the details were altered slightly—we aren't meant to engage with all that's missing in the flat and plastic, if more positive, representation we see.

When Islam does become more visible in *The Night Of*, it is usually associated with Nasir's parents. In fact, the headline of one article about the show even proclaimed, "*The Night Of* has humanized American Muslim families"[45] because of the way it presents Naz and his relationship with his parents. On the program, we see visualizations of Naz's parents' faith—his mother works in a shop seemingly selling hijabs and other types of scarves, for instance—and a tension exists in the program around whether to present these Muslim parents as out of touch or as the kind of concerned parents one might find in any other American drama. The audience is often given a glimpse of how Naz's arrest and incarceration affect them—they cannot reconcile the stories they hear of the life Nasir lived behind their backs with the young man they thought he was. His mother, Safar, in particular struggles with the knowledge that Nasir did and dealt drugs, had premarital sex, and lived a life that ran counter to the values of both her home country of Pakistan and the religion she thought they shared, Islam. At one point she asks Nasir's lawyer, "Did I raise an animal?" as she seeks to come to terms with the possibility that her son may be found guilty of murder. The focus on Nasir's parents once again highlights the disjuncture and disconnection that can sometimes exist between the experiences of immigrant parents and those of their children. Eventually, Naz is found not guilty of the murder and returns to his parents' home, an angry shell of himself, with the audience not knowing whether he will embrace the teachings of Islam or continue running from them. Interestingly, it is another crime show where we find a Muslim character who could have had any other background and yet whose faith is a central aspect of his identity.

Arastoo Vaziri, a forensic scientist on FOX's crime drama *Bones*, is an Iranian and a devout Muslim who prays five times a day. When he first arrives as an intern in the lab that is the heart of the show, Arastoo fakes a Jordanian accent in order to sound more newly arrived as he feels that will make his devotion to Islam seem less odd. He is concerned that his status as a scientist and his commitment to the scientific process will seem hollow or suspect if the extent of his devotion to Islam is known to this colleagues. Arastoo seems to understand that his connection and devotion to an "Eastern" religion, one that has been historically framed as antimodern and antirational,[46] might make his commitment to science suspect in some way. And he's shown to be right as his coworkers in the lab immediately engage in making anti-Muslim jokes at Arastoo's expense. Things change, quickly, one day when Arastoo slips into his regular speaking voice when engaged in a heated exchange with a colleague about whether his religion gets in the way of his work.

> **ARASTOO VAZIRI:** [Irritated without Jordanian accent] I am a scientist! Okay? Just like the rest of you. I can deal! So please just back off and let me do my job!
> **DR. CAMILLE SAROYAN:** Wow.
> **ARASTOO:** [With Jordanian accent] I apologize for my outburst.
> **CAMILLE:** Oh, you aren't even going to try to unring that bell, are you?
> **ARASTOO:** I have to pray.[47]

Arastoo was actually a controversial addition to the *Bones* cast, not because of his Muslim faith but rather because of the stereotyped way the show's producers chose to first present him. The subterfuge of Arastoo using a thicker accent to make his devotion to Islam more palatable to his colleagues was thought up by producers only after he had appeared on several episodes. In a *BuzzFeed* article about the character, *Bones* creator Hart Hanson admitted that the writers had fumbled Arastoo's introduction and scrambled to find a way to save the situation: "However, after the first three episodes featuring Arastoo, Hanson said the writers had to abandon their impulse to make him stereotypically foreign. 'I have to be both ashamed and proud when it comes to the character of Arastoo,' Hanson said—ashamed largely because Arastoo's Iranian accent was used for 'cheap humor.' Hanson decided that Arastoo had faked his accent so that his co-workers wouldn't question his faithfulness to Islam. 'Wouldn't it give us a pot to stir if this guy had put on the accent to deal with progressive discrimination?' Hanson said."[48]

After the fumbling of Arastoo's introduction and his relationship with Islam, *Bones* began highlighting his identity in ways that seemed designed to challenge the stereotypes that the early depiction played upon. One particularly poignant moment came when the lab was sent the remains of a 9/11 victim to examine. As Arastoo stands over the remains with several of his colleagues, a young white man from the American South asks, "Is this too difficult for you, Arastoo, because if it is I'd be more than happy to do as much as needed to

66   POP ISLAM

ease your load."[49] When asked why he thinks Arastoo might have a more difficult time working with the remains than the others, the young man responds, "Because . . . because you share the same religion as those men."[50] Arastoo's reply is filled with the history of hate and violence perpetuated in the name of Christianity, punctuated with his asking the young colleague if the men who committed violent acts in the name of Christ represented his faith. Of the 9/11 hijackers, Arastoo says, "This was not the work of religion. It was arrogance. It was hypocrisy. It was hate. Those horrible men who hijacked those planes hijacked my religion that day, too. They insulted my God. So, no, this isn't too difficult. It's a privilege to be able to serve this victim, to show him the care and love that was so absent that day."[51]

A moment of silence fills the scene after Arastoo finishes, broken by the same young man saying, "Thank you, sir. I'm sorry and thank you for taking the time to set me straight."[52] The scene is important for several reasons. First, it acknowledges the way Muslims are often imagined as monolithic in nature and then allows a Muslim to refute that stereotyping. Second, it reminds the audience that Islam is not the only religion that has spawned followers who commit acts of violence in its name. And, finally, Arastoo's short monologue echoes what so many American Muslims said in the aftermath of the September 11 attacks: "This is not our faith—those terrorists hijacked our faith when they hijacked those airplanes." For many, it had felt as though they were shouting that message into the void, as anti-Muslim sentiment and Islamophobia continued to rise in the United States. For Arastoo to state that so plainly on a prime-time television drama was an important moment. Arastoo is a devout Muslim who is also a scientist, two things that are not supposed to go together in the past Islamophobic narrative of who Muslims are. Arastoo is a Muslim man who makes visible his compassion for a victim of terrorism, something that Muslims are not imagined capable of doing. It was a small but powerful moment. In one of his pieces, poet Mark Doty has written that "any small thing can save you."[53] Perhaps it is these small moments of thoughtful representation that can begin the process of eroding centuries of stereotype and prejudice—at least when it comes to representations in popular media.

Arastoo is the exception to the rule when it comes to the representation of Muslim men on American television—rarely are they allowed to be visibly devout. Not even *Lost*'s Sayid is ever really shown to engage with Islam, though he is often shown discussing spirituality with various other characters on the program. Unlike most of their male counterparts, women *are* allowed to be more openly and more visibly Muslim on American television, but it has taken a while to get there.

THE SCRIPTED LIVES OF TV MUSLIMS

Historically, Muslim women have been portrayed as oppressed victims of Islam and Muslim men, as sexually suspect in some way or as collaborators in Islamic terrorism.[54] Rarely are they portrayed as thinking individuals with any sort of agency, particularly on American television. In her work on Muslim media representation post-9/11, Evelyn Alsultany has shown how the framing of Muslim women on informational programs has focused on "getting behind the veil" in order to understand the women locked away by the backward religion of Islam.[55] When Muslim women *have* been given any type of agency in American entertainment media, it has often been so they can heroically throw off their oppressive faith.[56] Whether Muslim women are oppressed or free, Islam is often imagined as their personal jailer. Jail features in the first season of ABC's anthology series *American Crime*, but the veil is the last thing its main Muslim character strives to break free from.

When viewers first meet Aliyah Shadeed on *American Crime*, it is as she sits with her brother, Carter, in a jail visitation room. Aliyah and her brother are both African American, and Carter has been arrested with his white girlfriend, the two accused of murdering a Marine Corps veteran. The duo are also accused of the brutal beating and rape of the veteran's wife who lies in a coma in the hospital. Aliyah is incensed that her brother, Carter, is being held, sure that it is the color of his skin that has him locked away. At one point she says to Carter, "You take their drugs. You sleep with their women. And then, they put you in their cage"[57] (the "they" here being white American society), to which Carter responds that, for all her piety, Aliyah is "merely" a convert to Islam—communicating that not only does he not share his sister's beliefs but he finds something inauthentic in them as well. Carter leaves her alone in her chair after she says she will help him find a lawyer if he humbles himself and if he gives up his white girlfriend. Carter had been married before he met said girlfriend, Aubry, and Aliyah implies he's been up to his neck in drugs and other illicit activities since coupling up with her. Sitting in her black hijab, demanding her brother be the man she imagines him to be, Aliyah is more harridan than victim.

The next time we see Aliyah, she is at worship in a mosque, surrounded by other worshippers. Rarely are American audiences given an inside view of a mosque, and on *American Crime*, there is no fanfare around the mosque's appearance; it is portrayed as benignly as any other religious space might be with the worshippers gathered together to pray. The show is remarkable not only for its portrayal of a mosque but also because that mosque belongs to the Nation of Islam (NoI). The NoI has been seen as an unorthodox branch of Islam, although some leaders have worked over the last several decades to bring

Fig. 2.3 As Aliyah Shadeed in *American Crime* speaks to community members in her local mosque, the camera pans around her, giving the viewer a look inside a space that is likely unfamiliar to them. The camera rests for a moment on a Qur'an that sits next to the podium from which Aliyah tells her fellow congregants that fighting for the freedom of one Black man is a fight for freedom for them all.

its teachings more in line with those of mainstream Islam.[58] Perhaps, more importantly for this discussion of Muslim representation is the NoI's historic antiwhite rhetoric,[59] with early leader Elijah Muhammad famously suggesting that white people were evil.[60] The NoI has preached the need for Black Muslims to keep themselves separate from white society,[61] a teaching Aliyah alludes to when she refers to Carter's sleeping "with their women." The issues of racism and Islamophobia are central to the argument Aliyah makes about her brother's incarceration as she sees in her brother's predicament the opportunity to fight the social injustice of systemic racism. "What's happening here is bigger than you," Aliyah says to Carter during one of her visits to him in jail. "This is about every Black man who cannot get justice. You need to represent. You need to be the voice for people who have no voice."[62] Aliyah's fight for her brother's freedom is not only personal but also political. For many American Muslim women, politics have been wrapped up with the personal all their lives.

Writing of the experience of Muslim women of color in the United States, Sylvia Chan-Malik suggests that Islam has at times served as a kind of "safe harbor" for its women believers—particularly for Black Muslim women who sought refuge from the violence they faced in hegemonically white America society.[63] Within Islam, Chan-Malik argues many American Muslim women

THE SCRIPTED LIVES OF TV MUSLIMS

found space for "affective insurgencies" that allowed them to resist racism, to resist white supremacy, and to resist patriarchy. Even within the NoI, which has held traditional views on gender roles for men and women, some American Muslim women found a way to harness expectations of womanhood and motherhood in order to resist the oppression and subjugation of Black women in America more broadly. Black women members of the NoI were seen as shoring up the masculinity of Black men at a time when white masculinity, and the white nuclear family, was seen as being in decline. Black women were seen by early NoI leaders as the anchor of belief in NoI homes.

In Aliyah, audiences see such an anchor. She is a strong, devout, and uncompromising Black Muslim woman who will do all it takes to ensure that her brother is not convicted of a crime she knows, in her heart, he did not commit. She draws strength from Islam as she fights for her brother's freedom. Aliyah is not passive; she is a woman of action who may turn to others for advice but who is confident in the path she is walking, although this was not always the case. As mentioned earlier, when we first meet Aliyah and Carter, Carter points out that Aliyah had converted to Islam. During their conversation, it becomes apparent that Carter finds something suspect in this conversion, that perhaps he does not find her belief authentic. We learn more about Aliyah's conversion later, when she shares her story with her brothers and sisters in the mosque as she educates them about Carter's plight. "When I learned to start doing for others, I dedicated myself to uplifting us, when I gave myself to our true god, our one true god Allah, that's when I finally found my freedom. The sky was truly blue, the temperature was right. I'm grateful for my freedom and I want freedom for all of us."[64]

For Aliyah, her membership in the NoI helped her construct a safe harbor that has allowed her to be more fully herself, more fully free. This was true for a number of Black American women who chose to convert to Islam out of a desire for "safety and spirituality."[65] However, Aliyah's fight for freedom for her brother is not an easy one, as the fight for freedom has not been easy for other Black Muslim women. In writing of the historic treatment of Black Muslim women in the United States, Kayla Wheeler writes that "Black Muslim women are often the last to be called upon to take formal leadership roles. When Black Muslim women do take centerstage, they often face vitriol, with little public support from anyone except other Black Muslim women."[66] Aaliyah fights to keep her brother's plight in the eyes of a public that might want to turn away and struggles to maintain the support of her community at times in this fight. She also faces regular Islamophobic and racist verbal abuse from the mother of the Marine murder victim. Rather than shrink away from this, Aaliyah welcomes it, holding it up as more evidence of the unjust world and system that would attempt to send her brother to death row. Aaliyah is at times hard and uncompromising, but she is devoted to her brother, even when he asks less devotion of her. She is not the helpless victim of a Muslim man or of her Islamic faith. She is a woman who is devoted to her brother and devoted, too, to seeing him escape from an unjust and racist justice system. Sibling devotion is also a sometime theme of another ABC drama, this one featuring Muslim women working inside the criminal justice system.

The first season of *Quantico* tells the story of an FBI agent accused of orchestrating a terrorist attack in New York City's Grand Central Station, but it's also the story of her experience as a cadet at the FBI's training academy in Quantico, Virginia. It's in the flashbacks to her time there that the audience learns that among her class were two Muslim twins, Nimah and Raina Amin. Though the women call the Detroit, Michigan, area home, they grew up in Lebanon during the civil war there. Raina is more conservative and more religious than Nimah; she also wears the hijab, while Nimah does not. The hijab, or veil, so central to arguments over the oppression of Muslim women by Islam, is also central to the story of these two FBI cadets.

The specter of the veiled Muslim woman has haunted the non-Muslim imagination, particularly in the historic West, for quite a long time. Edward Said pointed out how particular, gendered constructions of the imagined East and imagined West have been used to fuel European imperialism and American foreign policy.[67] Scholars Lila Abu-Lughod and Rafia Zakaria note that the idea that veiled, and therefore oppressed, Muslim women need to be rescued by non-Muslims propelled both war rhetoric and white feminist rhetoric.[68] Such framing has obscured understandings of the veil that give it a liberatory, and even feminist, meaning,[69] reducing Muslim women to little more than objects upon which religious convention and foreign policy is enacted. For some American women, though, to veil is to engage in an emancipatory act— freeing oneself from hegemonically white understandings of what it means to be American.[70] Sylvia Chan-Malik points out that "Islam can only be positioned as inherently oppressive through an elision of the choices and agency of Black women and other women of color who engage Islam as acts of racial and gendered insurgency."[71]

Is it progress that the veil is portrayed as something Raina Amin chooses to wear on *Quantico*, particularly as she wears it while training to join an American law enforcement agency? The Amin twins wound up at the FBI academy because Nimah decided she wanted to serve in this way, and Nimah's FBI recruiter convinces both women to join, with the caveat that they will pretend to be only a single person—Raina. This is to allow the recruiter to have more options when using the trainee agents in the field. While the two women trade playing Raina back and forth, they also trade wearing the veil. In a way, Nimah's decision to join the FBI forces her to wear the headscarf when her faith had not. The Amin twins would seem likely suspects in a terror attack, given the history of media portrayals of Muslims as terrorists, but Nimah and Raina are shown to be loyal to the United States during the show's first season. However, during an exchange with her recruiter, Raina reminds the woman that loyalty has been a difficult thing for some Muslims to hold on to in the aftermath of 9/11: "Every Arab man was targeted, questioned, followed, surveilled. They saw us not as humans, but as this hand of a monster that hated America. I saw people in my community act out in ways they never would have if they hadn't been treated so unjustly. Whatever you imagine people might have done, just don't lose faith in their humanity, because when you do, that's when you make the monster."[72]

Although the twins are working inside a federal law enforcement agency that has historically been dominated by white Americans, they are not forced to simulate and imitate "a white set of cultural practices and codes"[73] the way Muslim good guys on programs such as 24 have in the past. And unlike Arastoo on Bones, they are allowed to be angry about not only the way the 9/11 hijackers "hijacked" Islam but also the way non-Muslim Americans and the American government treated American Muslims in the aftermath of the attack. They are complicated Muslim women who are shown to be physically capable individuals who are oppressed more by the prejudice they face than any facet of their faith.

As with so much media portraying Muslim women, Quantico does fixate on the hijab. When using Raina's identity as their cover, the twins wear the hijab, though Nimah does not wear it outside Quantico. It is a way that Raina, who does wear hijab, can maintain her faith during their training. It also serves as a stark reminder to their colleagues of their religious identity, one that later leads to their being suspected of participating in terrorist activity. The issue of hijab, and what it stands for, actually serves as an obstacle in Raina and Nimah's relationship with one another. Nimah, who at one point declared herself an atheist, does not want to be tightly bound by the more conservative teachings of her faith, while Raina, at least during much of the first season of Quantico, finds them to be a source of comfort and strength. On the one hand, this debate over faith can highlight the twins' cultural difference to most of the audience, treating it almost as window dressing; on the other hand, however, the conversations the two have about their faith are between two Muslim women—they are not forced or facilitated by anyone else. It serves to challenge the idea that

Fig. 2.4 British actor and rapper Riz Ahmed was the first man of South Asian descent to win an acting Emmy and the first Muslim and South Asian actor to win an Emmy for a lead performance. Ahmed has also starred in the Star Wars anthology film *Rogue One* and the Amazon-backed drama *Sound of Metal*, for which he became the first Muslim man to be nominated for an Academy Award for Best Actor.

Islam is a monolith, that there is only one way to be Muslim, and that Muslim women unthinkingly take up the headscarf.

The programs featured in this chapter—*Quantico, American Crime, Bones, The Night Of,* and *Lost*—were watched by millions of people. These were not niche shows watched by a select or specialist audience. They made money for their creators and the networks that aired them, suggesting there is room on American television for shows that *do* challenge popular understandings of Islam and Muslim life. Additionally, the programs garnered award nominations and wins for their producers, with Regina King (*American Crime*) and Riz Ahmed (*The Night Of*) receiving particular praise for their portrayals of complicated Muslim characters. Their characterizations were more than just benevolent acts of multicultural media charity—Nasir, Arastoo, Aaliyah, and the Amin twins did not need someone else to speak up and defend their faith; they were capable of defending it when they needed to and criticizing it when they wanted to. But they all are Muslim characters whose narrative homes are on TV shows about crime or are crime adjacent, as in the case of *Lost*. On two of the shows, *Quantico* and *The Night Of,* they are also characters who were even seen as possibly suspect in relation to criminal activity. These are generally more nuanced representations than those of the past, but these are still Muslim characters who, no matter what they sacrifice, are not entirely above suspicion.

Many of the Muslim characters featured in American prime-time programming since *Lost*'s premiere have served at times as the narrative hearts of a program or as important supporting characters, presenting to audiences what can feel like accessible representations of the Muslim experience. The characters discussed in this chapter are not expendable to the narrative arcs of their programs, though there are moments when it feels as though their faith is. In the case of both Sayid and Nasir, their faith is sacrificed in an attempt to create male Muslim characters who are not threats because of their religion (though they might be threats for other reasons). There are moments when the faith of Aliyah on *American Crime* as well as that of Raina and Nimah on *Quantico* are seen as perhaps threatening, and yet, they are never forced on their programs to create distance between themselves and Islam the way Sayid and Nasir are. What emerges from this discussion of Muslim characters in American prime-time drama is the recognition of a seemingly gendered approach to more positive representations of Muslims and Islam, one that seems to strip Muslim men of their devotion while allowing Muslim women to turn to their devotion as a source of strength. Even in these more positive, more accessible representations, it seems that Orientalist ideas that devout Muslim men are in some way threatening may be at work. Even Arastoo, the unapologetically Muslim man on *Bones*, was first presented in such a way that his devotion was made to seem foreign in order for it to be made understandable to the show's audience. The most accessible Muslim men on prime-time television seem to be those with only a glancing connection to Islam; they are allowed to perform a kind of Muslim masculinity that is safe and nonthreatening to the viewing audience but that is divorced from faith or belief. Though these men are not portrayed as the stereotypical villain, these seemingly more accessible representations of Muslim men are, in their way, plastic and empty.

NOTES

1. *Lost*, "Pilot: Part Two," season 1, episode 2, dir. J. J. Abrams, written by J. J. Abrams and Damon Lindelof, ABC, September 29, 2004.

2. Ibid.

3. Abbas Kadhim, *Reclaiming Iraq: The 1920 Revolution and the Founding of the Modern State* (Austin: University of Texas Press, 2012).

4. *Lost*, "Pilot: Part Two."

5. Baram Amatzia, "The Iraqi Armed Forces and Security Apparatus," *Conflict, Security & Development* 1, no. 2 (2006), 113–23.

6. Sophia Rose Arjana, *Muslims in the Western Imagination* (Oxford: Oxford University Press, 2015).

7. Todd Green, *Presumed Guilty: Why We Shouldn't Ask Muslims to Condemn Terrorism* (Minneapolis: Fortress Press, 2018).

8. Samuel Huntington, "The Clash of Civilizations?," *Foreign Affairs* 72, no. 3 (1997): 22–49.

9. Nancy Wang Yuen and Cassidy J. Ray, "Post 9/11 but Not Post-Racial," *Contexts* 8, no. 2 (2009): 68–70.

10. *Lost*, "The Candidate," season 6, episode 14, dir. Jack Bender, written by Elizabeth Sarnoff, ABC, May 4, 2010.

11. Edward Said, *Orientalism* (New York: Vintage Books, 1979).

12. *Lost*, "One of Them," season 2, episode 14, dir. Stephen Williams, written by Jeffrey Lieber, J. J. Abrams, and Damon Lindlof, ABC, February 15, 2006.

13. Sarah Nilsen and Sarah E. Turner, "Introduction," in *The Colorblind Screen: Television in Post-Racial America*, ed. Sarah Nilesen and Sarah E. Turner (New York: New York University Press, 2014), 1–14, 4.

14. Robert Entman, "Representation and Reality in the Portrayal of Blacks on Network Television News," *Journalism Quarterly* 71, no. 3 (1994): 509–20; Entman, "Modern Racism and the Images of Blacks in Local Television News," *Critical Studies in Mass Communication* 7, no. 4 (1990): 332–45.

15. Howard J. Ehrlich, *Hate Crimes and Ethnoviolence: The History, Current Affairs, and Future of Discrimination in America* (New York: Routledge, 2018); Dana Mastro, Andrea Figuero-Caballero, and Alexander Sink, "Primetime Television: Portrayals and Effects," in *The Routledge Companion to Media and Race*, ed. Christopher P. Campbell (New York: Routledge, 2016), 89–98.

16. Jeremiah J. Garretson, "Does Change in Minority and Women's Representation on Television Matter?: A 30-Year Study of Television Portrayals and Social Tolerance," *Politics, Groups, and Identities* 3, no. 4 (2015): 615–32.

17. Dana E. Mastro and Bradley S. Greenberg, "The Portrayal of Racial Minorities in Prime Time Television," *Journal of Broadcasting & Electronic Media* 44, no. 4 (2000), 690–703; Elizabeth Monk-Turner et al., "The Portrayal of Racial Minorities on Prime Time Television: A Replication of the Mastro and Greenberg Study a Decade Later," *Studies in Popular Culture* 32, no. 2 (2010): 101–14.

18. Riva Tukachinsky, Dana Mastro, and Moran Yarchi, "Documenting Portrayals of Race/Ethnicity on Primetime Television over a 20-Year Span and Their Association with National-Level Racial/Ethnic Attitudes," *Journal of Social Issues* 71 (2015): 17–38.

19. Gail Coover, "Television and Social Identity: Race Representation as 'White' Accommodation," *Journal of Broadcasting & Electronic Media* 45, no. 3 (2001): 413–31.

20. Though a deep discussion of the concept of enlightened racism is beyond the scope of this chapter, those interested in taking a deep dive into American TV and enlightened racism should read Sut Jhally and Justin Lewis's book on the topic, *Enlightened Racism: The Cosby Show, Audiences, and the Myth of the American Dream* (New York: Routledge, 2019). The book is an analysis of audience responses to *The Cosby Show*, and though it is a bit dated, its finding that progressive narratives of racial solidarity and racial equality surrounding the show often masked the ways it trafficked at times in racial stereotyping and classism could prove useful to scholars interested in exploring current narratives of race and class on American TV.

21. John Eligon, "The 'Some of My Best Friends Are Black' Defense," *New York Times*, February 16, 2019, https://www.nytimes.com/2019/02/16/sunday-review/ralph-northam-blackface-friends.html.

22. Dana Mastro, "A Social Identity Approach to Understanding the Impact of Television Messages," *Communication Monographs* 70, no. 2 (2003): 98–113.

23. Nancy Signorielli, "Minorities Representation in Prime Time: 2000 to 2008," *Communication Research Reports* 26, no. 4 (2009): 323–36.

24. Ron Tamborini et al., "The Color of Crime and the Court: A Content Analysis of Minority Representation of Television," *Journalism and Mass Communication Quarterly* 77, no. 3 (2000): 639–53, at 649.

25. Ibid.

26. Michel Foucault, *Discipline and Punish: The Birth of the Modern Prison*, 2nd ed. (New York: Vintage Books, 1995).

27. Herman Gray, "Race, Media, and the Cultivation of Concern," *Communication and Critical/Cultural Studies* 10, no. 2–3 (2013): 253–58.

28. Amir Hussain, "(Re)presenting Muslims on North American Television," *Contemporary Islam* 4, no. 1 (2010): 55–75, at 3.

29. Saher Selod, "Citizenship Denied: Racialization of Muslim American Men and Women Post-9/11," *Critical Sociology* 41, no. 1 (2015): 77–95.

30. Hussain, "(Re)presenting Muslims on North American Television."

31. Ibid.

32. Faiza Hirji, "Through the Looking Glass: Muslim Women on Television— An Analysis of 24, Lost, and Little Mosque on the Prairie," *Global Media Journal—Canadian Edition* 4, no. 2 (2011): 33–47.

33. Rolf Hake, "Counter-Stereotypical Images of Muslim Characters in the Television Serial 24: A Difference That Makes No Difference?," *Critical Studies in Television* 10, no. 1 (2015): 54–72, at 68.

34. Hussain, "(Re)presenting Muslims on North American Television," 3.

35. "Enhanced interrogation techniques" was the euphemistic term officials in the George W. Bush administration used to describe their process for getting information from terrorists or terrorism suspects; many understood this as a sanitized way to describe what many saw as torture. For a deeper discussion of this issue, see Ruth Blakeley, "Dirty Hands, Clean Conscience? The CIA Inspector General's Investigation of 'Enhanced Interrogation Techniques' in the War on Terror and the Torture Debate," *Journal of Human Rights* 10, no. 4 (2011): 544–61; Michele Chwastiak, "Torture as Normal Work: The Bush Administration, the Central Intelligence Agency and 'Enhanced Interrogation Techniques,'" *Organization* 22, no. 4 (2015): 493–511.

36. Evelyn Alsultany, *Arabs and Muslims in the Media: Race and Representation after 9/11* (New York: New York University Press, 2012), 42.

37. Ibid.

38. Yvonne Tasker, "Television Crime Drama and Homeland Security: From Law & Order to 'Terror TV,'" *Cinema Journal* 4, no. 4 (2012): 44–65.

39. Alsultany, *Arabs and Muslims in the Media*, 69.

40. Eleanor Hersey discusses the way that *X-Files* sometimes worked with and around stereotypes in her 1998 article "Word-Healers and Code-Talkers: Native Americans in *The X-Files*" (*Journal of Popular Film & Television* 26, no. 3 [1998]: 108–19). Adrienne McLean's 1998 article "Media Effects, Marshall McLuhan, Television Culture, and 'Media Effects'" (*Film Quarterly* 51, no. 4 [1998]: 2–11) explores the problematic ways the idea of *The X-Files* as an exploration of "myth" can frame particular, negative, media experiences.

41. Aysha Khan, "'The X-Files' Draws Backlash with Islamic Terrorism Plot," *Washington Post*, February 17, 2016, https://www.washingtonpost.com/national /religion/the-x-files-draws-backlash-with-islamic-terrorism-plot/2016/02/17 /dc67733c-d5b3-11e5-a65b-587e721fb231_story.html.

42. *The Night Of*, "Samson and Delilah," episode 6, dir. Steven Zaillian, written by Steven Zaillian and Richard Price, HBO, August 14, 2016.

43. Kristen Warner, "In the Time of Plastic Representation," *Film Quarterly* 71, no. 2 (2017), https://filmquarterly.org/2017/12/04/in-the-time-of-plastic -representation/.

44. Ibid.

45. Lorraine Ali, "How HBO's *The Night Of* Has Humanized American Muslim Families," *Los Angeles Times*, August 28, 2016, https://www.latimes.com /entertainment/tv/la-ca-st-night-of-muslims-20160818-snap-story.html.

46. J. W. Lew, "The Deceptive Other: Mary Shelley's Critique of Orientalism in *Frankenstein*," *Studies in Romanticism* 30, no. 2 (1991): 255–83; Edward Said, "Orientalism Reconsidered," *Race & Class* 27, no. 2 (1985): 1–15; Scott Trafton,

Egypt Land: Race and Nineteenth-Century American Egyptomania (Durham, NC: Duke University Press, 2004).

47. *Bones*, "A Beautiful Day in the Neighborhood," season 5, episode 4, dir. Gordon Lonsdale, written by Janet Lin, FOX, October 8, 2009.

48. Ariane Lange, "What It's Like to Play a Muslim on Network TV," BuzzFeed, February 22, 2017, https://www.buzzfeed.com/arianelange /pej-vahdat-bones-arastoo.

49. *Bones*, "Patriot in Purgatory," season 8, episode 6, dir. Francoise Velle, written by Stephan Nathan, FOX, November 12, 2012.

50. Ibid.

51. Ibid.

52. Ibid.

53. Mark Doty, "Ararat," in *Fire to Fire: New and Selected Poems* (New York: HarperCollins, 2009), 65.

54. Lila Abu-Lughod, *Do Muslim Women Need Saving?* (Cambridge, MA: Harvard University Press, 2013); Myra Macdonald, "Muslim Women and the Veil: Problems of Image and Voice in Media Representations," *Feminist Media Studies* 6, no. 1 (2006): 7–23; Laura Navarro, "Islamophobia and Sexism: Muslim Women and the Western Mass Media," *Human Architecture: Journal of Sociology of Self-Knowledge* 8, no. 2 (2010): 95–11; Meyda Yegenoglu, *Colonial Fantasies: Toward a Feminist Reading of Orientalism* (Cambridge: Cambridge University Press, 1998).

55. Alsultany, *Arabs and Muslims in the Media*.

56. Jack Shaheen, *Reel Bad Arabs: How Hollywood Villifies a People*, 3rd ed. (Northhampton, MA: Olive Branch Press, 2015).

57. *American Crime*, season 1, episode 3, dir. Gloria Muzio, written by John Ridley, ABC, March 19, 2015.

58. Eric C. Lincoln, *The Black Muslims in America* (Boston: Beacon Press, 1961); Andrew Shryock, "Attack of the Islamophobes: Religious War (and Peace) in Arab/Muslim Detroit," in *Islamophobia in America: The Anatomy of Intolerance*, ed. Carl W. Ernst (New York: Palgrave Macmillan, 2013), 145–74.

59. Edward Curtis, "The Black Muslim Scare of the Twentieth Century: The History of State Islamophobia and Its Post-9/11 Variations in Islamophobia," in *Islamophobia in America: The Anatomy of Intolerance*, ed. Carl W. Ernst (New York: Palgrave Macmillan, 2013), 75–106; Lincoln, *Black Muslims in America*.

60. Amir Hussain, *Muslims and the Making of America* (Waco, TX: Baylor University Press, 2016).

61. A more in-depth discussion of the Nation of Islam can be found in chapter 6 of this book, which focuses on boxer Muhammad Ali. Ali was a onetime

member of the NoI and repeated Elijah Muhammad's framing of white people as devils during an interview with a British journalist in 1974.

62. *American Crime*, season 1, episode 4, dir. Joshua Marston, written by Diana Son, ABC, March 26, 2015.

63. Sylvia Chan-Malik, *Being Muslim: A Cultural History of Women of Color in American Islam* (New York: New York University Press, 2018).

64. *American Crime*, season 1, episode 4.

65. Chan-Malik, *Being Muslim*.

66. Kayla Wheeler, "On Centering Black Muslim Women in Critical Race Theory," Maydan, February 5, 2020, https://themaydan.com/2020/02/on -centering-black-muslim-women-in-critical-race-theory/.

67. Said, *Orientalism*; Edward Said, *Culture and Imperialism* (New York: Vintage Books, 2012).

68. Abu-Lughod, *Do Muslim Women Need Saving?*; Rafia Zakaria, *Against White Feminism: Notes on Disruption* (New York: W. W. Norton, 2021).

69. For a concise discussion of the histories and legacies of veiling, Teresa Heffernan's *Veiled Figures: Women, Modernity and the Spectre of Orientalism* (Toronto: University of Toronto Press, 2016), Rafia Zakaria's *Veil* (New York: Bloomsbury, 2017), and Liz Bucar's *The Islamic Veil: A Beginner's Guide* (New York: Simon and Schuster, 2012) are all worth reading.

70. Su'ad Abdul Khabeer, *Muslim Cool: Race, Religion, and Hip Hop in the United States* (New York: New York University Press, 2016).

71. Chan-Malik, *Being Muslim*, 181.

72. *Quantico*, season 1, episode 11, dir. Thor Freudenthal, written by Joshua Safran, ABC, December 13, 2015.

73. Hake, "Counter-Stereotypical Images," 68.

THREE

BIG SCREEN, SMALL STAGE

Negotiating Identity through Comedy

THE DAY AFTER DONALD TRUMP'S inauguration as the forty-fifth president of the United States of America, a brown man stood on a stage and gave a modified Nazi salute.

"It's fine," Aziz Ansari told the studio audience at *Saturday Night Live*. "As long as we treat each other with respect and remember that ultimately we're all Americans, we'll be fine." The Nazi salute was sneakily worked into Ansari's monologue as he began to talk about the way white supremacists had latched on to the Trump presidency. "The problem is, there's a new group. I'm talking about this tiny slice of people that have gotten way too fired up about the Trump thing for the wrong reasons. I'm talking about these people that, as soon as Trump won, they're like, 'We don't have to pretend like we're not racist anymore! We don't have to pretend anymore! We can be racist again! Whoo!'"[1]

Ansari's appearance on *SNL* happened not long after he'd wrapped production on the second season of his show *Master of None*, a semiautobiographical comedy exploring the realities of being a second-generation American. The program often deals with issues of race and identity and the choice of Ansari to host *Saturday Night Live* the day after Trump's inauguration seemed anything but coincidental. After all, Ansari himself is an American Muslim comedian whose family immigrated to the United States in the 1980s. Trump had campaigned on a political rhetoric that framed both Muslims and immigrants as threats to American stability and safety. Ansari telling people "we'll be fine" was an acknowledgment that, for many Americans in the aftermath of the 2016 election, things felt anything but fine.

Though Ansari's turn as host was tied to his show *Master of None*, he first found fame portraying the character of Tom Haverford on the NBC series

Fig. 3.1 Aziz Ansari hosted *Saturday Night Live* the day after President Donald Trump's inauguration. During his monologue, he reminded his audience to not demonize all Trump voters but also pointed out that there were many Americans who were concerned for their safety under a Trump presidency.

Parks and Recreation. Like Ansari, Tom was Muslim; however, Tom's religion was rarely discussed on the program. One of the mentions of Tom's religious identity came when he explained to the main character why he had changed his name to Tom Haverford: "My birth name is Darwish Zubair Ismail Gani. Then I changed it to Tom Haverford because, you know, brown guys with funny-sounding Muslim names don't make it far into politics."[2]

Guys with funny jokes, however, may make it far. At least on TV or in film. This chapter explores the intersection of comedy and representation. It considers how Muslim entertainers leverage jokes and comedic narratives to challenge stereotype and prejudice as well as reframe American understandings of who Muslims are. It also considers whose jokes become accessible to a mainstream audience and whose perspectives are less likely to result in Netflix or Comedy Central specials.

In writing of the social and cultural work scripted comedies do, David Scott Kastan notes that they have often been understood as media for moral reflection; particularly in Renaissance understandings, comedies have been spaces in which to engage with the worst of our natures and correct them. "Comedy," he writes, "is at once critical and corrective, holding the mirror up to degenerate nature so that the viewer may see and repudiate its images of human folly."[3] He also notes that comedies are vehicles for happy endings, even if those happy endings are often ones we cannot realize in our own lives. Aaron Green and

Annulla Linders suggest that Freud saw laughter as "a gateway to the unconscious," allowing us to access feelings that were normally closed off to us in some way. "Tapping into these neglected emotions allows us to experience a type of pleasure that would normally be inaccessible."[4] What we find funny, what gives us pleasure, what makes us laugh can often shape the symbolic boundaries of the communities and cultures we feel we belong to. For instance, when studying British and Dutch audiences, Sam Friedman and Geslinde Kuipers found evidence of a marked, classist reception of particular types of comedic stories—one that suggests that the idea that comedy unites us all as a mass community of fans, erasing boundaries of class in particular, might not be as true as we'd like it to be.[5] Joseph Meeker has suggested that comedy is "universal," that it is inherent to human experience and has been seen as an important part of American popular culture for quite a long while;[6] however, while we may all laugh, we do not all laugh at the same things or for the same reasons. Sometimes, a laugh is a moment of pleasure; sometimes, it's a moment of release. In the case of stand-up comedy, the semiautobiographical nature of the medium can provide moments of catharsis for the comedian holding the microphone.

Joanne Gilbert has noted that when up on the stage, stand-up comics are performing "self and culture," often serving up cultural critique through the lens of personal experience.[7] The critique can feel less biting when wrapped up in a personal narrative of struggle and redemption that leaves the audience roaring with laughter. Comics from marginal communities often frame themselves as victims in their jokes, and in doing so, they "may subvert their own status by embodying the potential power of powerlessness."[8] What have you got to lose when you're on the outside already? In the case of the female comics Gilbert is writing about, not a lot. Though she acknowledges that the self-deprecating humor of comics such as Phyllis Diller and Roseanne Barr has been seen as negative and as reinforcing stereotypes of what it means to be a difficult woman, Gilbert also suggests that the performances are often an act of resistance to stereotype. Women are meant to be laughed at; they are not supposed to laugh at or with us. As they crack jokes making fun of themselves or their "bitchy" natures, women comics are also often performing the anger and frustration that comes with existing in the world as someone seen as somehow lesser than the men in their lives and in their industry.

Aaron Green and Annulla Linders suggest that ethnic comedies also allow for such performances, giving the creators the opportunity to release anger, frustration, or angst they may feel over their often marginal place in society. "Comedy," Roger Henkle writes, "appears to express the need to let go, to give into something natural that has been too long repressed."[9] For Green and

Linders, such "letting go" in ethnic comedies holds the potential to upend racialized understandings of culture, identity, and social norms.[10] However, whether they actually do that is often the result of *who* is telling the joke as well as the setting for that telling. For instance, Raúl Pérez has shown how training differs between white comedians and comedians of color. White comedians are taught distance and denial strategies that allow them to engage in overt racial commentary and deny racism or racist intent,[11] while nonwhites are often encouraged to engage in racial stereotypes uncritically. White comedians are allowed to "let go" of their guilt; comedians of color, however, are asked to "let go" of their anger. Though we live in an era that has often been proclaimed to be "color-blind," Pérez argues that racism is not a thing of the past in comedic media; it is just expressed differently: "If color-blind racism tends to be concealed, racism in comedy is hidden in plain sight . . . [in stand-up comedy] racism is expressed in public and overtly, but its offensiveness is deflected, in part, by the use of strategies that make the performers seem 'not racist,' even as they say racist things."[12]

How does one navigate a space in which your identity, your religion, is often the butt of the joke? How do you carve space for yourself within an industry that has traded on racial, ethnic, and religious stereotypes for laughs? Do you embrace the bigotry and racism and roll it into your jokes the way Aziz Ansari did during his *Saturday Night Live* monologue? Do you offer comedic counter-framings? Do you write jokes highlighting cultural difference as a way to challenge stereotype and prejudice? For comedians and entertainers from minority backgrounds, the answer is often complicated and sometimes controversial.

In writing of comedy programs that showcase Black comics speaking of the Black experience to an assumed Black audience such as *Def Comedy Jam* or *Comic Justice*, Norma Shulman notes that "over and over again, in different ways, black comedians tell black audiences that things fundamentally have not changed in the United States since the days of slavery. The insults they must endure just have become subtler and less tangible."[13] They use the comedic stage to foreground their identities as Black Americans while connecting with the audience over their shared experience with racial injustice. While it is meant to connect Black Americans, it is a comedic space that does not want to think about or engage with the experience of white America.[14] It is a particular performance of jokes meant for a particular audience, not a universal one.

In 2007, the CBC premiered a program that was an attempt to create a more universal experience as it worked to convince viewers that Muslims could be just as Canadian as anyone else. *Little Mosque on the Prairie* was set in a fictional Saskatchewan town and focused on the lives of a Muslim community whose mosque was actually located inside a church. Created by Canadian Muslim writer Zarqa Nawaz, the show dealt with issues related to integration and religious interpretation. Many of the storylines, particularly in the first season, dealt less with cultural clashes between Muslims and non-Muslims than those between Muslims themselves. The "characters reflect the ethnic diversity of Muslims in Canada: a Lebanese Muslim, a Pakistani Muslim, a (Black) Nigerian Muslim, a (white) Canadian Muslim convert, a born-in-Canada mixed-race Muslim, and a Canadian-trained Imam,"[15] all of whom model a multicultural idea of not only what Canada is but also who Muslims are. The diverse cast, and the arguments over dogma they sometimes engaged in, served to challenge the idea of the homogeneous, "scary" Muslim other.[16] One critique of the program was that this multicultural portrait often seemed to champion an idealized idea of what a "moderate Muslim" might look like in the Canadian context, one who is "liberal" and "modern" and not extremist in any way.[17]

A situation comedy in the United Kingdom similarly attempted to present British Muslims as just as British as anyone else. The program premiered in 2012 on BBC and takes place in East Birmingham, called "the capital of British Pakistan" by the show's lead character Mr. Khan. *Citizen Khan* focuses on the life of the Khan family and aired during prime time, making it accessible to a wide swath of the British population. However, concerns arose over the stereotyped ways the Khan family seemed to be presented—the patriarch, for instance is loud and attempts to control the lives of his wives and two daughters, claiming to know what is best for them. The program has been criticized for what has been called its offensive, and simply not funny, representation of a British Muslim family. However, Saha Anamik has argued that the program follows in the footsteps of other British family comedies featuring bumbling and problematic father figures—it is in essence just another British family comedy of errors, only instead of the family being white and Anglican, it happens to be brown and Muslim: "The actual inventiveness of Citizen Khan might become more apparent if we consider its cultural political dimensions. Specifically I think about the value of grounding a representation of Asianness and Muslimness very explicitly—unashamedly so in fact—in this very British tradition of sitcom."[18] Saha suggests that, given the continued Orientalization and exoticization of Muslims and Muslim cultures in British media, presenting an Asian, Muslim family in a traditional British sitcom can present a "counter-hegemonic," or even subversive, framing of Muslims to British audiences. He notes, "I believe Citizen Khan 'transrupts' a nationalist discourse that paints Muslims as absolutely, irreconcilably different from British culture."[19] This is the opposite of what Hamza Arshad attempted to do with his YouTube series

84 POP ISLAM

Diary of a Badman, which played stereotypes to extremes in a way that ridiculed them and helped relieve the anxieties of British Muslims.[20]

The drive to make difference in some way invisible or palatable often drove the work of American Muslim comedians in the aftermath of September 11. The 2001 terrorist attacks seemed to be the manifestation of hundreds of years of warnings, hundreds of years of fear, hundreds of years of a social, political, and cultural discourse that had proclaimed that Islam and those who lived its tenets were a threat to the Western world. On a single, beautiful fall morning, centuries of Islamophobia and anti-Muslim sentiment seemed cataclysmically justified. The diverse lives of billions of Muslims around the world were erased that day by the actions of nineteen men affiliated with extremist al-Qaeda who many media pundits claimed exemplified the true face of Islam. Americans became increasingly wary of Arab or Muslim people or people who looked like they might be. In the aftermath, American Muslim comedians attempted to use humor and sarcasm to diffuse tensions when they performed; Amarnath Amarsingam noted that "Muslim standup comedians [break down] cultural barriers, [promote] interreligious and intercultural dialogue, as well as [tackle] the misperceptions of Muslim and Arab Americans in the United States."[21] They also, Amarsingam suggests, attempted to shape new "common sense" understandings of the Muslim experience, ones that foregrounded the ridiculousness of stereotypes and worked to foster cross-cultural understanding. Something similar happened in the aftermath of another cultural event, this one taking place in media spaces, not physical spaces.

In 2012, *Newsweek* published the latest in a string of cover stories about Muslim anger toward, or hate of, the West. Penned by controversial figure Ayaan Hirsi Ali, the cover story featured the headline "Muslim Rage" across the top of the magazine, with the subtitle "How I survived it; How we can end it" at the bottom. The response on social media was instantaneous, incandescent, and inventive. Twitter soon filled with the hashtag #MuslimRage as users turned the cover and its message into a joke. "Lost your kid Jihad at the airport. Can't yell for him. #MuslimRage," wrote one user; another tweeted, "i dont feel any rage. . . . does that mean i am not muslim?#someonegetmeadrink#MuslimR age."[22] Liz Sills points out that "when Ali's 'Muslim Rage' meets #MuslimRage, it also met a collectivity of individuals, emotions, and worldviews that makes the simple 'Them versus Us' propaganda into a complex network of perspective and understanding."[23] The cover story worked to homogenize all Muslims as scary, angry others; the social media response proved how ridiculous that homogenization is as Muslims from a wide variety of backgrounds and schools of thought pushed back at that stereotyping, with Sills suggesting, "Humor brings

Fig. 3.2 One of the many comedic takes on *Newsweek*'s "Muslim Rage" issue from 2012, several which went on to become memes circulated under the #MuslimRage hashtag on social media. This image and the creator's discussion of it can be found at the blog *Cartoon Muslim*. The specific post discussing this image is available at http://muhammadcomic.blogspot.com/2012/09/muslimrage-how-they-make-us-look-and.html

power."[24] In the case of the Muslim rage cover and social media, it was the power to fight back against stereotype and fear. Writing about American Muslim stand-up comedy post-9/11, Jaclyn Michael suggests that male and female Muslim comics "use humor to boldly challenge widely held social assumptions of Muslim America. Indeed, many of the new Muslim comedians are forthcoming with the socially critical goals of their comedy—they want to correct misinformed views that they feel distort the Muslim American identity."[25]

Jokes allow us to make bare difficult truths, wrap up prejudice and pain in laughter, and defuse tensions that may exist between those who have been othered and those doing the othering. The often tight space of a comedy club forces a particular type of closeness between the comedian and the audience, creating a short-term, and sometimes intense, relationship built on an ephemeral intimacy. The performer trusts the audience to listen and the audience trusts the performer to care for, and be careful of, them. Comedians who manage that relationship well often find themselves moving from stage to screen, though that transition has often been more difficult for comedians from minority

86

POP ISLAM

backgrounds. It's really only been in the last decade that Muslim performers have been able to successfully make this move—among the most successful has been Aziz Ansari.

Ansari rose to fame on the NBC mockumentary series *Parks and Recreation*. The show features a band of lovable misfits running the parks department in imaginary Pawnee, Indiana; among them is Tom Haverford, a well-dressed, fast-talking man who loves America and his Canadian wife (who married him to get a green card). Tom was often assumed by other characters to be an immigrant to the United States, although he (like Ansari) was actually born in the US and grew up in South Carolina. More than his race or ethnicity, what makes Tom standout in Pawnee is the smooth-talking way he gets himself into trouble as well as his many (often failed) attempts at entrepreneurship. Tom seems to luxuriate in his own laziness, at one point saying, "At the risk of bragging, one of the things I'm best at is riding coattails. Behind every successful man is me. Smiling and taking partial credit."[26] Tom does begin to bring his worst impulses for selfishness and snarkiness under control, eventually providing not just comedic support but also emotional support for other characters on the program. His admonition to the overworked women in the office to "Treat yo' self"[27] spawned countless internet memes. What is less obvious is Tom's Muslim background. It only comes up twice in the seven-season run of *Parks and Rec*, both references occurring in season 2. The first time it comes up is when Leslie Knope, the character played by Amy Poehler, asks Haverford where he's from:

LESLIE KNOPE: You're not from here, right?
TOM HAVERFORD: No, I'm from South Carolina.
LESLIE KNOPE: But you moved to South Carolina from where?
TOM HAVERFORD: My mother's uterus.
LESLIE KNOPE: But you were conceived in Libya, right?
TOM HAVERFORD: Wow. No. I was conceived in America. My parents are Indian.
LESLIE KNOPE: Where did the name Haverford come from?
TOM HAVERFORD: My birth name is Darwish Zubair Ismail Gani. Then I changed it to Tom Haverford, because you know, brown guys with funny-sounding Muslim names don't make it far into politics.
LESLIE KNOPE: What about Barack Obama?
TOM HAVERFORD: Okay, yeah, fine, Barack Obama. If I knew a guy named Barack Obama was gonna be elected president, yeah, maybe I wouldn't have changed it.[28]

BIG SCREEN, SMALL STAGE — 87

The exchange does two things: It acknowledges that Muslims are often imagined to be from someplace else, even if they were born and raised in the United States. It also makes visible to the audience how much people from minority backgrounds are forced to give up in order to be seen as less foreign, although in the case of Haverford, not even his adopted Anglo-sounding name gave him the patina of American authenticity he hoped it would. The second time Tom's Muslim heritage (Tom is a nonpracticing Muslim) comes up is in passing during a conversation at a dinner party being thrown by Leslie. And that's it for the entire run of the series. Perhaps it's a good thing that the writers did not make Islam central to Tom's characterization; it's easy to imagine how jokes dealing with Islam or Tom's Muslim identity could have gone wrong. However, the imperfect and accessible Tom could have helped further "transrupt" (to use Anamik Saha's term)[29] audience understandings of the people who work in and populate small town America. Instead, Tom is a Muslim in name only, and Islam is invisible. Something similar happened on HBO's *Silicon Valley*.

Much like *Parks and Rec*, *Silicon Valley* tells the story of a ragtag group of people who work together—this time in the tech world. One of the characters is a coder from Pakistan named Dinesh Chugtai, played by Kumail Nanjiani. Dinesh is a naturalized American citizen who says he was asked if he was part of al-Qaeda multiple times during his naturalization interviews. He most often spars with his Satanist coworker Bertram Gilfoyle, who is a Canadian immigrant, although, unlike Dinesh, he is not a legal immigrant. This comes up during a conversation Dinesh has with their coworker Jared as Gilfoyle is working nearby.

> **DINESH:** Hey, Jared, you know who else is Canadian? Justin Bieber, the Hitler of music.
> **GILFOYLE:** Do you have a problem with me being Canadian?
> **DINESH:** I do, actually. Do you have any idea how long it took me to become a citizen?
> **GILFOYLE:** Did it take you a long time? I'm glad I didn't do it then.
> **DINESH:** Typical lazy immigrant. These people think they can just walk into this country
> **GILFOYLE:** I did just walk into this country. My car broke down on the Ambassador Bridge. It took me an extra fifteen minutes to get across the border. Major hassle.[30]

As with Tom Haverford, Dinesh's religion rarely comes up in conversation or in jokes. Jokes are often made at his expense—focused on his bad luck with women, his weaknesses as a coder, and sometimes at how the way he lives in

88   POP ISLAM

California might clash with the Pakistani culture he grew up in—but there are almost no jokes made about his being a Muslim (though, like Tom, a non-practicing one) or about Islam itself. As with Tom Haverford on *Parks and Rec*, Dinesh is a Muslim character whose Muslim identity is obscured. That was not the case in Kumail Nanjani's feature film debut, *The Big Sick*.

The Big Sick tells the story of how Nanjiani met and fell in love with his white American wife, Emily, against the backdrop of her battle with a life-threatening illness. As Nanjiani is getting to know the woman who becomes his wife, his family is attempting to arrange his marriage to a good Muslim girl. The audience watches as he struggles to figure out how to tell his family this is not the path to love he wants to tread: he does not want to disappoint his observant Muslim parents, but he also does not want to live their life. It is a story many can relate to, Muslim or non-Muslim. That accessibility, however, came at a cost as his Muslim parents and the Muslim women they set Nanjiani up with in the film serve as little more than a backdrop against which his struggle over identity plays out. Critic Amil Niazi was particularly troubled by the portrayal of Nanjiani's mother and his brides-to-be in the film:

> The brown women in *The Big Sick*, from Nanjiani's meddling mother to his revolving door of brides-to-be, are such comical versions of real South Asian women that it felt—in a film that packs such emotional nuance into its leads—jarring. I understand that this is a very personal story for Nanjiani, and one of my biggest frustrations is when people of color (POC) are tasked by white people with being stand-ins for their entire culture rather than simply being allowed to tell their stories. Surely, he could have found room in his personal narrative to flesh out the characters of the brown women who make up such a core element of his story. Women who are so rarely otherwise seen in Hollywood.[31]

Even in a film written by an individual from Muslim background that at times challenges the historic stereotypes of Muslims, the Muslim women are rendered mute bystanders as someone else makes decisions about their lives. In both *Parks and Rec* and *Silicon Valley*, Islam is something gestured to but not really engaged with; in *The Big Sick*, it seems to be something Nanjiani is trying to run away from. There are comedians, however, who make their Muslim identities an integral part of the stories they tell.

Standing before an audience in Davis, California, comedian and writer Hasan Minhaj told joke after joke about growing up in the United States, the entire time foregrounding his identity as a minority in America: "Popping out of your mom is like real estate—it's all about location, location, location. I popped out here like, anybody brown, we popped out here we made it. We're the rappers that made it."[32] Famous for his work as a correspondent on *The Daily Show*, Minhaj is the son of Indian immigrants who moved to the United States after they were married. His Netflix stand-up special, *Homecoming King*, provided him a platform to discuss in frank and funny ways just how difficult it was to be a brown Muslim kid living in a majority white community like Davis after his mother went back to India to finish her medical degree: "I'm the only brown kid at my school, my dad is the only brown guy at work, so in a weird way, that brings us together and we have to do everything together . . . which sucks. Because, if you're with an immigrant father, you have to try to understand them and I still can't understand some of you guys to this day. Like, there are uncles here tonight, and none of you guys are smiling. I don't get it. You're gonna die, fucking laugh . . . you guys are always stressed and always tired."

Eventually, Minhaj moves away from jokes centered solely on his being the child of immigrants and actually begins to tell long, complicated jokes about what it's like to be Muslim. This arc begins as Minhaj explains that he married a Hindu girl, explaining to the audience, "Alright, some of you don't know, Hindus and Muslims are like the Montagues and Capulets of India,"[33] using the familiar narrative of Romeo and Juliet to explain the complicated religious and political divisions on the South Asian subcontinent and how they influence the lives of those who have left. When telling the audience how he convinced his father that marrying a Hindu woman was OK, Minhaj said he leaned on the myth of the American melting pot to make his case: "This is America, we can choose, we can pick and choose, what we want to adhere from the motherland here. Isn't like life biryani? Where you move the good shit towards you and push the weird shit to the side? Why do we got to adhere to this weird shit from back over there? He agrees, he's like 'That's a good point.'"

There are some things from the motherland Minhaj holds on to. Throughout his special, Minhaj code switches, at one moment uttering a phrase in Hindi with the text sometimes appearing on the screen behind him, before quickly translating it for the audience and moving on to the joke or story's main point. It is a hypervisible, hyperperformative moment. Dressed in casual street clothes and at times speaking in a way that would suggest Minhaj is fluent in hip-hop culture, he is a friendly, familiar face as he moves between Hindi and English. Su'ad Abdul Khabeer has written of how what she calls "Muslim cool" has emerged out of Black hip-hop culture in the United States and how, for non-Black Muslims, this "cool" can help them move away from Orientalist ideas of who they are while also making them seemingly more "approachable" at times.[34] When Minhaj gestures toward this Muslim cool in his comedy and

Fig. 3.3 In his Netflix special *Homecoming King*, Hasan Minhaj talked about what it's like to grow up as Muslim and brown in the United States. At one point, he tells the audience of how someone bashed in the windows of the family car after the September 11 attacks. Minhaj's father tells him that's the price for living in the United States, but Minhaj responds that his generation has the "audacity of equality."

in the way he dresses, he is attempting to reorient his audience to the idea that Muslims are American. Against this "cool" presentation, the moments when he foregrounds Hindi or his brownness or the fact of his parents' status as immigrants, Minhaj reminds his audience that the Muslim "other" they have been so primed to fear often sounds like them, dresses like them, and shares their struggles. Minhaj's stand-up special is framed by his struggle to find his place in the United States, his struggle to understand where he, as a brown Muslim son of immigrants, fits. This becomes all too clear when he tells the story of his family's experience during 9/11.

> When 9/11 happened I was a sophomore in high school and my dad sits everyone down at the dinner table. He's like, "Alright, Hasan, whatever you do, do not tell people you are Muslim and do not talk about politics." I was like, "Alright, Dad, I'll just hide it, cool." This just rubs off. Sitting there, phone rings, I run to the phone, but my dad had a good first step and he beats me to the phone. "Hello," and I grab the second phone, "Hello?" and I hear a voice. "Hey! Hey you sand nigger, where's Osama?" He looks at me. "You can hear me, right, you fucking dune coon, where's Osama?"[35]

Minhaj tells this story as the American flag is shown on the screen behind him, the audience learning that the phone call ends with the caller making it clear he knew where his family lived and threatening to kill them. He tells the audience that when he looked at his father he "saw his mortality" and that he, Minhaj, was a coward because he said nothing to his father in the aftermath of the call. When someone does come to their house and breaks all the windows in the family's car, Minhaj is filled with rage, and it is as he is walking up and down the street looking for the people who did this that he sees his father sweeping up the shattered glass. When he asks his father what he is doing, his father responds in Hindi, which Minhaj translates for his audience: "These things happen and these things will continue to happen. That's the price we pay for being here." Minhaj says that's the moment he realized he and his father truly were from two different generations; his father's generation is willing to endure some racism in order to live the American dream, while Minhaj's generation has "the audacity of equality" and expects more of their fellow Americans.

Mehdi Semati has argued that within the current global political framework, "the racist imagination does not appeal to 'race' to posit the inferiority of an Other based on biology but to 'cultural differences' and their insurmountability."[36] Much of what Minhaj tears apart in his *Homecoming King* special is the idea that cultural differences are insurmountable. By code switching and by performing an identity that is informed by his parents' homeland but also by his American childhood, Minhaj is suggesting that Muslims are as American as anybody else. As children, they wish for presents they never get. As teenagers, they work to keep their parents off the phone when they are talking with their friends. As adults they figure out how to navigate the disappointment that can come when they don't live up to their parents' expectations of them. These are all human experiences—ones that are, yes, shaped by Minhaj's background as the Indian American Muslim son of immigrants but ones that connect him to everyone else in the audience laughing along with him. Minhaj demands that the audience see his difference, engage with it, and still see him as American.

Experiences of racism and Islamophobia and how different generations respond to them were also themes of the Comedy Central special *Goatface*. The special featured Minhaj as well as comedians Asif Ali, Fahim Anwar, and Aristotle Athiras. All four are the Muslim sons of immigrants to the United States and the special often pokes fun at experiences that bind them together. In one sketch, Minhaj serves as the host of a game show called "Baba Knows Best," in which the other three comedians parody immigrant fathers.[37] During the five-minute sketch, the "fathers" throw shoes at cutouts of their "children," stand stoic in the face of major life events, and eventually break down and cry when their own fathers seemingly tell them they love them. As with Minhaj's *Homecoming King* stand-up special, there is a loose, almost hip-hop vibe to

Goatface, one that is fun and accessible. But even with the shared feeling and sketches highlighting shared experiences, the diversity of the comedians' experiences are also important throughlines to *Goatface*. There are short stand-up interstitials inserted between some of the sketches where the comedians have a chance to talk specifically about their own diverse experiences. As mentioned earlier, Hasan Minhaj's parents immigrated from India and Asif Ali's family background is also Indian, while Fahim Anwar's parents are from Afghanistan, and Aristotle Athiras's parents are Iranian. In the short stand-up pieces, and in a few of the sketches themselves, their difference from one another is highlighted, helping to push back against the homogenization of Muslims as being from one place and living the same sorts of lives. *Goatface*'s foregrounding of all of this helps make visible to the non-Muslims watching the diversity of the American Muslim experience.

The success of Aziz Ansari, Hasan Minhaj, and Kumail Nanjiani seems to have proven that American audiences are willing to hear uncomfortable truths about life in the United States as long as there is laughter involved. Samah Choudhury has argued that these three comics have partly found fame as their humor signals they are modern subjects who are at home in secular society.[38] After *Homecoming King* won a Peabody Award, Minhaj was offered his own weekly late night–esque program on Netflix. Premiering in late 2018, the weekly, half-hour-long *Patriot Act with Hasan Minhaj* saw Minhaj break down everything from the American relationship with Saudi Arabia to the global impact of the NRA. Minhaj's Muslim identity rarely comes up on the program, but it would seem his willingness to tell funny stories about life as an American Muslim helped him get it and helped positioned him as someone who could reliably interpret modern life. Since the work of Ansari, Minhaj, and Nanjiani has become so visible (and seemingly profitable), other Muslim comedians are being offered opportunities to get their jokes before a wider audience, including Ramy Youssef and Mo Amer. Youssef created and stars in the award-winning Hulu program, *Ramy*; Amer stars in the semiautobiographical *Mo* on Neflix, cocreated with Youssef.

However, not all Muslim comedians are quite as visible.

While male Muslim comedians are finding their way into high-profile media spaces, female comics have had less mainstream success. Much as with their non-Muslim compatriots, female voices are overshadowed by male voices, are often overlooked, or simply not seen as profitable. Though there are Muslim women comedians who have gained popularity in Canada or the United Kingdom, American Muslim women have had a harder time gaining mainstream success and certainly have not been provided the same kinds of platforms as

Fig. 3.4 During a comedic roast competition, Dina Hashem's opponent continually told jokes that took aim at her religious or ethnic heritage. Over the course of thirty minutes, Hashem had to listen as Eli Sairs repeated Islamophobic and anti-Muslim narratives that ultimately won him the contest.

their male counterparts. One of those comedians is New Jersey native Dina Hashem.

Hashem is a comedian based in New York City. She has appeared on several Comedy Central programs and, in 2017, did a set on *Conan* on TBS: "I'm an Arab lady. Whenever people talk about the problems facing Arab women, I think it's usually about the religion or the laws, or Trump now. No one talks about the body hair. I came here to tell you about it. Like, I grew up in a Muslim family, we couldn't talk about anything sexy like that, I had to figure out on my own what was normal for a growing girl."[39]

Hashem's jokes swung back and forth between those that were broadly general in nature—dating on Tinder—and those very specifically pulled from her life. "I'm from New Jersey. My dad left when I was very young, he's lived in the Middle East my whole life for some reason and he's called on the phone and given me the same speech every time. He goes: 'Dina . . . ,' I can't do an Arab accent, so just imagine your favorite enemy of the state. He'll be like, 'Dina, you have to be a good Muslim so that one day we can reunite together in Heaven.' I'll be like, 'Really? You won't even reunite in New Jersey.'"

A month before she appeared on *Conan*, Hashem competed against white male comedian Eli Sairs for the RoastMasters national championship in New York City. The two went head-to-head in three rounds of insult filled jokes. A comedic roast focuses on one individual, generally a celebrity, as a group of friends, fans, and admirers tell funny stories meant to embarrass the honoree just a little. While the jokes featured at roasts have always been a bit off-color and outrageous, Hallie Cantor writing for *Vulture* noted how they began trafficking much more frequently in humor some might find outright offensive.[40] At the same time, roasting reached past celebrity and was picked up by touring comics. It also became popular in some parts of the internet; in fact, there is even a forum on reddit dedicated solely to roast humor.[41] So the space that Hashem and Sairs entered for the RoastMasters championship was one where the expectation was that they would tear one another apart. And they did. However, while Hashem actually insulted Sairs, the person, during the battle, Sairs throughout insulted Hashem, the Muslim, as exemplified in his very first joke of the battle: "Dina, Dina is a Muslim. It's crazy that she sent a drone over here to ruin our lives. She does have some credits. You may know her from crashing . . . her truck into people in Manhattan last week."[42]

Hashem responded in her signature dry style: "Eli, Eli looks like his mom wrote him notes to get him out of gym class. You look like Mrs. Doubtfire if Robin Williams played her today."[43] As she started her joke, though, the audience was still laughing over Sairs's joke suggesting she was a terrorist. Almost every joke Sairs made during the roast was related to Hashem's identity as a Muslim woman, connecting that identity to violence or terrorism. And Hashem, in order to compete, had to stand there and take it. "When you talk like this," Sairs said, as he imitated Hashem's style of delivery, "people think something is more clever than it actually is. Something seems more impressive if it was written by a retard . . . like the Qur'an."[44] The battle featured several such vile "jokes" before Sairs was declared the winner, his brand of familiar, racist humor finding safe harbor with the audience. It was that type of racist and Islamophobic thinking that Negin Farsad hoped to challenge during her *The Muslims Are Coming* comedy tour.

Negin Farsad is an Iranian American who labels herself a "social justice comedian."[45] She also directed and produced the 2008 film *Nerdcore Rising*, which explores the genre of nerdcore hip-hop. In 2013, she released another movie, this one codirected with comedian Dean Obeidallah, which chronicled *The Muslims Are Coming* comedy road show. Farsad and Obeidallah got together some of their Muslim comedian friends and took them on a trip through the American South and Southwest, with the goal of using laughter to fight prejudice. In addition to the free comedy shows they put on during the tour, they also engaged in public outreach, doing things like setting up an Ask A Muslim booth in one city and playing a game called "Name That Religion" with passersby in Birmingham, Alabama. In the game, individuals were given a quote from a holy book and asked to decide whether it came from the Old Testament, the New Testament, or the Qur'an. When asked about one quote suggesting that a woman who did not bleed on her first night of marriage should be stoned, all of the respondents shown the quote assumed it came from the Qur'an. When Farsad asked one woman why she had answered Qur'an so quickly, the woman said, "Because, you know, women, the women are subjected to men," to which Farsad responded, "It is the Old Testament. Deuteronomy, dude."[46] One thing particularly interesting about the film is that when moments like that happen rather than lingering too long in a joke one could make related to the misperception, the film often cuts to an expert who helps explain why such a perception exists. Farsad and Obeidallah are trying to not only resist stereotype or even rage against it; they are attempting to educate.

Since the film's premiere, Farsad has launched her own podcast, *Fake the News*, as well as begun appearing as a panelist on NPR's pop culture quiz show, *Wait, Wait Don't Tell Me*. She's also appeared on news programs during segments related to Islam or Muslim life. Farsad discussed the aftermath of one of those news appearances during a set she performed for *Live from Here* in 2018: "I was on MSNBC recently because I am the voice of a generation and we were there talking about our ruler and after the show someone tweeted at me '@neginfarsad is clearly the Jewish nerd on the panel.' And I'm actually an Iranian-American Muslim like all of you, and so, to be called a Jewish nerd, it felt like an upgrade, you know? It was really exciting."[47]

Farsad then explained that she attempted to correct the man's mistake, pointing out she was "the Muslim nerd," but what she said did not matter to the man. "He responded, 'I'm sorry, but you're clearly a Jewy-McJewface.' And I thought it was so interesting that he was so insistent that I be Jewish, like 'I'm sorry I took your anti-Semitism away from you, but I feel like Islamophobia is a really good substitute.' You know what I mean? It's like a packet of stevia, you guys."[48]

In that short story, Farsad highlighted what many scholars have argued— that there is a link between antisemitism and Islamophobia as well as the idea that certain religions have become racialized so that people think they can know a person's faith by simply looking at them.[49] Writing of the ways in which the histories of antisemitism, Islamophobia, and racism are all bound up with one another, Nabar Meer notes that "racialized categories have saturated cultural portrayals of Muslims and Jews, endowing each with characteristics"[50] that were meant to mark them as different from their Christian neighbors. Those racialized differences bound them together as people who were not Christian and, therefore, were often seen as unknowable and threatening in

Fig. 3.5 During a stand-up set on *Late Night with Seth Meyers*, Zainab Johnson told jokes about growing up in a large Muslim family and breaking up with a former friend who said racist things about her hair and about how her family thought she was going to "come dribbling out the closet."

some way. Meer suggests that "what this means is that the category of race was co-constituted with religion."[51] The man who called Farsad a "Jewy-McJewface" acted out a racialized connection between antisemitism and Islamophobia that has existed for centuries. "I wanted to point out to him, though," Farsad told the audience, "that Jewy-McJewface is actually an Irish name. Like if you really wanted to get me you'd call me Goldstein Bagelface Dollarsign or whatever."[52]

The connection between race and religion is unavoidable in the comedy of Zainab Johnson. "Hi! Yay! Yay! Yay! Give it up for my afro," Johnson urged the audience during a set she performed on *Late Night with Seth Myers*. "It excites me because I had a shaved head for seven years, I was never late anywhere."[53] Like Dina Hashem and Negin Farsad, Johnson has ties to New York City. The African American comedian grew up in in Harlem, where she was raised in a Muslim household with her twelve siblings. "My mom wanted 20, she made it to 13. When I was in 2nd grade she had kid number 10, and I was like, 'This has got to stop.'"[54] Much of Johnson's comedy revolves around her identity as a Black woman—touching on everything from the pressure she feels to marry a Black guy (because none of her siblings has married a Black person) to the stereotype that Black people are late. On her album, *Model Citizen*, she often discusses how her identity as a Black woman intersects with her experiences as a Muslim.

I don't look Muslim. You can't look at me and tell I'm Muslim so it's very easy for me to fly. My name could give it away, though, Zainab: most popular female Islamic name. Middle Eastern men meet me, they get excited. They're like, "Oh my, oh my god, Zainab, that is my mother's name. That is my sister's name. That is my first, my second, and my third wives' names, Zainab." Zainab is an esteemed name. Zainab was the prophet's wife. Zainab is the reason all Muslim women cover up. My last name, though, is Johnson. Straight from the plantation.[55]

The story about her name serves to remind her audience that she is Black, Muslim, and American—all at the same time. By gesturing to the racial profiling many Muslims experience in airports, Johnson set the joke within the historic cultural framework of Muslims as people to be feared while suggesting, as she makes them laugh, she is not someone the audience needs to fear. She then, just a few moments later, shows how that fear has also conditioned her to respond in particular ways to other Muslims. "Like, I'm not afraid of the country," Johnson said while talking about a visit to Dubai, "but, you know, we see so much . . . our media presents it in such a way I just didn't really know what was going to happen."[56] Her nervousness upon her arrival was amped up by a customs agent who muttered about America under his breath as he looked through her things. "And then as soon as he opened my passport, he was like, 'Zainab, welcome home, Zainab.'"[57] Johnson pauses as she lets the audience engage with the story she's just told The story the joke communicates is that Muslims are diverse. Zainab's discussion of her name, her Black identity, and her experience traveling to Dubai helps make that visible to her audience. Through her comedy, Johnson shows how, in the words of scholar Sylvia Chan-Malik, "Islam acts as an insurgent ethos"[58] in her life, providing her a way of working toward her own understanding of freedom within the culture that she lives. The insurgent work of Johnson, Dina Hasem, and Negin Farsad is well known within the comedy community, but they have not had the broad, mainstream success that Aziz Ansari, Kumail Nanjiani, and Hasan Minhaj have had to date. The three women have made their lived experiences as Muslim women accessible through their jokes, but that accessibility has not necessarily translated into mainstream visibility.

The performers discussed in this chapter represent a fraction of the American Muslim comedians working today. Virtually every week, there are news stories about how a Muslim comedian somewhere is "changing perceptions" or "breaking down walls" and it's almost always a different comedian being profiled. And, though at least one article framed comedy as a "softer way to build bridges,"[59] comedy done well is rarely soft. Or safe. Particularly for individuals from minority communities for whom racism, xenophobia, or Islamophobia are

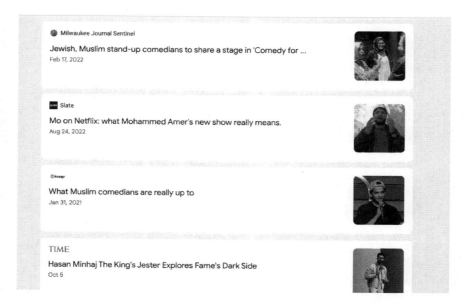

Fig. 3.6 News outlets regularly publish stories about Muslim comedians. Many of these stories are designed to highlight how the comedians use comedy to fight stereotype while also suggesting that the individuals are just as American as anyone else.

a regular part of daily life. Working to resist stereotyping and prejudice in front of an audience, making yourself vulnerable, and opening up the possibility of the crowd turning against you—all of that is the opposite of safe. Green and Linders suggest that comedy is a space where people who have been marginalized can express anger and frustration over their treatment by society, suggesting the possibility that dangerous vulnerability might be worth the release for some.[60] If Michel Foucault is right, and visibility can trap us into performing in ways expected of us rather than in ways that are authentic to ourselves, perhaps comedy is one way some can escape that trap. Muslim comedians are becoming increasingly visible in the United States, though it is too early to tell whether their comedy will be able to hold "the mirror up to degenerate nature"[61] and force Americans to reckon with the Islamophobia and anti-Muslim sentiment that shapes their understandings of Islam. What it does suggest is that Muslims who are not framed as terrorists or oppressed victims or despotic tyrants can gain a foothold in American popular media when given the chance to create media. Kumail Nanjiani's ability to create media has propelled him to pop culture stardom. This chapter began with a discussion of *Saturday Night Live*, and it now closes with another.

In October 2017, Nanjiani hosted *SNL*. Standing before the audience in Studio 8H in Rockefeller Center, he reminded them that Islamophobia still exists: "Islamophobia is really on the rise right now, it never really went away, but it's really having a moment right now. Islamophobia is really like Will and Grace, you know it was huge a while ago and we thought it was gone and done and now it's back and bigger than ever!"[62]

Nanjiani's hosting stint came months after President Trump's Muslim travel ban was put in place and after several attacks on Muslim individuals, or individuals who looked Muslim, and a mosque bombing in Minnesota. Though Islam and Nanjiani's Muslim identity rarely make an appearance on *Silicon Valley* and served as little more than a prop in his film *The Big Sick*, issues related to racism and Islamophobia filled Nanjiani's *SNL* monologue: "My fantasy is when someone is racist to me I want danger to befall them, immediately. And then, I wanna rescue them, just to see the confused look on their face. Like I want them to be, 'Go back to India, haha' [looks to right] 'Wolves!' And then I fight off all the wolves and they're like, 'We were racist to you and you still saved us.' And I go, 'That is the way of my people'"[63]—his people, in this instance, being Pakistani Muslims. Nanjiani could easily have avoided the issue altogether in his monologue or only lightly touched on it before moving on to something else. Instead, he spent all seven minutes cracking jokes about racism and Islamophobia in the United States. As far as accessible popular media spaces in America go, it doesn't get much bigger than the *SNL* stage. Except for maybe the Marvel Cinematic Universe, which Nanjiani is now part of thanks to his casting in the film *The Eternals*.

What is striking about both Nanjiani and Aziz Ansari is that they are individuals of Muslim background who are not religiously Muslim. While comedians like Hasan Minhaj, who is a religiously observant Muslim, are increasingly becoming visible, the seeming hesitancy on the part of media producers to show a Muslim man seriously, deeply engaged with his faith identified in the previous chapter appears to be true of Muslim comedians as well, at least when they appear in scripted comedies. (Although, Ramy Youssef's Hulu show, *Ramy*, seems to suggest that might be changing.) Muslim men have long been imagined as violent, irrational others driven by a slavish devotion to the tenets of Islam—the media examined thus far would suggest that one way media producers have worked to humanize Muslim men and make them seem less of a threat, is to divorce them from their faith. Nanjiani worked against that in his monologue weaving together jokes that showed he was clearly well steeped in American culture but that also made visible his identity as a minority living in that culture. That it was during his monologue, which was really more of a short stand-up routine, is telling. Nanjiani was allowed to discuss issues related to Islamophobia as himself; Nanjiani's scripted characters, though seemingly sharing his ethnic and religious background, have not been allowed that same freedom.

NOTES

1. *Saturday Night Live*, "Aziz Ansari/Big Sean," season 42, episode 12, dir. Don Roy King, written by Chris Kelly, Sarah Schneider, Bryan Tucker, and Kent Sublette, NBC, January 21, 2017.

2. *Parks and Recreation*, "The Stakeout," season 2, episode 2, dir. Seth Gordon, written by Rachel Axler, NBC, September 24, 2009.

3. David Scott Kastan, "All's Well That Ends Well and the Limits of Comedy," *ELH* 52, no. 3 (1985): 575.

4. Aaryn Green and Annulla Linders, "The Impact of Comedy on Racial and Ethnic Discourse," *Sociological Inquiry* 86, no. 2 (2016): 243.

5. Sam Friedman and Giseline Kuipers, "The Divisive Power of Humour: Comedy, Taste and Symbolic Boundaries," *Cultural Sociology* 7, no. 2 (2013): 179–95.

6. Joseph W. Meeker, "The Comedy of Survival," *North American Review* 257 (1972): 2; Lawrence E. Mintz, "Standup Comedy as Social and Cultural Mediation," *American Quarterly* 37, no. 1 (1985): 71–80.

7. Joanne Gilber, *Performing Marginality: Humor, Gender, and Cultural Critique* (Detroit, MI: Wayne State University Press, 1997).

8. Ibid., 317.

9. Roger B. Henkle, "The Social Dynamics of Comedy," *Sewanee Review* 90, no. 2 (1982): 200.

10. Green and Linders, "Impact of Comedy on Racial and Ethnic Discourse."

11. Although, that does seem to be changing. As of this writing, *Saturday Night Live* fired one of its new members for the 2019–20 season after it was revealed he had a history of making racist and sexist jokes.

12. Raúl Pérez, "Learning to Make Racism Funny in the 'Color-Blind' Era: Stand-Up Comedy Students, Performance Strategies, and the (re)Production of Racist Jokes in Public," *Discourse and Society* 24, no. 4 (2013): 479.

13. Norma Schulman, "The House That Black Built: Television Stand-Up Comedy as Minor Discourse," *Journal of Popular Film and Television* 22, no. 3 (1994): 108.

14. Ibid.

15. Shelina Kassam, "'Settling' the Multicultural Nation-State: *Little Mosque on the Prairie*, and the Figure of the 'Moderate Muslim,'" *Social Identities* 21, no. 6 (2015): 610.

16. Sandra Cañas, "*The Little Mosque on the Prairie*: Examining (Multi) Cultural Space of Nation and Religion," *Cultural Dynamics* 20, no. 3 (2008): 195–211.

17. Kassam, "'Settling' the Multicultural Nation-State."

18. Anamik Saha, "*Citizen Smith* More Than *Citizen Kane?* Genres-in-Progress and the Cultural Politics of Difference," *South Asian Popular Culture* 11, no. 1 (2013): 97–102, at 99.

19. Ibid., 100.

20. Abdul Azim-Ahmed, "Faith in Comedy: Representations of British Identity in Muslim Comedy," *South Asian Popular Culture* 11, no. 1 (2013): 91–96.

21. Amarnath Amarsingam, "Laughter Is the Best Medicine: Muslim Comedians and Social Criticism in Post-9/11 America," *Journal of Muslim Minority Affairs* 30, no. 4 (2010): 466.

22. These and other #MuslimRage tweets can be found at NPR's reporting on the meme: Bill Chappell, "'Muslim Rage' Explodes on Twitter, but in a Funny Way (Yes, Really)," The Two-Way, September 17, 2012, https://www.npr.org /sections/thetwo-way/2012/09/17/161315765/muslim-rage-explodes-on-twitter but-in-a-funny-way-yes-really.

23. Liz Sills, "Hashtag Comedy: From Muslim Rage to #MuslimRage," *Re-Orient* 2, no. 1 (2017): 170.

24. Ibid., 173.

25. Jaclyn Michael, "American Muslims Stand Up and Speak Out: Trajectories of Humor in Muslim American Stand-Up Comedy," *Contemporary Islam* 7, no. 2 (2013): 129–53.

26. *Parks and Recreation*, "Born and Raised," season 4, episode 3, dir. Dean Holland, written by Aisha Muharrar, NBC, October 6, 2011.

27. *Parks and Recreation*, "Pawnee Rangers," season 4, episode 4, dir. Charles McDougall, written by Alan Yang, NBC, October 13, 2011.

28. *Parks and Recreation*, "The Stakeout."

29. Saha, "*Citizen Smith* More Than *Citizen Kane?*," 100.

30. *Silicon Valley*, "Articles of Incorporation," season 1, episode 3, dir. Tricia Brock, written by Matteo Borghese and Rob Turbovsky, HBO, April 20, 2014.

31. Amil Niazi, "'The Big Sick' Is Great, and It's Also Stereotypical toward Brown Women," Vice News, July 7, 2017, https://www.vice.com/en_us/article /zmvmp3/the-big-sick-is-great-and-its-also-stereotypical-toward-brown-women.

32. *Hasan Minhaj: Homecoming King*, comedy stand-up special, dir. Christopher Storer, written by Hasan Minhaj, Netflix, May 23, 2017.

33. Ibid.

34. Su'ad Abdul Khabeer, *Muslim Cool: Race, Religion, and Hip Hop in the United States* (New York: New York University Press, 2016).

35. Ibid.

36. Mehdi Semati, "Islamophobia, Culture and Race in the Age of Empire," *Cultural Studies* 24, no. 2 (2010): 256–75.

37. *Goatface: A Comedy Special*, "Does Baba Really Know Best?," dir. Aristole Athiras, written by Asif Ali, Fahim Anwar, Aristotle Athiras, and Hasan Minhaj, Comedy Central, November 27, 2018.

38. Samah Choudhury, "What Makes Humor Muslim?," in *American Examples: New Conversations about Religion*, vol. 1 (Tuscaloosa: University of Alabama Press, 2021).

39. *Conan*, "Jean-Claude Van Damme/Barkhad Abdi/Dina Hashem," dir. Billy Bollotino, written by Levi MacDougall, TBS, December 5, 2017.

40. Hallie Cantor, "The Roast: A History," Vulture, June 17, 2011, https://www.vulture.com/2011/06/the-roast-a-history.html.

41. Anna Kasunc and Geoff Kaufman, "'At Least the Pizzas You Make Are Hot': Norms, Values, and Abrasive Humor on the Subreddit r/RoastMe," *Proceedings of the International AAAI Conference on Web and Social Media* 12, no. 1 (2018).

42. The Stand NYC, "The RoastMasters @NYCF 11.10.17 Championship Match: Eli Sairs (C) vs. Dina Hashem," filmed November 2017, YouTube video, 34:46, posted November 2017, https://www.youtube.com/watch?v=BrjBljSDWug.

43. Ibid.

44. Ibid.

45. Negin Farsad, "Negin Farsad: Comedian, Writer, Actor, Director," accessed July 20, 2023, http://neginfarsad.com/.

46. *The Muslims Are Coming!* dir. Negin Farsad and Dean Obeidallah, Vaguely Qualified Productions, New York, 2013.

47. *Live from Here*, "Negin Farsad," filmed October 2018, YouTube video, 7:17, posted October 2018, https://www.youtube.com/watch?v=bYYuKzE-2HI.

48. Ibid.

49. Nabar Meer, "Racialization and Religion: Race, Culture and Difference in the Study of Antisemitism and Islamophobia," *Ethnic and Racial Studies* 36, no. 3 (2013): 385–98.

50. Ibid., 388.

51. Ibid., 389.

52. *Live from Here*, "Negin Farsad."

53. *Late Night with Seth Myers*, "Pete Davidson/Mary Lynn Rajskub/Zainab Johnson/Ben Sesar," written by Ben Warheit, NBC, September 27, 2018.

54. Ibid.

55. Zainab Johnson, *Model Citizen*, Super Artists, Inc., B01CB5VKHI, 2016, digital download.

56. Ibid.

57. Ibid.

58. Sylvia Chan-Malik, *Being Muslim: A Cultural History of Women of Color in American Islam* (New York: New York University Press, 2018), 186.

59. Aqilah Allaudeen, "A Muslim Woman Comic Walks into a Bar: Changing Perceptions through Jokes," *Mother Jones*, September 19, 2019, https://www.csmonitor.com/The-Culture/2019/0918/A-Muslim-woman-comic-walks-into-a-bar-Changing-perceptions-through-jokes.

60. Green and Linders, "Impact of Comedy on Racial and Ethnic Discourse."

61. Kastan, "All's Well That Ends Well," 575.

62. *Saturday Night Live*, "Kumail Nanjiani/P!nk," dir. Don Roy King, written by Bryan Tucker and Kent Sublette, NBC, October 14, 2017.

63. Ibid.

FOUR

IDENTITY AND RELIGION IN REALITY TV

THE GREAT BRITISH BAKE OFF is known for many things—disastrous Victoria sponges, melting ice cream confections, and contestants who, even when being kicked off the show, are graceful, generous, and kind in defeat. The program, produced by Love Productions, was a huge hit in Great Britain when it premiered in 2010. It captured the hearts of American audiences when it was broadcast on PBS the following year. The program's winners have included housewives and architects, university students and grandmothers, but none garnered the media attention that series 6's winner did.

Nadiya Hussain, who was born and raised in Luton but whose parents had immigrated to the United Kingdom from Bangladesh, was the first Muslim contestant to be crowned Britain's Best Baker. The show had featured Muslim contestants before her series, but Hussain was the only one to make it all the way to the end. She won over the judges with elaborate confections that included a peacock made of chocolate and a finale wedding cake made using her wedding jewels for her husband because they did not have a fancy cake when they were married in Bangladesh. News stories written about Hussain's win at the time waxed poetic about how it "defies prejudice in Britain" and how it "serves up the perfect rebuttal to Theresa May's xenophobic rhetoric."[1] When asked in a *Guardian* interview after her win how she felt about the fact that news media (and even some politicians) were holding her up as someone who shattered stereotypes, Hussain said, "Going in, the things that worried me were not these deep issues like: 'I have to represent all Muslims.' What bothered me was more that I didn't want to go in there and sound unintelligent or get my bakes wrong."[2]

Fig. 4.1 *The Great British Bake Off* winner Nadiya Hussain did the media circuit after winning the coveted prize. She appeared on an episode of *The Graham Norton Show* where she talked about her experience with arranged marriage and how she knew her husband was the one for her.

Even if Hussain didn't go into the competition thinking about how her appearance (and success) on the program might reflect on British Muslims, her kind demeanor made the hijab-wearing woman in the bakeoff tent seem approachable. The glimpse the show provided into Nadiya's life outside the tent as a wife and a mother made her an audience favorite, particularly among young Muslims who often don't find positive representations of Islam on British television. This was something Hussain acknowledged in that *Guardian* interview: "Growing up, I didn't see that many Muslims on TV and we don't see many now. But essentially I am a mother and that's the job I know best. For me, it's important to instill in my children that they can do whatever they like, that no matter what their religion and colour, they can achieve what they want through hard work. And it's nice to be able to do the same for a wider audience. If I have—amazing."[3]

Those glimpses into Hussain's life, as well as into the lives of other contestants, is a big part of the program's appeal. *The Great British Bake Off*, while concerned with things like cake and biscuits, is a reality show, one that provides insight into not only what makes a "scrummy" dessert but also the *real* lives of its contestants. As in the United Kingdom, there have been Muslim contestants who have taken part in American reality TV and found success. If, as MTV's

The Real World suggested, reality TV gives us insight into "what happens when people stop being polite and start getting real" (unlikely given the scripted nature of most reality programs), this chapter considers what audiences are told about the *real* experience of American Muslims when they appear on programs such as *Top Chef, Project Runway*, and *America's Next Top Model*.

In 1992, MTV revolutionized prime-time TV with the premiere of its program *The Real World*. The show was produced in a kind of documentary style and featured seven strangers thrown together in an apartment in New York City. The show chronicled their struggles to find a way to live together as they also worked to find their way in New York. Annette Hill has suggested that "reality TV is located in border territories, between information and entertainment, documentary and drama."[4] The first several seasons of *The Real World* seemed to engage in a kind of genre boundary crossing, as the naturalistic documentary style made the sometimes soap opera–worthy storylines feel both real and entertaining. Early seasons dealt with not only relationship drama—both romantic and platonic—but also issues of race, gender, and sexuality. Perhaps the most famous storyline involving a serious issue concerned *The Real World: San Francisco* cast member Pedro Zamora. Zamora was not only one of the first openly gay men to be featured on prime-time TV, but he was also one of the first people living with AIDS to gain such visibility as well. Program creator and producer Jonathon Murray said of choosing to set the show's third season in San Francisco and of casting Zamora, "As a gay man who had lost friends to AIDS, I felt it was important."[5] Zamora's inclusion in the series made an epidemic that seemed far distant from most of American experience real. However, even if groundbreaking, *The Real World* was not the first program to give audiences an up-close look at American lives.

In 1974, PBS premiered a program called *An American Family*. Widely considered by many to be the first reality television program to air in the United States, *An American Family* followed the upper-middle-class Louds family in California over the course of a year. Jonathon Bignell says what made the program a success was that it gave audiences what felt like a real look into the life of an American family—showing it warts and all.[6] This early foray into what would come to be called reality TV had much more in common with documentary filmmaking than it did with the dating and cooking competition shows that would come to dominate the genre in the 2000s. This connection to documentary style lends reality TV a feeling of authenticity, with the people appearing in such programs seen as authentic if their appearance seems truthful and honest.[7] In the case of *An American Family*, this authenticity, this honesty of representation, captured the disintegration of the family and the parents' eventual divorce. It got real decades before MTV's *The Real World*.

Something on TV feeling real is very much wrapped up in the way it is presented to us, and in the case of people's lives, Hill notes that "the way real people and their stories are represented on television is closely linked to how we judge the truthfulness of visual evidence."[8] The types of documentary photographs and films that informed the production of *An American Family* have primed us to expect that what we see when we are dealing with every day people is the truth. When it comes to reality TV, particularly formats that promise viewers insight into the human condition in some way, if it is documenting reality, then it is true. If an audience thinks that the people on-screen are performing, not engaging organically with what is happening in the moment, then the less truthful the program seems. In writing of the dynamics of *Big Brother*—which, like *The Real World*, traps strangers in a house together but, unlike it, has castmates vote one another out of the house each week—Nick Couldry notes that, in order to succeed, contestants have to seem authentic.[9] Whether we accept something we see as *authentic* depends on whether that thing feels true or honest to our own personal experiences.[10] Of course, what experiences and identities audiences have access to is rarely decided by the people appearing on reality TV programs but, instead, by program producers and their ideas of what they think audiences expect from a show. One of the critiques that has been leveled at reality programming is that, like much of the larger media landscape, minorities rarely make appearances on the programs, or when they do, their representation is marked by stereotypes. Grace Wang points out that "while reality TV programs open up a space for greater representation of racialized minorities, these shows also adhere to, and authenticate, racialized narratives and stereotypes by embodying them in the characters of 'real' people."[11] As producers and casting directors seek to create diverse, multiracial, and multiethnic casts, the need to produce simple and understandable narratives for each character means they often use easily accessible and often racist stereotypes to flesh out the stories of their cast.[12] Because the programs promise to offer up a slice of reality, seeing Asian individuals portrayed as "technical robots" or Black women as hypersexual drama queens or Black men as angry and violent makes them seem to be *authentic* representations of the Asian or Black experience because the person embodying the stereotype is supposedly a *real* person.[13] Robin Boylorn reminds us that reality TV is a "supposed lens into the everyday experiences, thoughts, and actions in the lives of participants"[14]—which lends the representations found there a weight they perhaps do not deserve.

For James Wong, reality TV "allows us to gaze at others,"[15] although he argues that this is not simply an issue of being seen but also an issue of how we choose to behave, or choose to perform, when we know we are being watched. Michel Foucault suggested that an individual does not need to know they are being seen for their behavior to become circumspect; it is simply enough to know that they *could* be disciplined for stepping out of line that keeps them from deviating too far from social expectations for their behavior.[16] This fear of being disciplined is potent and real for contestants on reality TV as they are often trapped by the conventions of the genre as they must live up to the expectations of their particular identities or "risk being sent home."[17] In her discussion of Hung Huynh, a Vietnamese American winner of Bravo's *Top Chef* competition, Grace Wang shows how his win was predicated on his willingness in the finale to shirk his classical French training in order to produce a meal that the judges felt had more soul; for them, that meant it should be more tied to Vietnamese cuisine.[18] To the judges, and possibly the audience, Huynh's performance as a chef over the course of the series was not authentic enough because it was not seen as Asian enough. It is only when he embraces what is seen as his *authentic* Asian heritage that he is showered with accolades and declared the best chef of the season.

Reality TV has made television more diverse, suggests Mark Orbe, but not necessarily better (or less racist). Programs that feature diverse casts often manipulate situations to create or heighten interracial tensions, which can also make racial stereotypes feel more real because viewers watch the stereotyped conflict play out for them on their TVs.[19] There is rarely any sort of kumbaya, come together, "we're all one" narrative in programs featuring diverse casts as reality TV positions race as a point of contention between multiracial cast members because conflict is good for ratings.[20] Individuals are often placed in a situation where they are expected to both represent and defend their race or ethnicity, with the cast members often openly chaffing at being placed in such a situation.[21] However, there's no guarantee that even when reality TV producers purposefully create programs meant to break down the stereotypes we hold of each other that they will find much purchase with American audiences— especially if the program becomes a political football, as happened with TLC's *All American Muslim*.

In 2011, a reality program featuring American Muslims aired for a short while on the cable channel TLC. Following in the footsteps of *An American Family*, *All American Muslim* promised a documentary-esque look into the lives of five families living in Dearborn, Michigan, with the aim of showing just how American they were. One family featured a cop, another a football coach, and

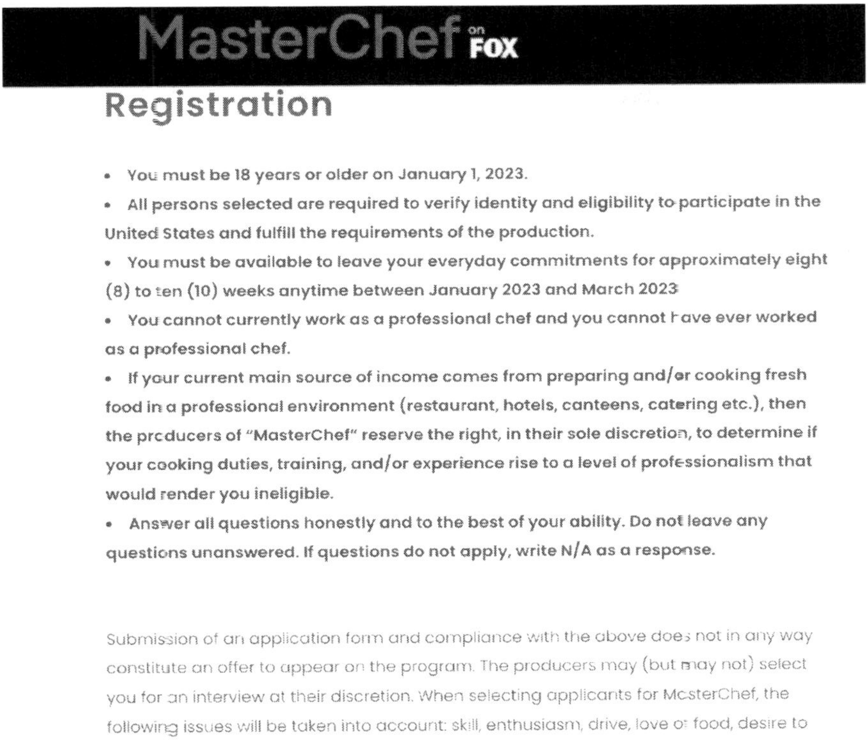

MasterChef on FOX

Registration

- You must be 18 years or older on January 1, 2023.
- All persons selected are required to verify identity and eligibility to participate in the United States and fulfill the requirements of the production.
- You must be available to leave your everyday commitments for approximately eight (8) to ten (10) weeks anytime between January 2023 and March 2023
- You cannot currently work as a professional chef and you cannot have ever worked as a professional chef.
- If your current main source of income comes from preparing and/or cooking fresh food in a professional environment (restaurant, hotels, canteens, catering etc.), then the producers of "MasterChef" reserve the right, in their sole discretion, to determine if your cooking duties, training, and/or experience rise to a level of professionalism that would render you ineligible.
- Answer all questions honestly and to the best of your ability. Do not leave any questions unanswered. If questions do not apply, write N/A as a response.

Submission of an application form and compliance with the above does not in any way constitute an offer to appear on the program. The producers may (but may not) select you for an interview at their discretion. When selecting applicants for MasterChef, the following issues will be taken into account: skill, enthusiasm, drive, love of food, desire to

Fig. 4.2 Reality shows often post casting calls on their program websites. This one for FOX's *MasterChef* suggests that producers are looking for contestants who do not have much professional cooking experience. Those who go on the show are often forced to cook with unfamiliar ingredients.

still another an event planner. The show was produced in a post-9/11 climate that had seen a continual rise in anti-Muslim sentiment and was partly meant to challenge the idea that Muslims are un-American or a threat to the safety of the United States. *All American Muslim* did prove to be a threat, however, to TLC's bottom line.

Not long after the program premiered, anti-Islam activists began to call for the show's cancellation. The effort was led by conservative Christian group the Florida Family Foundation and called on consumers to boycott companies that advertised during the program. The organization claimed that *All American Muslim* was "propaganda clearly designed to counter legitimate and present-day concerns about many Muslims who are advancing Islamic fundamentalism

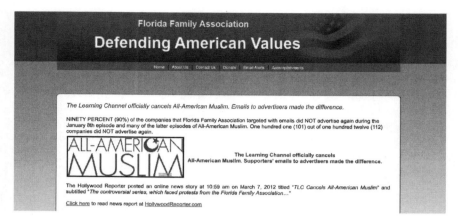

Fig. 4.3 The Florida Family Association organized a boycott against TLC for its airing of *All-American Muslim*. The FFA boycott was successful, and the show was pulled from the air.

and Sharia law."[22] The boycott was supported by figures such as Pamela Geller, whose work Nathan Lean has labeled part of the "Islamophobia industry."[23] The "controversy" surrounding the program continued to grow and Lowe's became the first big advertiser to pull its ads from TLC in response to the Florida Family Foundation's activism. Soon, other companies followed suit, and concerned about the loss of revenue and the program's low ratings, TLC canceled *All American Muslim* after one season.

In writing about the manufactured controversy surrounding *All American Muslim* for the *New Yorker*, Amy Sorkin suggested that "we are in a dangerous place when people can be told, to their faces, that they are not real—that their identities make no sense, and that they are impossible Americans."[24] She was referencing a conversation between two cast members about what it means to be a good Muslim in America, but Sorkin could very well have been writing about the public's broad understanding of the place of Muslims in American society. The boycott of *All American Muslim* was fueled by centuries of misrepresentation that suggests Muslims are people to be feared, that it is "impossible" for them to become full members of Muslim-minority nations. The experiences of the Muslim families featured in *All American Muslim* were either too real or not real enough to circumvent entrenched stereotype and prejudice.

The reality programs explored in this chapter—*Project Runway*, *America's Next Top Model*, *Top Chef*, and *MasterChef*—are competition programs. Unlike *All American Muslim*, the shows are focused on the performances of the Muslim cast, not their everyday lives; although, their lives outside the competition do often become part of their narratives. When they do, they are often forced to position themselves as just as American as anyone else, highlighting once again that their religion marks them as possibly "impossible Americans." This often becomes visible when Muslim contestants are forced to do something that might run counter to the teachings of their faith. This regularly happens in relation to food.

Most Muslims do not eat pork. Pork, like alcohol, is considered haram, forbidden, in Islam. Pork being forbidden becomes a problem when you are competing to be the "best home cook in America," particularly when a challenge requires you to cook breakfast as Amanda Saab was forced to do when a contestant on FOX's *MasterChef*. Saab was the first hijab-wearing woman to appear on an American cooking show.[25] A social worker from Dearborn, Michigan, and the daughter of immigrants from Lebanon, Saab told the Muslim Girl website that she took up cooking to manage the trauma and grief in her life: "After I began my career in social work, I needed an outlet; a way to process the traumas and grief that I had witnessed. I would come home to prepare dinner and would feel better. I soon realized that cooking was my way to process my day, my creative outlet, my 'me time.'"[26] Her love of cooking landed her a spot on season 6 of *MasterChef*, wowing the judges with dishes that she described as "East meets West." It wasn't until episode 7 of Saab's season, however, that she would be faced with a challenge that served as a challenge to her Muslim identity.

The show features a series of challenges contestants must compete in to advance to the next week. In addition to team challenges and pressure test challenges, the show features what it calls "mystery box" challenges—these, as you might imagine, surprise the contestants with an ingredient they must use in a dish. During Amanda Saab's season, one of these mystery box challenges featured bacon and asked the chefs to create a breakfast dish alongside judge Graham Elliot. Though Saab wore hijab throughout her appearances on *MasterChef*, this was the first time her religion overtly became part of her competition storyline as viewers watched Saab mull over what to do. In the end, Saab cooked the bacon without tasting it or knowing how done it should be, the judges praising her for her perseverance. On her blog, *Amanda's Plate*, Saab wrote how proud she was to be able to complete the challenge.

> I made a stuffed french toast with a maple bacon nut crumble, berry compote, and two berry coulis'. I separated the blueberries and raspberries so I could have two brightly colored sauces.

Yes, you read that correctly. Maple bacon nut crumble! I cooked bacon for the first time ever and from what I know I did a good job at it! Chef Gordon Ramsay walked by and tasted it and smiled!!!

I was proud of my dish! I cooked with a protein I've never cooked with before and had a beautiful plate![27]

Though Saab managed to produce a dish she was proud of, the bacon-breakfast situation raises two questions: First, should Saab have been asked to cook an ingredient that is forbidden by her religion in the first place? Second, should Saab's grace under fire be something we celebrate? Why is it that the Muslim contestant is faced with a problematic ingredient and then is praised for politely rising to the occasion after being placed in what is an Islamophobic situation? This is not simply a contestant facing an ingredient they've never cooked, such as sea urchin or beef tongue—this is an instance of the producers and the judges knowing that pork products are prohibited in Islam and forcing a contestant to choose between her faith and her position on the program, as though a program that forces knife-wielding contestants to cook elaborate meals in a short amount of time needed much more drama.

MasterChef is far from the only competition cooking show to do this; contestants on Food Network's *Chopped* have also been forced to cook ingredients that are religiously forbidden. What is being forced into view in these moments is the conflict in the United States between secular and religious traditions; particularly, religious traditions that are not seen as part of the mainstream American story. In terms of the American Muslim experience, the "positioning of Islam as otherness allows one to create and give substance to a common space, defined in a reactive manner by values and traditions presumed to be opposed to those of Islam."[28] During those moments when a Muslim contestant is forced to cook an ingredient that is haram, they are being othered and if they are successful with their dish, they are celebrated for overcoming that otherness. They are celebrated for succeeding in a public space that defaults to excluding them, not including them.

There has rarely been a thoughtful engagement with minority identity on programs that feature multiracial or multiethnic casts. Programs such as *The Bachelor, The Real World,* and even *MasterChef* seem to approach the casting of contestants of color more with an eye toward paint-by-numbers diversity than a real consideration of what a diverse cast might reflect back to audiences. The diverse participants who do appear on such programs are often expected to stand in as representatives for their identity group,[29] a reality that was not lost on Saab: "In my experience, many stereotypes have been quickly dispelled as people get to know me. I believe my presence in the culinary world is breaking stereotypes that Muslim women are oppressed and cannot follow their passions. Here I am culinary world! I am free!"[30]

Saab's hope was that her appearance on *MasterChef* would signal to those watching that a hijab-wearing woman can be free from oppression. News outlets certainly took a celebratory tone when covering her experience on *MasterChef*, with one NPR headline crowing, "In 2015, TV Broke Ground by Showing Relatable Women in Hijab,"[31] with one of those relatable women being Saab. But even relatable Muslim women have a hard time escaping stereotype, as the case of another female chef shows.

Fatima Ali left her family in Pakistan when she was eighteen in order to pursue her dream of becoming a chef.[32] She found success in New York City and became the first Pakistani woman to become a *Chopped* Champion on Food Network (after a round in which she had to create a dish using a pork olive loaf that she, like Saab with the bacon, could not taste). As with Hung Huynh before her, the *Top Chef* judges questioned whether Ali's heart was really in her food because she did not often cook dishes influenced by her cultural and ethnic heritage. Time and again, the judges would praise Ali's technique or her skill but suggest her food lacked passion because it did not feel authentic to them. After several episodes with the judges telling her she should create a dish that more *authentically* reflects her background, Ali is forced into a situation where she has to cook a fried chicken biryani, something that takes days—not the twenty-four hours the chefs have—to develop its full flavor. In a recap of the episode, *Food & Wine* writer Carolyn Lipka notes of Ali that "because she is one of the first people to ever really represent the foods of Pakistan and that region on *Top Chef* the pressure on her to live up to a cuisine that Padma knows in and out is clearly weighing on the young contestant."[33] Ali's worry is proven to be well founded when Indian American judge Padma Lakshmi says to her, "You do such a good job cooking western food. Why can't you cook *our* food like that?"[34] It would be an attempt to meld South Asian flavors with American nachos that would lead to her downfall, with the judges calling the flavors of her steak and lentils nachos "muddled."[35] It is Lakshmi who eventually tells Ali to "please pack your knives and go" at the end of the episode.

While on the show, Ali expressed her frustration more than once with the judges' evaluation of her cooking as being somehow less authentic than that of other contestants. Lakshmi was particularly hard on Ali during the competition, often seeming frustrated with what she and the judges felt was lackluster and soulless food cooked by the young chef. Ali died in January 2019 after a quick and public battle with a rare type of bone cancer. While Ali was being treated, she and Lakshmi seemed to grow quite close, with photos often

114 POP ISLAM

showing Lakshmi with Ali as she received or recovered from treatment. Lakshmi often referred to Ali as "little sis" in social media posts about the two of them hanging out. After Ali's death, Lakshmi penned an essay for *People* magazine meant to be a tribute to her *Top Chef* "little sis." In the essay, she acknowledged that she had been hard on Ali while she was a *Top Chef* contestant.

> I first got to know Fatima through her food. I was hard on her—not with my judging but with the tenor of my feedback. Not only did I think she could take it, but I knew she wanted me to give it to her straight. I could feel how focused she was. I challenged her openly to do better because I knew she could. I saw my younger self in Fatima. We connected as immigrants and as women of color working in food. We both knew we needed to fit in while staying true to our roots. But we had more than shared backgrounds. She was different. When the show aired in 2018, I saw the other side of her—how funny she was, how keenly she got the psychology of the contest.
>
> It's a trait you have to possess to succeed, and I knew Fatima had it and would go far.[36]

Ali did not win her season of *Top Chef*, eliminated in week nine of the fourteen-week competition, but she was voted the "fan favorite" by viewers of the program, suggesting that while the judges might have sometimes found Ali inauthentic, the viewing public did not.

The reality Ali on *Top Chef* and Saab on *MasterChef* were meant to represent on their respective programs was the same—one that celebrated cultural mixture while also suggesting that there are some things that are so intrinsic to an individual's identity that to not display them is to behave in an inauthentic manner. During the breakfast challenge, Amanda Saab was praised not only for cooking bacon for the first time ever but also for using turmeric in the waffle she served with it, something the judges praised her for because it was a way for her to include her heritage in her food. Saab was celebrated because she seemed real, at least real as the judges understood her to be in relation to her religious and ethnic identities. It wasn't until Fatima Ali began to cook dishes inspired by her Pakistani heritage that the *Top Chef* judges decided she was finally being true to herself. For both women, their religious and ethnic identities were the arbiters of their authenticity, whether or not they were the things Saab or Ali wanted to focus on. The commentary of the judges—including Padma Lakshmi—reflected a seemingly Eurocentric understanding of difference. Ali was a skilled, classically trained French chef whose food was judged inauthentic because it was not different enough. Ali's choice to cook Western food, food that was judged to be not true to her identity because she was not from the

Fig. 4.4 Ayana Ife's first unconventional challenge design was celebrated for its movement and creativity by the *Project Runway* judges. She wrote about the look and winning the challenge on Instagram after the episode aired. (Courtesy Ayana Ife)

historic West, made her seem fake—a sin on a TV program that promises to traffic in the real. If the world of cooking competition shows revolves around a notion of realness dependent on ideas about what authentic ingredients are and how authentic foods taste, how does one judge authenticity in an industry built on fantasy?

Fashion is a space where traditions are challenged. Fashion-forward designs challenge aesthetic conventions—rarely is modesty a concern. The 2017 season of fashion design competition show *Project Runway*, however, made modesty a central concern, at least for one contestant. Ayana Ife is a Black Muslim woman who grew up in Utah. She was also a contestant on season 16 of *Project Runway*, making it all the way to the finals. However, early in her season, Ife struggled to find her footing when going up against the other designers. Though in her introductory segment, Ife explained that she wanted to introduce cool modest fashion to American audiences, it took a few challenges for Ife to convince *Project Runway* judges that her work was worth a closer look And it was the "unconventional materials" challenges that made the judges and viewers really pay attention to what Ife was producing.

Generally, *Project Runway*'s unconventional material challenges are viewed with trepidation by contestants as they are asked to create high-fashion looks from nonfabric materials. Many a competitor has cried when their mélange of plastic, wires, and muslin fails to come together in a cohesive look. Ayana Ife would not be one of them. During the first unconventional challenge of season 16, Ife produced a fringed, long sleeved maxi dress out of essentially garbage that the judges praised for its "texture" and "movement." That episode's guest judge, *Marie Clarie* editor in chief Anne Fulenwider, said of the garment, "The dress was deeply chic, and I didn't even know that she was trying to design modest fashion!"[37] Another winning look was a Little Bo Beep–esque pink ruffled avant-garde piece topped with a giant bow, and a later unconventional materials challenge saw Ife shatter road reflectors and paint plastic mesh in order to create a ball gown that won the approval of the judges, including designer Zac Posen. "This is hot," he told Ife. "This is bold, this is big . . . in general I think this is superb work."[38]

As with Amanda Saab on *MasterChef*, Ife wears hijab, and many of her designs featured head coverings in some way, designed to show that they could be fashionable accessories alongside fancy bags and sky-high heels. Hijabs were featured on several models who walked in Ife's *Project Runway* finale fashion show, including the model who closed the collection. As she strode down the runway in a gold embroidered confection of tulle, the model also rocked a turban-like head covering made of the same material as her dress. During judging, judges Heidi Klum and Zac Posen talked about how Ife's designs were modest but didn't necessarily *feel* modest. "It didn't feel like it was a show where everything was covered up," Klum said of Ife's collection. "And they're still sexy," added Posen. "And they're an empowered sexiness, and I really like that."[39]

For Ife, modesty was something she wove into her designs and into her presentation of herself as a designer. In a way, the coolness of this modesty was in the same vein as that of the Muslims featured in the Mipsterz video "Somewhere in America." The 2013 video features Muslim women, most of whom wear some form of hijab, as they navigate what seems to be life in New York City. Set against the backdrop of Jay-Z's song "Somewhereinamerica," the video shows hijabis on skateboards, running through Central Park, riding motorcycles late at night, and practicing their fencing skills in a studio somewhere. The women, with their fashionable clothes and their carefree attitudes, are the epitome of cool. Su'ad Abdul Khabeer has called this kind of public performance of coolness "Muslim Cool." It arose from the Black American Muslim experience, and when "done across race, it is indubitably informed by a racial politics of cool in which Blackness and cool are synonyms and sites of youthful exploration and abandonment."[40] The Mipsterz video serves as such a site. It was celebrated both on social media and in some more mainstream media outlets, with one *Guardian* headline explaining, "Miptsers: like hipsters, but Muslim,"[41] as though it should come as a surprise that one could be both a hipster and a Muslim at the same time (not an impossible American, but perhaps an impossible hipster?). However, not everyone was enamored of the picture of Muslim life the video portrayed. Writing for *Islamic Monthly*, Sana Saeed expressed frustration around the idea that Muslims might need to "fix" their image through such media: "What we as Muslim women don't need in trying to *own* our spaces in our small and large communities is the *use of our image* for the purposes of *fixing our image*. More specifically: we don't need to use a ('positive') superficial representation of us to combat other ('negative') superficial representations."[42]

Echoing Evelyn Alsultany's warning about the good Muslim / bad Muslim binary, Saeed wrote that the video was just as likely to reinforce stereotypes as it was to challenge them as it seemed to suggest that you can be modest *and* hip at the same time. What the *Guardian* headline had celebrated, Saeed pointed to as problematic. It's a critique that could also be applied to Ayana Ife's appearance on *Project Runway*. While Ife made for a personable and friendly Muslim reality star, she still presented a type of modest Muslim identity designed to be pleasing to those outside the faith. She fit inside the "good Muslim" label of the good Muslim / bad Muslim binary because her pretty, modest designs were things that could be worn by anyone, the only thing that marked them as specifically Muslim at times was the inclusion of hijabs in some of the designs. Her accessible modesty made Ayana Ife's Muslim identity nonthreatening to her fellow contestants and the people watching *Project Runway*; it made her seem authentic to the judges and to the audience alike. Modesty did not shape the experience of one Muslim reality contestant, however, though some viewers thought it should.

Sandra Shehab is a well-known Instagram model and founder of SHEE Cosmetics.[43] her account features photos of her wearing designer clothes in settings around the world. In 2018, she made news after being chosen to compete on *America's Next Top Model* (*ANTM*). The program brings together anywhere from fourteen to twenty amateur models, forces them all to live in one house together (a la *The Real World*), and puts them through a series of challenges and photo shoots meant to turn them into the next supermodel. (Although, it should be noted, few of *America's Next Top Model* winners actually shoot into superstardom.) The winner is promised a modeling contract with an elite agency and a spread in a major fashion magazine along with a cash prize. The show is as focused on the fights among the contestants as it is on their actual performance in front of the camera or on the runway. A number of challenges seem designed to push the models out of their comfort zones and have included having the women pose with insects and spiders or in coffins placed in the ground.

As might be expected of a program looking for the "next top model," many challenges also force the models to preen before the camera in swimsuits and lingerie that leave little to the imagination. This has posed problems for contestants concerned with modesty in the past, most famously during a season 1 photo shoot for a jewelry brand. That first season of *ANTM* featured two models concerned with modesty—Robin Manning, a Black woman, and Shannon Stewart, a white woman. Both refused to participate in certain activities because of their Christian faith and neither woman would pose nude for the jewelry shoot. Manning was sent home at the end of the episode for this decision, although Stewart ended up being season 1's runner up.

Modesty did not seem to be an outward concern for Sandra Shehab as she competed on *ANTM*. Praised for her "stunning" beauty, Shehab had both judges and contestants alike fawning over her; one contestant even said she "envied" Shehab for her looks. A number of the photo shoots Shehab participated in while on the program required that she wear outfits that, while perhaps not as skimpy as they could have been, would likely fail to live up to the expectations of many understandings of what it means to be modest. One striking image showed Shehab defiantly standing with her hands on her hips, staring into the camera while modeling a nude-colored bra and underwear set. It seemed to be daring the viewer to suggest that she was in any way oppressed. While she was not the first Muslim to compete on the program Shehab was the first Muslim to openly discussion her faith and her identity during the competition. Several times while competing Shehab talked about her religion, particularly as it related to her decision to remain a virgin until marriage. Islam was never treated as a problem on the program because Shehab never discussed it as though it stood in the way of her success. However, during an interview after she was eliminated from the program, she did hint that there were times when she was concerned with how what she was doing might be received by Muslim viewers: "Muslim girls don't model. That's not what we do, you don't see a lot of Muslim girls out there modeling, so it was pretty tough; I had to do some crazy things that I wasn't really used to . . . the whole acting thing, when I was so, with that guy, I was like 'I know I'm going to get a lot of backlash about that.' Being in a bathing suit, I'm always in a bathing suit, that's nothing crazy, but I know I'm going to get stuff about that."[44]

Shehab does not wear a headscarf and, with her dark-haired good looks, she could pass for one of Kim Kardashian's sisters; she is an accessible and commercial representation of Muslim women. One that might easily sit alongside the representation of Muslim life offered up in the Mipsterz video. Shehab's commercial appeal is actually what got her sent home in the end, as judge (and show creator) Tyra Banks told her that she was "absolutely stunning" but not necessarily the right fit for editorial modeling. However, Shehab was told she had the looks to become a successful commercial model.[45] The image that led to Shehab's dismissal from *ANTM* showed her in a gold bikini, covered in gold paint, as she stood in front of a rather beefy looking man covered in the same gold paint. Once again, Shehab stares into the camera, daring the viewer to suggest she isn't good enough to be there. In an Instagram post she wrote after her elimination, and in which she shared the photo that got her eliminated, Shehab wrote, "I want all you Muslim girls out there to understand it's okay to model and follow your dreams." A year after her elimination from *America's Next Top Model*, online publication *About Her* suggested Shehab "should be on your radar for 2019" as the aspiring model launched a number of different fashion-related endeavors. It also reminded readers of Banks's comments that Shehab could "make a lot of money" as a commercial model,[46] suggesting that Shehab's potential for success might lie in her ability to become a consumable good herself.

Reality TV programs are packaged for consumption. June Deery has argued that reality TV "represents the triumph of the market, the notion that everyone as well as everything has is price and that people will do pretty much anything for money."[47] As people tuned in to watch singers compete for a recording contract, magicians for a Las Vegas show, or rock stars to be the next lead singer of INXS, companies saw the ratings for these programs as a commercial goldmine. However, advertisers do not only seek to place commercials in a particular block of reality programming; they also seek to place their products in the programs themselves. Deery points out that this is not a new process, but the promise of the real that frames reality programming makes such product placement particularly potent.[48] Increasingly, the products for sale are the reality contestants themselves.

A number of reality programs now offer winners the opportunity to partner with a company in order to sell something related to their particular specialty. For instance, winners of *Project Runway* have partnered with companies such as JCPenney and Bluefly in order to produce and sell ready-to-wear lines inspired by their high-fashion finale collections. *MasterChef*'s winner often creates a cookbook to be sold to the show's audience and the chefs who compete on

Fig. 4.5 In an introduction video for Sandra Shehab's season of *America's Next Top Model*, judge Tyra Banks described Shehab as having "the face of gods." It was after a photo shoot shot by Banks, in which Shehab modeled in a bikini while covered in gold paint, that she was eliminated from the competition. Banks told her that she could have a successful commercial career if she wanted it.

Top Chef have parlayed their wins into lucrative business partnerships or have even launched their own restaurants after competing on the show. The Muslim competitors who appear on these programs are cast because they are good for narrative content but also because they are consumable. Their work, their ideas, and their lives can be consumed by an audience that is often asked to become involved in the show narrative by visiting a website, discussing the program on social media, or voting for a fan favorite contestant. The contestants are as much a product as the show itself, which makes the inclusion of Muslims all the more interesting as it suggests that producers or marketers think that Muslim contestants can be appealing to a broad swath of the American population.

In an article on two Muslim reality programs, Evelyn Alsultany notes that while the increase of American Muslims, as well as Americans of Middle Eastern background, on reality television can be read as a positive step forward in the representation and inclusion of these groups, it is important that viewers and scholars critically engage with such reality representations. Alsultany asks, "What do the representational strategies of such shows tell us about how and whether these groups are accepted in the vision of a multicultural America?"[49] Of the cast of *Shahs of Sunset*, Alsultany writes that the show "sidesteps Islam and plays into Orientalist discourse by evoking associations with royalty, rather than religion."[50] The cast is made up of wealthy Iranian Americans who live in Los Angeles, home to one of the largest Iranian communities in the United States. Their lives are portrayed in a soap operatic way, as they fight and make up over and over again, with all the drama taking place against sparkling and sumptuous backdrops. The framing of the show is similar to that of *Keeping Up with the Kardashians*—the reality TV program that follows the wealthy and well-connected Kardashian family as it goes about its day-to-day life—with the *Shahs* cast "portrayed as rich obnoxious narcissists."[51] It's that wealth and all that it affords them that helps situate the *Shahs of Sunset* as American—the difference leaned into here to market the show, and mark the "shahs" as multicultural Americans, being less about religion or ethnicity and more about socioeconomic difference.

The lifestyle of the *Shahs of Sunset* cast is centered on extravagant consumption as the cast themselves become consumable goods by way of their appearance on the program. Alsultany points out that the *Shahs* cast is often seen talking about the differences in freedoms experienced by Iranians living in Iran and those living in the United States, with many of the cast members discussing how proud they are to be American. That patriotism, coupled with the cast's wealth and consumption, turns them into the embodiment of the mythical American dream. This helps make the Muslim members of the *Shahs of Sunset* cast accessible in ways that Iranian Muslims appearing in media generally have not been; these are not Muslims to fear, but Muslims to perhaps aspire to be. Serving as aspirational role models helps situate the *Shahs of Sunset* as authentically American.

In contrast, the Muslim contestants on *Master Chef, Top Chef, Project Runway,* and *America's Next Top Model* discussed in this chapter were seemingly only accepted when their difference from mainstream American culture was highlighted and treated as authentically multicultural on the programs in which they appear. Their difference, and the value that difference added to the program, helped mark them as members of a multicultural America but *only* when they were willing to make that difference part of the narrative of the program. The determining question seemingly is: Can the difference be marketed and sold as part of the show? If the answer is yes, that difference is embraced and even celebrated. By appearing on reality television programs, contestants open themselves up to a kind of continual surveillance, first as participants and then, after the program's end, as figures of continued focus for the fandoms associated with the shows. It is not the authoritative panopticon of Jeremy Bentham or even Michel Foucault that keeps its watchful eye on the contestants but the always-on media environment in which we all live and in which we are all meant to be continually visible, continually available, and continually consuming.

When *The Real World* premiered on MTV, it promised viewers a look inside the *real* lives of a group of strangers. Since then, American audiences have watched reality shows featuring plastic surgery and makeovers, beach battles and big brothers, amazing races and singing phenoms. Reality television has moved from being a kind of prime-time docudrama promising insight into the lives of its cast to becoming almost another sporting event as audiences cheer for their favorite designer or model or home cook. We root for contestants; we cheer as some win and as others fall. In a way, their success becomes evidence that perhaps we can find success of our own if we just keep pushing on. "These programs are a retelling," June Deery writes, "of the American dream wherein any individual can make it big—which usually translates as rich—never mind their initial circumstances."[52]

Perhaps it shouldn't seem revolutionary, but the fact that Muslims in America appear on these programs as likable, sympathetic individuals who are trying their damnedest to achieve their dreams is worth mentioning. However, the contestants' participation and characterization is often wrapped up in narratives that seem to reinforce the idea of a good Muslim / bad Muslim binary, the idea that some Muslim identities are safe and others may not be. And notably, the most successful Muslim reality show contestants in the United States have all been women. Considering the wealth of research suggesting that Muslim men are regularly framed as threatening others to be feared, it's important to consider how their absence from much of American reality TV might implicitly reinforce that idea.

One last Muslim reality show star is worth mentioning, although he is not an American Muslim.

When the makeover show *Queer Eye* relaunched in 2018, it featured five new cast members, one of whom happens to be a British Muslim man of Pakistani background. Whereas reality TV's gay men have often been portrayed as outrageous or audacious,[53] Tan France actually works against that framing. In his impeccably tailored clothing and with his quiet demeanor, France presents as a gay Muslim man who is reserved, thoughtful, and kind. The British fashion designer's appearance works against the stereotypes of Muslim men as angry, rabid, or irrational, as not in control of their emotions or themselves. As his four other castmates buzz about the home of the individual they'll be working with that week, France stands as the calm eye in the midst of a rambunctious, and caring, hurricane. That thoughtfulness and care often bleeds into his conversations with the subjects of *Queer Eye* makeovers, as France talks openly with them about issues of prejudice, stereotype, and misunderstanding. In the second episode of *Queer Eye*'s first season on Netflix, France and crew work with Neal, an Indian American man who has closed himself off from his friends and loved ones. Neal discusses his fears of disappointing his parents, who are immigrants to the United States, with the new Fab Five. At one point, Tan and Neal stand in Neal's closet looking at a dowry suitcase Neal's mother gave him and the two seem to bond over having overbearing, but well-meaning, South Asian mothers.

> **TAN:** This is some beautiful stuff . . .
> **NEAL:** It's not a dowry, she just told me to hold onto it.
> **TAN:** I love that you fell for that bullshit. Do you feel pressure with this in the house to marry someone Hindu?
> **NEAL:** I don't feel that much pressure anymore, I mean I kinda just separated myself from it.
> **TAN:** I feel the same. Listen, my family still asks, "So, when are you going to marry a nice girl?" And I'm like, "Uh, I've got something to tell you, Mum."[54]

However, even though France is Muslim, he rarely discusses issues of belief or the tenets of his faith. This is perhaps appropriate given the format of his TV show, but as with the male Muslim characters who appear in prime-time TV programs, France never moves beyond being nominally Muslim on *Queer Eye*. Unlike Ayanna Ife on *Project Runway*, who wore a headscarf while appearing on the show and who often spoke about how Islam influenced her approach to fashion, Tan France in *Queer Eye*'s first few seasons was not given the same space to share how his faith informs his life, perhaps because the stereotype of the dangerous Muslim man looms over even his gentle performance of Muslim identity. This is something he seemed to acknowledge when discussing his early difficulties participating in the show in an interview with *Men's Health*:

> I'm never going to represent everyone. . . . All I can do is be myself and do my best to conduct myself well. That will hopefully encourage people to see my people in a more positive light. . . . But other than that, I don't see myself as representative at all. I do what I do, and I hope that encourages people to say, "Oh, well, we don't see all Pakistanis this way, we don't see all South Asians this way, but we like that he's not what we see in the press." . . . Basically what I'm saying is, not all brown people are terrorists.[55]

In that same interview, France talked about how one of his apprehensions about participating in the show was the thought that he would somehow have to stand in as a representative of all Muslims or all Pakistanis or all brown gay men. It was the realization that he could escape that trap that allowed him to embrace his role on *Queer Eye*. "I just got to be me," France said, "and that's why I thought, 'OK, I can do this, and at no point will I profess to speak for people. I am myself and myself only.'"[56] Though he only speaks for himself, France is still one of the only Muslim men to appear on American reality television, reminding us once again that even as some Muslim identities become more visible in American popular media, others remain obscured.

NOTES

1. Dan Bilefsky, "Muslim Winner of Baking Contest Defies Prejudice in Britain," *New York Times*, October 8, 2015, https://www.nytimes.com /2015/10/09/world/europe/muslim-winner-of-baking-contest-defies-prejudice -in-britain.html; Simon Kelner, "Nadiya Hussain Serves Up the Perfect Rebuttal to Theresa May's Xenophobic Rhetoric," *Independent*, October 8, 2015, https:// www.independent.co.uk/voices/great-british-bake-off-nadiya-hussain-serves -up-the-perfect-rebuttal-to-theresa-mays-xenophobic-a6686601.html.

2. Homa Khaleeli, "Bake Off Winner Nadiya Hussain: 'I Wasn't Thinking about Representing Muslims, I Was Thinking about My Bakes,'" *Guardian*, October 12, 2015, https://www.theguardian.com/tv-and-radio/2015/oct/12 /bake-off-winner-nadiya-hussain-muslims-britain.

3. Ibid.

4. Anette Hill, "Reality TV: Performance, Authenticity, and Television Audiences," in *A Companion to Television*, ed. Janet. Wasko (Malden, MA: Wiley Blackwell, 2005), 449.

5. Stacy Lambe, "How 'The Real World' Star Pedro Zamora Humanized AIDS (Flashback)," *E! Online*, June 21, 2018, https://www.etonline.com/how -the-real-world-star-pedro-zamora-humanized-aids-flashback-104687.

6. Jonathon Bignell, "Realism and Reality Formats," in *A Companion to Reality TV*, ed. Laurie Oulette (Malden: MA, Wiley Blackwell, 2014), 97–115.

7. Hill, "Reality TV."

8. Ibid.

9. Nick Couldry, "Reality TV or the Secret Theater of Neoliberalism," *Review of Education, Pedagogy, and Cultural Studies* 30, no. 1 (2008): 3–13.

10. Hill, "Reality TV."

11. Grace Wang, "A Shot at Half-Exposure: Asian Americans in Reality TV Shows," *Television & New Media* 11, no. 5 (2010): 450.

12. Katrina E. Bell-Jordan, "Black, White, and a Survivor of the Real World: Constructions of Race on Reality TV," *Critical Studies in Media Communication* 25, no. 4 (2008): 353–72.

13. Ibid.; Robin M. Boylorn, "As Seen on TV: An Autoethnographic Reflection on Race and Reality Television," *Critical Studies in Media Communication* 25, no. 4 (2008): 413–33; Bell-Jordan, "Black, White, and a Survivor of the Real World."

14. Boylorn, "As Seen on TV," 423.

15. James Wong, "Here's Looking at You: Reality TV, Big Brother, and Foucault," *Canadian Journal of Communication* 26 (2001): 33–45.

16. Michel Foucault, *Discipline and Punish: The Birth of the Modern Prison*, 2nd ed. (New York: Vintage Books, 1995).

17. Wang, "Shot at Half-Exposure," 406.

18. Ibid.

19. Mark P. Orbe, "Representations of Race in Reality TV: Watch and Discuss," *Critical Studies in Media Communication* 25, no. 4 (2008): 345–52.

20. Gray Cavender, "In Search of Community on Reality TV," in *Understanding Reality Television*, ed. Su Holmes and Deboray Jermyn (New York: Routledge, 2004), 154–72.

21. Bell-Jordan, "Black, White, and a Survivor of the Real World."

22. Florida Family Foundation, "The Learning Channel Officially Cancels All-American Muslim. Emails to Advertisers Made the Difference," accessed June 15, 2022, https://floridafamily.org/full_article.php?article_no=108.

23. Nathan Lean, *The Islamophobia Industry: How the Right Manufactures Fear of Muslims* (London: Pluto Press, 2012).

24. Amy Davidson Sorkin, "The Attack on 'All American Muslim," *New Yorker*, December 13, 2011, https://www.newyorker.com/news/daily-comment/the-attack-on-all-american-muslim.

25. Lucas Peterson, "Masterchef's Amanda Saab Is the First Woman in a Hijab on an American Cooking Show," Eater, May 21, 2015, https://www.eater.com/2015/5/21/8640161/masterchefs-amanda-saab-is-the-first-woman-in-a-hijab-on-an-american.

26. *Muslim Girl*, "Meet the First Headscarf-Clad Chef on Primetime Television," May 20, 2015, http://muslimgirl.com/12349/meet-first-headscarf-clad-chef-primetime.

27. Amanda Saab, "MasterChef: Breakfast and TV Dinners," *Amanda's Plate*, June 15, 2015, http://amandasplate.com/masterchef-breakfast-and-tv-dinner.

28. Nadia Marzouki, *Islam: An American Religion* (New York: Columbia University Press, 2017), 6.

29. Orbe, "Representations of Race in Reality TV."

30. *Muslim Girl*, "Meet the First Headscarf-Clad Chef on Primetime Television."

31. Neda Ulaby, "In 2015, TV Broke Ground by Showing Relatable Women in Hijab," NPR, January 1, 2016, https://www.npr.org/2016/01/01/461490153/in-2015-tv-broke-ground-by-showing-relatable-women-in-hijab.

32. Bravo TV, "Top Chef: Fatima Ali," accessed July 21, 2023, http://www.bravotv.com/people/fatima-ali.

33. Carolyn Lipk, "'Top Chef' Colorado Recap: Episode 6 – 'Now That's a Schnitzel,'" *Food & Wine*, January 11, 2018, https://www.yahoo.com/news/apos-top-chef-apos-colorado-035942501.html.

34. *Top Chef*, "Now That's a Lot of Schnitzel," season 15, episode 6, dir. Ariel Boles, Bravo, January 11, 2018.

35. *Top Chef*, "Bronco Brouhaha," season 15, episode 9, dir. Ariel Boles, Bravo, February 1, 2018.

36. Padma Lakshmi, "Padma Lakshmi Pens Emotional Tribute to Her 'Angel' Fatima Ali," *People*, January 29, 2019, https://people.com/food/padma-lakshmi-essay-fatima-ali-tribute/.

37. Megan DiTrolio, "How 'Project Runway' Contestant Ayana Ife Is Making Conservative the New Cool," *Marie Claire*, September 21, 2017, https://www.marieclaire.com/fashion/news/a29578/ayana-ife-modest-muslim-fashion-designer/.

38. *Project Runway*, "Driving Miss Unconventional," season 16, episode 10, dir. Rich Kim, Lifetime, October 19, 2016.

39. *Project Runway*, "Finale Part 2," season 16, episode 14, dir. Ryan Bunnell, Lifetime, November 16, 2017.

40. Su'ad Abdul Khabeer, *Muslim Cool: Race, Religion, and Hip Hop in the United States* (New York: New York University Press, 2016), 145.

41. *Guardian*, "Mipsters: Like Hipsters, but Muslim," April 10, 2016, https://www.theguardian.com/society/shortcuts/2016/apr/10/mipster-muslim-hipster-exploitative-marketing-term-growing-urban-trend.

42. Sana Saeed, "Somewhere in America, Muslim Women Are 'Cool,'" *Islamic Monthly*, December 2, 2013, http://theislamicmonthly.com/somewhere-in-america-muslim-women-are-cool/.

43. Sandra Shehab (@sandrashehab), Instagram profile, accessed June 15, 2022, https://www.instagram.com/sandrashehab/feed/?hl=en. Since appearing on *America's Next Top Model*, Shehab has retired her missshehab Instagram account for one published under her full name, though she does still use that account name on TikTok.

44. Andrea Wurzburger, "Drew Elliott Sits Down with Contestant Who Was Made for Instagram, but Not the Top Model Competition," VH1, February 28, 2018, http://www.vh1.com/news/350767/americas-next-top-model-exit-interview-sandra-shehab/.

45. *America's Next Top Model*, "Beauty Is Social," season 24, episode 8, dir. Tony Kroll, VH1, February 27, 2018.

46. Roula Allam, "Getting to Know the Former 'America's Next Top Model' Contestant Sandra Shehab," About Her, accessed June 15, 2022, https://www

.abouther.com/node/17026/entertainment/celebrity/getting-know-former
-%E2%80%98america%E2%80%99s-next-top-model%E2%80%99-contestant-
sandra.

47. June Deery, "Reality TV as Advertainment," *Popular Communication* 20, no. 1 (2004): 2.

48. Ibid.

49. Evelyn Alsultany, "The Cultural Politics of Islam in U.S. Reality Television," *Communication, Culture & Critique* 9 (2016): 596.

50. Ibid., 602.

51. Ibid.

52. Deery, "Reality TV as Advertainment," 13.

53. A deep examination of the representation of gay men (or other members of the LGBTQ community) is beyond the scope of this chapter; however, there are a number of books and articles that have been published on this issue. Among them, Ron Becker's *Gay TV and Straight America* (New Brunswick, NJ: Rutgers University Press, 2006); Larry Gross's *Up from Visibility: Lesbians, Gay Men, and the Media in America* (New York: Columbia University Press, 2001); and Roger Streitmatter's *From Perverts to Fab Five: The Media's Changing Depiction of Gay Men and Lesbians* (New York: Routledge, 2009).

54. *Queer Eye*, "Saving Sasquatch," season 1, episode 2, Netflix, February 7, 2018.

55. Philip Ellis, "Tan France Reveals He Almost Quit 'Queer Eye' during the First Season," *Men's Health*, July 13, 2019, https://www.menshealth.com/entertainment/a28384902/tan-france-almost-quit-queer-eye/.

56. Ibid.

FIVE

A GLOSSY ISLAM

Muslim Lives in Fashion Magazines

IN THE FALL OF 2016, social media was atwitter as *Playboy* announced that its October issue would feature a photo of a hijab-wearing Muslim woman. The hijabi in question, Noor Tagouri, is a journalist who became fairly well known in the United States for her desire to become the first hijab-wearing news anchor on American television.[1] The social media conversation that erupted around *Playboy*'s announcement swung between support of Tagouri and the seeming embrasure of a Muslim woman by a legacy media outlet and frustration that appearing in a magazine that objectifies women was seen as a legitimate path toward acceptance.[2] One commentator in the UK's *Independent* saw nothing to celebrate in the image: "I don't see what there is to celebrate when a hijabi woman—member of an already maligned part of society—makes the 'revolutionary' choice to join forces with a sexist establishment that has debased other women by reducing them to sexual objects for generations."[3]

What the controversy over Noor Tagouri's appearance in *Playboy* highlighted was the debate within some Muslim communities about how to challenge stereotyped representations of Muslim women. Some want to be accepted on their own terms—whether conservative or liberal, hijab wearing or not, they want to be accepted as who they are with no qualifiers and without feeling they have to embrace aspects of mainstream culture they may find problematic. Others, however, see things like the inclusion of Tagouri in *Playboy* as a step toward that unqualified acceptance. One Muslim woman noted on a Facebook post about the way Muslim women are appearing in mainstream media that "representation needs to happen now, and at least the more modest look from the Muslim influence is providing an alternative to the skimpy outfits that are usually promoted in western media."[4] The commentator seemed to be

A GLOSSY ISLAM

Fig. 5.1 After her photo appeared in *Playboy*, Noor Tagouri was profiled by BBC News. In the piece, she discussed her heritage as an American Muslim of Libyan background. Tagouri also explained why she decided to pose in *Playboy*, saying that she feels it is important for American Muslim women to be seen in diverse media spaces.

suggesting that Tagouri's representation in *Playboy* matters not only because it allows a Muslim woman to visually enter a mainstream media space as herself but also because her representation there provides an alternative vision of what it means to be a modern woman. The push and pull between increased visibility in mainstream media and a desire for acceptance on their own terms often sees Muslim women accepting what many feel are nonideal representations in the short term in the hopes of more nuanced representation in the long term. The debate over Tagouri's appearance in *Playboy* also brought to light different understandings of what empowerment might look like for Muslim women.

If visibility is a trap as Michel Foucault suggests, then this chapter considers what traps of representation Muslims fall into in fashion magazines. It examines the push and pull between the desire for visibility and the desire for acceptance as it appears on the pages of these publications. Fashion magazines are glossy playgrounds of consumption—between stories of dream vacations, female powerhouses, and the hottest trends for the season are full-page advertisements attempting to convince the reader that she needs a glittering diamond bracelet or that a particular perfume will make her irresistible or that buying the latest designs from Dolce and Gabbana will transform a plain Jane into a regal queen. This chapter examines the Muslim women who appear in these media, what

Fig. 5.2 Jean Joseph Benjamin Constant's painting *The Favorite of the Emir* is reflective of images of women of the Orient painted during the 1800s. Such images often reflected Orientalist understandings of women as hypersexualized. (Courtesy of the United States Naval Academy Museum)

stories are told of Muslim life there, and what experiences may be overlooked or ignored. It considers what the magazines communicate about the realities of being a Muslim woman as well as how those stories are situated within the broader historic context of Muslimah representation.

Orientalist art often depicts women of the East swathed in veils or reclining nude or seminude on a couch covered in colorful fabrics, or existing in a type of suspended boredom in a harem full of other women. Amina Yaquin suggests the connection of Muslim women to harems portrays them as a kind of sexual property. It suggests that they are women who do not challenge orthodox beliefs or traditional cultural practices and, therefore, acquiesce to patriarchal practices that leave them prisoners of their own homes.[5] Lila Abu-Lughod notes that the tradition of keeping the lives of men and the lives of women separate in some interpretations of Islam has produced an obsession with the "secret lives of Muslim women."[6] This obsession has been nurtured by exoticized tales of the harem or stories of what secrets lie behind women's veils, all of which obscure the real, lived communities that women create in the private sphere—communities that serve as networks of care as women discuss such everyday issues as the management of the home and the raising of children. Such

A GLOSSY ISLAM 131

environments can also serve as social spaces of protection for women who have no family, are elderly, widowed, or are in some other way socially vulnerable.[7] Orientalist narratives have turned such networks into spaces of licentiousness, where strange sexual acts are performed for a male audience.[8] The harem, in this imagining, is a female space that is easily penetrated by men.

That specter of penetration—at least visually—is apparent in the odalisques that Orientalist artists loved to paint. Odalisques were the female slaves or concubines who inhabited imperial harems. As Mohja Kahf notes, when odalisques began to emerge in Western literary representations of the East, they were portrayed as "abject and angry or virginal and victimized, but always an oppressed creature."[9] This was not always the way Muslim women had been imagined, Kahf suggests, but emerged as a result of East-West interactions of the eighteenth and nineteenth centuries: "When the Orient was Orientalized (to paraphrased Edward Said), when a vast and complex body of knowledge about the Islamic Other developed simultaneously with Western subjugation of that world, the image of the Muslim woman most familiar in the West today emerged."[10]

The odalisques were fetishized as objects to be rescued from enslavement, only to be mastered not by the Muslim tyrant who had enslaved them but by the Western men imagined as freeing them. Perhaps the most famous representation of an odalisque is Jean-Auguste-Dominique Ingres's painting *Grande Odalisque*.

The work shows a nude woman reclining on a bed of pillows and silks, her back to the viewer with her face turned to meet the gaze of those who would look on her. She holds a peacock feather fan in one hand and has a patterned fabric turban wrapped around her brown hair. Her skin and eyes are light, and sitting near her feet is what appears to be a long opium pipe. It is an image that exudes sensuality, pleasure, and, in its way, danger. Though such images began as representations of one type of female experience, the hypersexualized framing of these particular women eventually began to frame understandings of women of the Orient more broadly. They were often portrayed in media—both visual and text based—as hypersexualized threats or hypersexualized victims. This Orientalist framing has influenced more recent mediated understandings of what it means to be a Muslim woman as well, with Muslim women often portrayed as either the oppressed victim of Muslim men, and Islam, or as a sexual threat to the West.

The oppressed victim is the Muslim woman who shows up most frequently in news stories about Muslims living somewhere "over there." They were the women in the sky-blue burkas who were used to justify the war in Afghanistan;

Fig. 5.3 Jean August Dominique Ingres's *Odalisque in Grisaille*. An unfinished grayscale repetition of Ingres's famed *Grand Odalisque*. The Met says that such reproductions were designed to make it easier for the image to be reproduced in black-and-white printing, but there is no record of why this reproduction was being created. (Courtesy the Met and the Catharine Lorillard Wolfe Collection, Wolfe Fund, 1938)

they are the Saudi women who only recently were granted the ability to drive and the Muslim women who grow up in cultures that practice female genital mutilation. They are the Muslims whose experiences are held up to show Western audiences just how different and unmodern Muslim cultures can be and are very often used to justify some sort of intervention in the country in which they live.[11] The visual representation of submissive and oppressed Muslim women developed during European colonization of Muslim countries and was used to help justify Europe's imperial expansion.[12] The idea was that Muslim women needed saving from a patriarchal Islam that kept them trapped in their homes and virtual slaves of the men in their families; these women were imagined as lacking the agency to decide much in regard to their lives.[13] This framing showed up again in stories about the so-called war on terror. Esmaeil Zeiny and Nouraini Yusof explain that it appeared in narratives of Muslim women talking about their lives that were designed to "elicit sympathy from the Western readers" and justify wars meant to, at least partly, liberate Muslim women from cultural captivity.[14]

In the run-up to the war in Afghanistan, news media were filled with images of Afghan women in the ubiquitous sky-blue burka. Carole Stabile and Deepa Kumar point out that the need to rescue these women from the Taliban, and from the burka, was among the justifications for the war.[15] The media picked up this political talking point and began running stories about the oppression of Afghan women, stories that denied the women agency "by rendering women the passive grounds for an argument aimed at imperialist domination, the discourse of protection used by politicians and media alike—like the very fundamentalism it purported to attack—denied women any agency in the decision-making processes that affected their everyday lives and futures."[16]

The media's representation of Afghan women is similar to how the peoples and cultures of the Middle East have historically been represented in American political, cultural, and media rhetoric. Melani McAlister has pointed out how framings of the Middle East have portrayed it as an "acceptable area for the exercise of American power" while also serving to represent the "Middle East as a stage for the production of American identities."[17] The Middle East and the conflicts, imagined and real, the United States finds itself involved in there "have been central to in the construction of U.S. global power."[18] This happened in Afghanistan, where the fight against the Taliban was partly framed as a mission to "protect" Afghan women from oppressive Afghan men and help the United States position itself as a champion of human rights. American power was displayed in the ability of US forces to liberate the Muslim women of Afghanistan. In her framing as oppressed victim, a Muslim woman is never allowed the space or the ability to free herself from that which is imagined as imprisoning her.

The framing of Muslim women as a sexual threat portrays them as not simply passive victims of the men around them; instead, these Muslim women are the *victimizers* of hapless males. Sophia Rose Arjana has noted how Orientalist explorers described Muslim women as being impossibly immoral, "exhibiting unrestrained sexuality in public."[19] This unrestrained sexuality made them monstrous; Arjana suggests that in Orientalist texts "female Muslim monsters, like their male counterparts, were symbols of fear."[20] The fear, of course, being that such vixens might seduce the rational West and help bring to life a situation in which divisions between East and West were not as impenetrable as colonizers or other kinds of conquerors claimed them to be. The worry over the possibility of such boundary transgressions predates Europe's age of expansion,

134 POP ISLAM

as Suzanne Akbari states that during the medieval period, the Orient was seen as "beautiful and dangerous" because of the potential of Muslim cultures to assimilate Western Christian travelers into their fold.[21] The Orient was seen as a seductive place with an anything-goes attitude, and its women were imagined as the embodiment of this attitude. Behind the veil, such a narrative seemed to suggest, lay a succubus in wait. But the sexual threat posed by Muslim women is not only centered on their possible seduction of unsuspecting Westerners; it is also often related to their relationships to Muslim men.

In their discussion of narratives of violent women, Laura Sjoberg and Caron Gentry point out that in the twentieth century, a Muslim woman who is framed as violent in relation to stories on the war on terror is often suggested to be violent because "she is sex-crazed or in a sexual relationship with a male terrorist" or because she was neglected by her father growing up.[22] In this instance, Muslim women become framed as irrational actors who are driven mad by sex in some way and can pose a danger to us all. If it is not explicitly sex that is the danger, then it is the relationships that might produce sexual encounters that we are told to worry over. In a Runnymede report on the experience of Muslim schoolgirls in the United Kingdom (in light of the recruitment of several by the Islamic State to travel to Syria and join the group), Heidi Mirza notes that Muslim schoolgirls are often caught up in a gendered web of expectation in the United Kingdom in which their identities are reduced to their wearing of the headscarf. Their experiences of Islamophobia and social exclusion have made the young women amenable to the romance and even motherhood offered to them by the caliphate—which, in turn, causes people to treat them as a threat to the stability of the United Kingdom.[23] A high-profile example of this particular narrative was found in season 4 of the FOX series 24. The season focused on the threat posed to the United States by a terrorist cell, one with vague connections to an unnamed Middle Eastern country. Members of the cell included the Araz family and although the husband is the more active member of the cell, his wife, Dina, features most frequently in the story. She is a true believer in the terrorists' anti-American cause, framed as a Muslim she-wolf who will fight for her husband and her son. Her relationship to those two Muslim men makes her a threat to national security. In the end, she sacrifices one of them to save the other and is killed by the cell whose ideology she was sworn to uphold. Noor Tagouri's *Playboy* spread did not frame her as a seductress, nor did it suggest that her sexuality might pose a threat to national security. But much of the controversy was centered on sex.

Tagouri's spread appeared in an issue devoted to "renegades," and while part of the outrage was over Tagouri's decision to appear in the magazine in an attempt to seem like a "normal" American, there were other concerns over the way a soft porn magazine seemed to be framing a conversation about modesty. Saira Mahmood, writing about Tagouri's appearance in *Playboy* for Muslimah Media Watch, suggests that "the porn industry also makes use of violent, Orientalised tropes in its depiction of Muslim women—often resorting to putting non-Muslim women (like Mia Khalifa) in hijab to serve as fetishes."[24] In a way, through her appearance in *Playboy* to promote modesty as a valid life choice, Tagouri helped feed into that fetishization of Muslim women, journalist Hannah Allam writing that "the focus on Tagouri's headscarf annoyed Muslims who've grown tired of a so-called 'hijabi fetish' they believe reduces smart and talented women to the scraps of fabric over their hair."[25]

However, writer Hina Tai pointed out how the controversy that erupted over Tagouri's decision was not helpful in changing the way Muslim women are represented in media. "We are continuously paralyzed by old conversations on hijab, modesty, and Muslim women's bodies. Noor in *Playboy* is not the controversy. This controversy is the controversy," Tai wrote.[26] In her story about the controversy, Allam suggested it made visible discussions about the ethics of representation: "The uproar over Tagouri speaks to a wider debate over Muslim representations. After years of being confined to a handful of stereotypical roles—think bombers and oil barons—Muslims are becoming increasingly visible in other roles onscreen and online. . . . But the wider exposure is forcing a discussion of Islamic ethics in public appearances and whether there's an issue of too much of a good thing."[27]

The question at the heart of Tagouri's appearance in *Playboy* seemed to be: Can it be empowering for a member of a historically disempowered community to subvert stereotype by appearing in a media space that thrives on stereotype?

In addition to the oppressed victim and the sexual threat framing of Muslim women, there is a third framing that has emerged in some modern media portrayals—that of the empowered reformer. This framing is often wrapped up in neoliberal ideas about the power of the individual to change not only themselves but also society; it is also often tied up with feminist notions of what empowerment is. In writing of Islamic critiques of Western feminism, Sara Salem notes that "the act of defining constitutes an exercise of power that creates certain women's experiences as patriarchal and others' as emancipatory."[28] Women who live religious lives are not often imagined as having emancipatory experiences this is especially true of Muslim women. Within the framework of Western feminism, religious women are understood as "a homogeneous block who cannot or will not see the inherent patriarchy in religion."[29] The women framed as empowered reformers within this context are those who

136   POP ISLAM

see the patriarchy and are often publicly struggling against it. Writer Rafia Zakaria suggests that this Western notion of both feminism and empowerment traps feminism, and the individuals it proclaims to emancipate, in essentialized framings of who they are or who they might become: "Feminists today face the great challenge of transformation: an embrace of the adversarial while knowing that adversaries are not enemies, an embrace of community that does not require endless compromises by those with the least power, and a realism that accepts women as they are and where they are."[30]

In response to this, feminists working in Black communities and in the field of postcolonial studies have attempted to create feminist frameworks that make space for their own lived experiences, frameworks in which agency and emancipation do not have to be boiled down to homogeneous ideas grown out of a Western ideology. Islamic feminism, Sara Salem writes, "constitutes a field that can be broadly defined as an attempt to exercise power over knowledge production and meaning making within Islam."[31] She suggests that scholars like Fatima Mernissi and Kecia Ali have looked to texts such as the hadith and the Qur'an for reinterpretation in order to understand how gender inequality is facilitated within some Islamic traditions and where it might be challenged. It's important to note that the idea of what constitutes Islamic feminism is not a settled thing,[32] with a secular Muslim feminism often seeming to have arisen before a more religiously grounded Islamic feminism in some contexts.[33]

The Muslim women framed as empowered reformers, however, are not often situated so they are seen as working within the framework of Islam; rather, they are portrayed as somehow outsiders to Islam. If they are framed as working within Islam, then they are portrayed as Muslim Joans of Arc, only instead of fighting off an outside threat, they are often fighting off the threat posed to women by the very faith itself. While Noor Tagouri could be placed in this category by some, a more potent example might be activist and journalist Mona Eltahawy.

Eltahawy labels herself a "FEMINIST GIANT" on Twitter, particularly when she engages with the critics and trolls who sometimes go after her for her support for women's rights or her outspoken thoughts on sexual liberty. On her website, she says she "calls herself a proud liberal Muslim,"[34] which opens Eltahawy up to criticism from both conservative Muslims and some on the left who think she should disavow Islam altogether. The activist and former journalists is savvy, however, and plays her critics off one another in order to push her ideas about what sort of reforms Islam needs to undergo in order to be more welcoming to and safer for women. She has been particularly powerful in pushing conversations about sexual assault or sexual abuse that might otherwise be ignored. In 2018, she joined a chorus of Muslim women sharing their stories of abuse using the #MosqueMeToo hashtag in social media.[35] Given her visibility and notoriety, Elthaway's use of the hashtag to share her own experiences amplified the conversation and made it more visible to people who might have otherwise ignored it. Eltahawy's own experiences as a survivor, and her willingness to discuss her assaults, allowed her to position herself as an expert—someone who could not only contribute to the discussion personally but also comment on it as observer. Her work as both a journalist and an activist has garnered her international praise and attention, with her book *Headscarves and Hymens: Why the Middle East Needs a Sexual Revolution* in particular positioning her as someone who understands what needs to happen in order to upend what she sees as the sexual oppression of Muslim women in Islam.[36]

Eltahawy does not position herself as a specifically Muslim feminist, though she points to amina wadud as a spiritual mentor of sorts. wadud has written extensively about the issue of gender within Islam and is among the most visible and well known of the scholars considered to be working in the field of Islamic feminism. She is one of the founding members of Sisters of Islam, an organization that seeks to promote women's rights within an Islamic framework,[37] and she has suggested that full equality for women within Islam will only happen with a fundamental transformation in the way the religion is taught and practiced. wadud often makes her argument by turning to the Qur'an itself, noting in one article that "many people—both women and men—have often been acculturated into accepting this false notion of male superiority and thereby disregarding equality rather than seeing it as essential to their creation."[38] In 2005, wadud gained public attention after leading a mixed gender prayer service that organizers said was going to help usher "Islam into the 21st century."[39] In an interview with scholar Kecia Ali, wadud discussed how she makes the decision to do things that might be seen as controversial or as destabilizing to some:

> Everywhere I get pushed up against the wall, I'm looking for the magic
> button in the wall that will cause the panels to slide open and allow me to
> enter the next room. It's not as if I don't sometimes feel backed up against
> the wall; I just try not to succumb to it, except to recognize my discomfort
> and acknowledge that the only way I would be discomforted is through not
> accepting a reality. . . . The lack of a fixed location has allowed me to entertain,
> intellectually and academically and politically in terms of my activism, how
> to move the parameters that people are trying to establish in such a way as to
> limit the possibilities for other human beings to likewise experience that kind
> of life.[40]

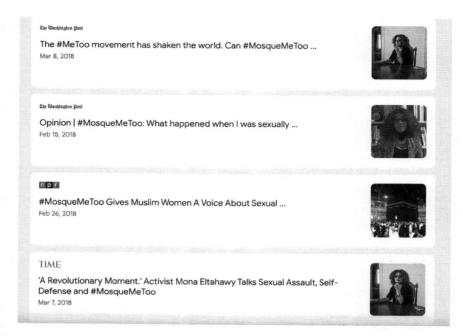

Fig. 5.4 Activist, writer, and journalist Mona Eltahawy helped launch the #mosquemetoo hashtag in 2018 after sharing her experience of being sexually assaulted in a masjid. Much of the early coverage of the hashtag as it trended focused on Eltahawy's story as reporters sought to contextualize it against the backdrop of the larger #MeToo movement. #MeToo was sparked by activist Tarana Burke in 2006 and began trending in Twitter in 2017.

Like wadud, Eltahawy has talked about how she has maneuvered spaces in order for her perspective to be heard. She's also stated that she thinks Islam needs to be reimagined to be more inclusive of the experience of women, often using stories of her own personal experiences to support her argument. It's this openness that many people, Muslim and non-Muslim, find appealing about Eltahawy's activism, and she's grown a large following in social media.

This short discussion of Eltahawy's activism is meant to point out that she is the type of empowered reformer who often appears in media coverage of Muslim women. She garners attention when her activism falls comfortably into the neoliberal idea of the empowered reformer, one focused on the agency and autonomy of the individual, or when her activism highlights issues that fit within an Orientalist framing of Islam, such as the idea that Islam poses a threat to the sexual liberty of Muslim women. When her feminist activism fits neatly within a Western framework, she is celebrated; if she challenges the tenets of Western feminism, however, news media are less likely to cover what she has said. That's also the case at times when her activism is focused on the work of other Muslim activists. An example would be when Eltahaway used Twitter to try to raise the issue of Saudi Arabia's treatment of Saudi feminists—suggesting the kingdom is treating feminism as a kind of terrorism waged against the Saudi state. Unlike her activism around sexual liberation, her activism on behalf of Saudi feminists garnered much less media attention, as did the activism of the Saudi feminists themselves.

As problematic as the media's framing and treatment of some reformers can be, there is also the issue of the language of empowerment itself. Rafia Zakaria has noted how it is often deployed by development agencies to push a particular idea of female freedom, one that imagines that it is largely "an economic issue, one that can be separated from politics."[41] However, it was not always associated with the ability to make money. As Zakaria and her coauthors note in their report *Emissaries of Empowerment*,[42] the term entered the development lexicon via women from the Global South who understood empowerment as the transformation of gender norms, the escape from oppression, and the ability to politically mobilize as a force. But it become connected to the ability to make money, to "earn a living," once development became an industry. Empowerment as it most often appears in American media is very much situated within a Western, neoliberal understanding of what that term means—closing off other ways of being or becoming empowered, often veiling the work of activists and reformers who take a different approach.

Muslim women have been used in various political discourses as props, often imagined to be veiled away from society by their religion and by literal veils. This discourse of oppression and repression obscures the diversity of experience of Muslim women and reduces them to little more than two-dimensional caricatures. Such Orientalist framings of Muslim women have appeared in a wide variety of media, including magazines.

Women's magazines can serve to fuel the imagination of their readers. Lorna Stevens and Pauline Maclaren suggest they create "dreamworlds" of shopping, where women can imagine the kinds of things they'd like to own and consume and how those might shape the women they hope to be.[43] For Julia Twigg, "Patterns of consumption become increasingly significant in the narration of the self and the formation of social identities, performing an integrative function within a common culture lifestyle."[44] To be a modern woman is to consume. The ads that propel those patterns or dreamworlds, however, can communicate to women that, even though they are sought as consumers, they should take up less room in the world than men. They can serve to both expand and constrict the worlds women may imagine themselves part of, but that was not always the case.

The first successful women's magazines, Amy Beth Aronson argues, did not simply feature journalists or advertisers telling women how to live—many of their articles were edited and authored by women.[45] The readership actively participated in shaping the understanding of domesticity (the focus of the magazines) that appeared on the publications' pages. The lives reflected in the magazines were informed by real women and so also reflected lived cultural understandings of the role of women in society. In a way, these magazines served as a vehicle for a public conversation about what it meant to be a woman. This idea is echoed in Brita Ytre-Arne's examination of women's magazines in Norway. Her work considers the way the glossies might serve as a kind of alternative public sphere, as they do communicate ideological information related to class and the role of women in society.[46] In fact, Merja Marta notes that women's magazines often attempt to reflect the values of their readers or, importantly, the values their readers strive to represent.[47] They may communicate ideological information, but readers don't necessarily look for confirmation of their own beliefs in magazines; sometimes they are looking for *alternatives* to their beliefs.

In one examination of *Seventeen* magazine, the authors found that the representation of women's roles in society featured in the magazine reflected the understandings most prevalent in the culture at one particular time. During particularly feminist moments, the women featured in the magazine took on a more empowered framing; when backlash toward feminism emerged in American culture, such as during the 1980s, the representation of women in the magazine was less empowered and powerful.[48] While women's magazines have helped shaped popular understandings of the role women play in a society, they are also spaces where cultural debates may take place. At the same time, women's magazines can also communicate to their audience what it means to be beautiful, reinforcing cultural standards that may be oppressive or stereotyped. American and European understandings of beauty are shaping global beauty standards in a way that often erases the experience of women of color. Although, in her study of race in teen magazines, Durham found that the magazines were featuring more diverse models, although the representations remained imperfect at best: "Race was a trope that yoked consumerism to a multicultural enterprise signifying unity, political progress, and social cohesiveness. It functioned in these beauty texts to support a dominant ideology of assimilation, where difference was minimalized and marginalized in a beauty culture defined primarily by consumerism."[49]

Table 5.1. Out of the mainstream fashion magazines examined for this project, only *Cosmopolitan*, *Marie Claire*, and *Teen Vogue* featured stories about Muslims. Some of the other fashion magazines occasionally featured editorials shot in a Muslim nation, such as Morocco, or might publish a travel story about a country such as Egypt, but they did not write about Muslim life.

Outlet	Number of Articles	Time Period Covered
Cosmopolitan	32	2013–16
Marie Claire	16	2007–16
Teen Vogue	88	2014–16

All of these, the legacy of nineteenth-century Orientalism, the media misrepresentations of Muslim women, and the place of women's fashion magazines in American culture, shape the questions guiding this chapter: How are Muslims framed in fashion magazines? Which Muslim lives are visible in them and which are missing?

To begin digging into these questions, I examined three fashion magazines that featured articles and essays about or produced by Muslim women writers. Originally, I had hoped to include a wider swath of the American fashion magazine industry, but only *Teen Vogue*, *Marie Claire*, and *Cosmopolitan* regularly covered issues related to Islam or Muslim life up to 2016, when I ended the gathering of material that would make up my archive for this chapter.[50] The articles for analysis were found by searching the websites of the three magazines using the terms *Muslim* and *Islam*. Every article the search uncovered published through 2016 was included for analysis. This means for *Cosmopolitan*, thirty-two articles were analyzed; for *Marie Claire*, sixteen; and for *Teen Vogue*, eighty-eight. No time frame beyond my end-date was specified, as I was interested in seeing not only how Muslims were covered in these magazines but also the scope of the coverage and how that coverage may have changed over time. I did make note, during my analysis, of whether articles first appeared online or were reprints from the physical magazine.

Out of the three magazines examined, *Teen Vogue* is particularly interesting. It published the most articles in the shortest time frame, but more interesting is the reputation the publication is gaining for its treatment and coverage of social justice issues. Though covering such issues has been a mission of *Teen Vogue* for some time, its reporting became increasingly visible in the aftermath of Donald Trump's election as US president. Its coverage of social justice issues is frequently shared in social media, with some suggesting that a magazine designed for a youth readership might be doing a better job of critiquing the

142   POP ISLAM

racism, sexism, and xenophobia that circulate in society than more mainstream
news outlets. Unfortunately, since this analysis was conducted, Conde Nast,
the magazine's publisher, stopped publishing a hard copy of the magazine,
though it still exists as an online publication.

Articles from the three magazines were examined to understand the themes
that emerged in the coverage of Islam and Muslims. What the analysis uncovered was an emphasis in the earlier articles on reporting narratives that
perpetuated Orientalist understandings of Islam and Muslims; however, over
the course of time, the articles published in the magazines seemed to pull away
from the stereotyped coverage of the past. *Teen Vogue*, in particular, published
a number of articles that directly challenged some of the earlier, prejudicial
reporting on Islam and Muslim communities. Three major themes emerged
during the analysis: the idea that Islam is "a threat to women," that "Muslim
women are victims of Islamophobia," and that they can "shatter stereotypes."
The magazines tended to rely heavily on the tropes of Muslim women as victims
or Muslim women as in some way empowered in the stories they published.

In 1991, Sally Field starred in the made-for-TV movie *Not without My Daughter*. The film was based on the book by Betty Mahmoody, both chronicling
Mahmoody's quest to get herself and her daughter away from an abusive husband in Iran. Betty De Hart has suggested that such "maternal melodramas"
reinforce Orientalist framings of Muslim men as abusive and serve to warn
Westerners away from racial and cultural mixture.[51] In writing of the book the
movie was based on, Megan Goodwin noted that Islam was presented in it as "a
specific, bodily threat to white American womanhood and urges the embodied
rejection of Islam as fundamentally anti-American."[52] In both the film and
the book circulates the narrative of the women oppressed via Islam, although
the woman in question happens to be a non-Muslim. Some of the earliest articles examined in this research, all published in *Marie Claire*, featured similar
themes, all seeming to communicate that Islam and its believers are a threat to
women. In fact, in a strange flip of the "Not without My Daughter" idea, one
article chronicled the way Saudi women can be forced to divorce their husbands
by male relatives if they think a divorce and remarriage is in the best interest of
the family, with the article suggesting that a good, devout Saudi Muslim woman
is forced to follow the dictates of her father even when she leaves the home.

The threat Islam posed to a woman's happiness was chronicled in another
piece, authored by Asra Nomani. Nomani is a journalist who has become a
controversial figure for some Muslims (she notably published a piece for the
Washington Post detailing why she, as a Muslim, voted for Donald Trump).
In her *Marie Claire* story, Nomani detailed how the pressure to marry a good

Muslim South Asian man in order to please her family and her religion caused her emotional and mental distress: "To me, abiding by the dictates of my culture and religion meant finding a love that would be halal, or legal, according to Islamic law. As a girl, I had learned to live by the hudood, or sacred boundaries, of traditional Muslim society: I never dated, and I never went to the junior high school dances. My senior year at Morgantown High, standing by my red locker, I politely refused the class president when he invited me to the prom. 'I can't,' was all I could say. And I couldn't. It would be haram—unlawful."[53]

Unlawful interactions between men and women were the focus of another *Marie Claire* article, this one from 2007. It highlighted how some interpretations of Islamic teachings put women in crisis situations even more in danger. The focus was on the development of a search and rescue crew in the mountainous region of Pakistan that was made up of all women. The article centered on the religious mandate that men and women who are not related should not interact: "Alam and her colleagues in Pakistan and Tajikistan are the first Muslim women in today's Islamic world to risk their lives this way to save others. 'Our men can be very conservative,' says Alam. 'They won't let a man who is not a relative touch their women—even if it means letting her die.'"[54]

The article began with the story of a fire in Saudi Arabia that killed schoolgirls who tried to escape the blaze. They were trapped in the building because they were attempting to leave it without headscarves on and school staff would not let them leave uncovered. Though the *Marie Claire* article worked to celebrate the accomplishment of the Pakistani women, it did so while framing other Muslim women as victims of Islam, pointing out that "in many Islamic countries, custom dictates that a woman or girl cannot be viewed or touched by a man outside the immediate family, even if that man is a doctor—or a rescue worker trying to save her life."[55]

This theme of Islam, and Muslim men, being a threat to women is not a new one. Arjana has traced the way this idea arose during the Middle Ages and continues to shape our understanding of Islam, while Abu-Lughod pointed out the way it was used to help justify the launching of the United States' 2001 war in Afghanistan.[56] The early magazine articles fit within this framework, perpetuating a reductionist and Orientalist understanding of Muslim women as victims. Victimization was central to another frame that appeared in the archive, but this rarely framed Islam as the threat. Instead, it was the fear of Islam that threatened the lives of Muslim women.

The majority of the articles that used this frame were published in 2015 and 2016 and seemed, at times, to be a response on the part of the magazine to address either earlier coverage that may have been Orientalist in nature (in the case of *Marie Claire*) or simply was nonexistent (in the case of *Cosmopolitan*). Many of the stories simply chronicled the rise of anti-Muslim hate crimes, such as a *Teen Vogue* piece that noted that "the attacks ranged from vandalism to arson and included a firebombing of a mosque in California and a severed pig's head being left at a mosque in Philadelphia last year."[57]

Quite a few of those articles tied that rise in anti-Muslim speech and acts to the poisonous political rhetoric of the 2016 presidential campaign—which often featured Republican candidates, particularly Donald Trump, arguing that Islam was a threat to America. One *Teen Vogue* article detailed how members of a GOP LGBTQ group hosted a party that was billed as a "rally against radical Islam" and was organized by noted anti-Islam activist Pamela Geller and controversial conservative figure Milo Yiannopoulos.[58] The piece went on to suggest that members of one stigmatized minority group should not be reinforcing the stigma associated with another.

The experience with Islamophobia and anti-Muslim activists took a personal tone in a number of the articles and essays. One first-person essay published by *Cosmopolitan* featured Amani al-Khatahtbeh, a well-known Muslim media figure, writing to a hypothetical future daughter, thinking out loud about the kinds of questions her daughter might ask in light of the election of Donald Trump as president and the seeming rise in Islamophobia associated with it.

> I don't know how old you'll be when you start asking me these questions. Maybe it'll be when you're in sixth grade, the same grade I was in the first time I felt scared enough to lie about my religion. Maybe we'll have to talk about it a little sooner, if you break my heart and run to me after elementary school one day because a classmate called you a racial slur for the first time, the same way I ran to my dad when someone insulted my "people" in fourth grade. Maybe you'll enjoy privileges I didn't have and you'll be shielded from all of that until later on—until the day that you might decide to start wearing a headscarf, and you complain to me about people suddenly asking you if you speak English.[59]

Several articles explored the impact of Islamophobia on the everyday lives of Muslims. One story in *Teen Vogue* explored how Muslim women who wear headscarves were considering taking off their hijabs in order to be less visibly Muslim in public. Another *Teen Vogue* piece considered the way the political discourse centered on discussions of "radical Islam" perpetuates Islamophobia, which can cause anxiety in Muslims and make them feel unsafe: "Calling it 'radical Islam' shows a lack of understanding of the actual religion, and promotes generalizing Islam, Muslims, and terrorism in one lumped category.

Doing so might seem like trivial semantics, but in an age of rampant Islamophobia and violent backlash against Muslims, it's imperative to clarify meanings and choose our words carefully."[60]

The stories focused on the ways Muslims are victimized by Islamophobia and its proponents seemed designed to make visible to readers the way American Muslims are made to feel like strange others in the country in which they live. If we consider women's magazines—and fashion magazines are a subset of women's magazines—as spaces where particular ideologies are communicated, then an increased focus on the way Muslims are victimized by anti-Muslim speech and actions would suggest the ideology the magazines are pushing is increasingly one of understanding and inclusion. What can push that ideology of inclusion further than framing Muslim women as people who shatter stereotypes?

Debate has sprung up from time to time in social media about images showing Muslim women wearing hijabs designed to look like American flags. After the Boston marathon bombing, the Muslim Political Action Committee circulated an image of a Muslim woman set against a dark, empty background wearing a flag hijab. Though she did not wear such a headscarf in her *Playboy* photo, Noor Tagouri was shot against a mural painted on a brick wall to look like a waving American flag. For the Women's March on Washington in January 2016, the artist famous for Obama's "Hope" poster created images meant to communicate the diversity of America's female population—one of those posters featured a Muslim woman in an American flag head covering. What the evocation of the American flag, and the patriotism it symbolizes, is meant to do is convince the viewer that the person associated with it is American. A number of fashion magazine articles attempted to do this work as well.

During the 2016 Summer Olympics in Rio de Janeiro, Brazil, two American Muslim women made headlines. One was Ibtihaj Muhammad and the other Dalilah Muhammad. Both women medaled at the games—Ibtihaj Muhammad as the first American Muslim hijabi to compete and win a medal and Dalilah Muhammad as the first American woman to win gold in the four-hundred-meter hurdle event. *Teen Vogue* covered the triumphs of both women, noting how they were helping change Americans' understandings of what it means to be Muslim. During an interview with the magazine, Dalia Muhammad explained what she hoped her accomplishment would mean for Muslim women: "My medal is a symbol of that determination. The same determination I apply in my everyday life. As far as the progress for Muslim woman in sports I hope to see many more. I hope to at least break the stereotype of what a Muslim woman looks like."[61]

Fig. 5.5 Before the 2016 Olympics, CBS Evening News profiled Ibtihaj Muhammad. During the story, Muhammad coached anchor Elaine Quijano through some fencing basics.

The emphasis in these stories was on the way the women shattered the stereotypes of what it means to be a Muslim woman. This narrative of Muslims shattering stereotypes was actually the theme most widely deployed in the coverage of Islam and Muslim life in the three magazines; however, at times, that ability to shatter stereotypes was more wrapped up in consumerism than patriotism. One story in *Marie Claire* epitomized this intersection of identity and consumption.

The article, "Shopping in Dubai," featured two Emirati women—one who worked in public relations, the other in event management—whom the magazine labeled "chic." A reporter then followed these chic Muslim women on a shopping excursion to the Mall of Emirates.[62] While the story suggested the women "could be two of your closest friends," it also emphasized the long, black abayas the women had to wear in public; in fact, the shopping story was centered on the pair's attempt to find fashionable abayas that might follow religious custom but that also allowed the women to show off a little individuality. When asked if they ever found the abaya restricting, one of the women said, "We're proud to wear the abaya. It represents our culture. We can look glamorous and good and still be covered up."[63] The idea that the women were shattering stereotypes is played up not only in their proclamation of pride in the abaya (particularly the designer abayas they comb through in the article) but also in the admission early in the story that they are fans of the American TV show *Desperate Housewives*.

That Muslim identities might get wrapped up with consumption in these magazines should come as no surprise, they are designed to sell products and lifestyles; however, consumption was often focused on pushing an agenda of inclusivity in the magazines. One *Teen Vogue* article explored the way a young Muslim social media star was using makeup to challenge notions of modesty within Islam, while a *Cosmopolitan* story profiled a niqabi (a niqab is a black garment that covers a Muslim woman from head to toe) hip-hop dance troupe that was attempting to challenge the perceptions of what covered women are able to do. That seeming need to challenge perceptions was only heightened as a political rhetoric developed during the 2016 US presidential campaign, which framed Muslims as a threat to the country. *Teen Vogue* published an article during the primary season that featured Muslim women talking about how important it is, to them, to shatter the stereotypes perpetuated about their religion and themselves: "The latent Islamophobic sentiment in the post-9/11 era has had a tremendous impact on our identities as Muslim millennial women. Growing up Muslim in America during such a unique moment in our country's history has really shaped who we are today. We connect with society based on a deep love and appreciation for our faiths and an eager desire to reclaim our identities even in the face of adversity."[64]

Considering the long history of the portrayal of Muslim women as oppressed individuals with no agency, the stories published in the fashion magazines that show them breaking out of that mold, that show them actively challenging that framing, suggest that media portrayals may be moving away from tired and prejudice-producing Orientalist stereotypes.

This chapter considers the story being told about Islam and Muslim life in three fashion magazines. Against a historic backdrop that has framed both the religion and the believers as things to be feared and avoided, it considered what Muslim experiences are made visible on the pages of American glossies. Evelyn Alsultany suggests that "a negative stereotype is defused not with a 'better' stereotype, but with a diverse field of images"[65]—this chapter considers if such a field exists in fashion magazines and, if so, what that might look like and communicate. Of the three magazines examined in this analysis, *Teen Vogue* had the most diverse mix of stories and sources. The articles there were also the most likely to be situated within a larger social justice framework—often linking the plight of American Muslims to that of other minority groups, in particular racial minorities. At the same time, these stories are being published in fashion magazines—media designed specifically to sell the reader consumption. Next to stories about hijabi fashionistas or the elaborate black robes purchased by women in Dubai are ads for consumable objects—perfumes, handbags, shoes—that are meant to mark the bearer as a modern woman. What is the price of accessibility, then? What is the price of visibility in these media spaces? To be seen on the pages of fashion magazines must Muslim women be shattering stereotypes? Must they be defining themselves as consuming citizens?

Yes and no. Certainly, the majority of articles published across the three magazines tended to rely on the idea that Muslims—particularly Muslim women—are shattering stereotypes. The stories often suggested the individuals were more progressive or funny or interesting than the reader might imagine. It was as though the articles were saying to their readers, "See, Muslims are just like you; they aren't scary at all." The perhaps unintended consequence of such a framing is that same narrative does the work of also suggesting that any Muslim who is not as progressive or as Westernized or who is not as wrapped up in cultures of consumption might be somehow suspect. This was amplified in *Marie Claire* and *Cosmopolitan* by some of the earlier pieces that perpetuated Orientalist or Islamophobic understandings of the lives of Muslim women.

The picture emerging from *Teen Vogue* is more complicated, more nuanced, and more contextualized. While all three magazines included in this analysis have sought Muslim commentators and reporters to help improve their coverage of Muslim communities, *Teen Vogue* has been the most aggressive and featured the most contributions from Muslim writers. The articles produced by such writers have covered things like radicalization in Muslim communities, how to talk about ISIS without being Islamophobic, and, yes, profiled Muslim individuals who are shattering stereotypes about Islam. In fact, at the 2016 SXSW conference, the magazine received praise in social media for an event it cohosted on the refugee crisis and Trump travel ban—one of the event's moderators was Muslim Girl editor in chief and *Teen Vogue* contributor Amani Al-Khatahtbeh. Al-Khatahtbeh has been featured as one of those stereotype shatterers, but she has also written about difficult issues facing Muslims living in non-Muslim countries.

While the picture beginning to emerge of Muslims in fashion magazines may not be perfect, it does seem to be moving toward a more nuanced reflection of Muslim life. However, there are voices and experiences that are left out. Religiously conservative perspectives rarely appear in these magazines; when conservatives do appear, they are often framed as foils for the more progressive understandings of Islam featured in the magazines. It's likely the mission of these magazines does not make them the appropriate place for a real consideration of such perspectives. However, given their target audience of young women and their ability to drive ideological understandings of culture, it's worth considering whether they should work to create a more inclusive picture of Muslim life.

The idea of Muslims, particularly Muslim women, as victims of their religion and as victims of Muslim men does seem to be receding from coverage. (Although this framing does pop up in reporting on the actions of groups like ISIS and how they target Muslims as well as how their actions affect the way people in the West see Islam.) That is not to say that the framing of Muslims as victims has disappeared completely; instead, stories that frame Muslims as victims most often pointed the finger at Islamophobes as the threat. While it is important to make visible the hate and violence many Muslims experience in the United States, as well as trace its circulation in media and political discourse, media producers must be careful to not trade one frame of victimization for another. To be a victim of Islam or a victim of Islamophobia is to still be a victim and often creates a mediated understanding of Muslim women that can strip them of their agency and autonomy and perpetuate the idea that they need saving. If visibility, as Foucault suggests, opens us up to surveillance and limits the types of identities we feel free to perform, then understanding the identities Muslims see in popular media is crucial to understanding how they navigate a culture that has frequently treated them as others to be feared or others who should feel fear. The type of content produced by an outlet like *Teen Vogue* is rare; most magazines do not provide the space for such thoughtful or critical reflections on identity and othering, with the images of Muslim women appearing in most fashion magazines being more glossy fantasies than anything else. However, sometimes the fantasy can become a glossy nightmare of representation.

Social media lit up again in early 2019 over an appearance by Noor Tagouri in a mainstream magazine. This time, however, the debate was not over whether Tagouri should have appeared in the publication—this time the ire of social media users was turned toward the publication itself. It began after Tagouri shared a video of herself opening up the February 2019 issue of *Vogue* magazine and flipping to a photograph showing her standing in profile. In the tweet accompanying the video, Tagouri wrote "I'm SO heartbroken and devastated. Like my heart actually hurts. I've been waiting to make this announcement for MONTHS. One of my DREAMS of being featured in American @VogueMagazine came true!!"[66]

The cause of her devastation? *Vogue*'s misidentifying her in the caption accompanying the photograph. Instead of saying the model was "Noor Tagouri," the magazine identified her as "Noor Bukhari." Tagouri is an American Muslim of Libyan background; Bukhari is a Pakistani actress and model. The two women share nothing beyond a name, a religion, and the fact they both wear headscarves. In a Twitter thread that followed the tweet featuring the video, Tagouri wrote, "Misrepresentation and misidentification is a constant problem if you are Muslim in America. And as much as I work to fight this, there are moments like this where I feel defeated."[67] In writing of Vogue's mistake, author and scholar Rafia Zakaria suggested that "in that enduring misidentification... lurks a horrible truth of how America chooses to treat Muslim women who wear the headscarf: To many Americans, one veiled Muslim woman is interchangeable for the next."[68] Zakaria also points out that research has shown that such misidentification, or outright harassment in some instances, is generally a low-cost faux pas, writing "whether done out of animus or carelessness, misidentifying those who already face alarming levels of harassment in the United States is likely assessed to be free of social cost or moral censure."

As discussed earlier, Muslim women—particularly those who choose to veil themselves in some way—are often imagined as having no personal agency. They are seen as oppressed or passive subjects who cannot choose their own path in life or even something as seemingly simple as what to wear when leaving their house. Even when it seems they do something to challenge that idea— like, say, appearing in *Playboy* or *Vogue*—problems related to misrepresentation, stereotype, and othering pop up. Tagouri is far from the only American Muslim woman to deal with these issues; she just happens to be among the most visible and among the most accessible to a broad public to do so.

In writing about her concept of "plastic representation," Kristen Warner suggested that because of the history of misrepresentation, people of color are often placed into a situation where any type of nonstereotypical representation is automatically seen as a good thing—even if that representation does not meaningfully engage with what it is like to be Black in America or, for the purposes of this book, Muslim in America. She argues that media producers who engage in multiracial casting—be it for a photo shoot or a television production—that are focused on the "quantity of difference" rather than the "dimensionality" of that difference help produce representations that "can feel—in an affective sense—artificial, or more to the point, plastic."[69] A producer can mask myriad problems with the representation of a Black or Muslim character if that character is given a nonstereotypical framing, such as an unexpected occupation or, in the case of a Muslim character, allowing them to proclaim a love of pork or alcohol that is understood to be forbidden in Islam. Plastic representation, Warner says, "can be understood as a combination of synthetic elements put together and shaped to look like meaningful imagery, but which can only approximate depth and substance because ultimately it is hollow and cannot survive close scrutiny."[70] After laughing at the joke about a Muslim loving pork comes the realization that the joke, though showing a Muslim doing something unexpected, is itself predicated on stereotype. It cannot exist if it does not assume that the stereotype communicates some truth about what it means to be Muslim and, therefore, serves to reinforce the stereotype, not challenge it.

Noor Tagouri is an American Muslim success story. And yet if Rafia Zakaria is to be believed, Tagouri remains "interchangeable" with other headscarf-wearing women in the American imagination. Her appearances in *Vogue* and *Playboy*, though at times groundbreaking and certainly personally meaningful, are in their way empty as it could have been any headscarf-wearing woman in that photo in *Vogue* or another Muslim "rebel" photographed for *Playboy*. If glossy magazines help create dreamworlds for their readers, then those worlds are often still filled with Orientalist understandings of who Muslim women are—even when the Muslim women appearing in the publications are meant to upend Orientalist stereotypes. They are glossy, diverse, and yet frequently empty representations of the Muslim experience.

NOTES

1. Lauren Loftus, "All Eyes on Noor: Local Woman Wants to Be the First Hijabi Anchor on American TV," *Washington Post*, June 18, 2015, https://www.washingtonpost.com/news/arts-and-entertainment/wp/2015/06/18/all-eyes-on-noor-local-woman-wants-to-be-first-hijabi-anchor-on-american-tv/.

2. Aymann Ismail, "Muslims Should Praise Hijabi Journalism Noor Tagouri, Not Criticize Her," *Slate*, September 27, 2016, https://slate.com/human-interest/2016/09/playboy-photographed-muslim-american-woman-noor-tagouri-in-her-hijab.html; Zehra Rizavi, "Noor Tagouri Responds—But Is Playboy the Medium for Muslim Women's Empowerment?," *Altmuslim*, September 30, 2016, https://www.patheos.com/blogs/altmuslim/2016/09/noor-tagouri-responds-but-is-playboy-the-medium-for-muslim-womens-empowerment/.

3. Nishaat Ismail, "I Fail to See Why I Should Celebrate a Hijab-Wearing Muslim Woman Appearing in Playboy for the First Time," *Independent*, September 26, 2016, https://www.independent.co.uk/voices/noor-tagouri-first-hijab-wearing-muslim-woman-playboy-magazine-hugh-hefner-bunniers-celebrate-first-time-a7330806.html.

4. This comment appeared on a post on the Muslim Voices Facebook page on January 1, 2017, and was contributed by a Facebook user named Sarah Choudhury.

5. Amina Yaqin, "Inside the Harem, Outside the Nation," *Interventions: The International Journal of Postcolonial Studies* 12, no. 2 (2010): 226–38.

6. Lila Abu-Lughod, "Zones of Theory in the Anthropology of the Arab World," *Annual Review of Anthropology* 18 (1989): 289.

7. Carine Bourget, "Complicity with Orientalism in Third-World Women's Writing: Fatima Mernissi's Fictive Memoirs," *Research in African Literatures* 44, no. 3 (2013): 30–49.

8. Diya Abdo, "Uncovering the Harem in the Classroom," *Women's Studies Quarterly* 30, no. 1/2 (2002): 227.

9. Mohja Kahf, *Western Representations of the Muslim Woman: From Termagant to Odalisque* (Austin: University of Texas Press, 1999), 6.

10. Ibid., 8.

11. Carol A. Stabile and Deepa Kumar, "Unveiling Imperialism: Media, Gender and the War on Afghanistan," *Media, Culture & Society* 27, no. 5 (2005): 765–82; Rafia Zakaria, "Prisoners of Paradigm," in *On Islam: Muslims and the Media*, ed. Rosemary Pennington and Hilary Kahn (Bloomington: Indiana University Press, 2018), 51–56.

12. Esmaeil Zeiny and Noraini Md Yusof, "The Said and the Not-Said: New Grammar of Visual Imperialism," *GEMA Online Journal of Language Studies* 16, no. 1 (2016): 125–41.

13. Lila Abu-Lughod, "Do Muslim Women Really Need Saving? Anthropological Reflections on Cultural Relativism and Its Others," *American Anthropologist* 104, no. 3 (2002): 783–90; Abdo, "Uncovering the Harem in the Classroom."

14. Zeiny and Yusof, "The Said and the Not-Said."

15. Stabile and Kumar, "Unveiling Imperialism."

16. Ibid., 770.

17. Melani McAlister, *Epic Encounters: Culture, Media, and U.S. Interests in the Middle East since 1945*, updated ed. (Berkeley: University of California Press, 2005), 3.

18. Ibid., 4.

19. Sophia Rose Arjana, *Muslims in the Western Imagination* (Oxford: Oxford University Press, 2015).

20. Ibid.

21. Suzanne Conklin Akbari, *Idols in the East: European Representation of Islam and the Orient, 1100–1450* (Ithaca, NY: Cornell University Press, 2009).

22. Laura Sjober and Caron E. Gentry, "Reduced to Bad Sex: Narratives of Violent Women from the Bible to the War on Terror," *International Relations* 22, no. 1 (2013): 68.

23. Heidi Safia Mirza, "'Dangerous Muslim Girls? Race, Gender and Islamophobia in British Schools," in *The Runnymede School Report: Race, Education and Inequality in Contemporary Britain*, ed. Claire Alexander,

A GLOSSY ISLAM   153

Debbie Weekes-Bernard, and Jason Arday (London: Runnymede Trust, 2015), 40–43.

24. Saira Mahmood, "Noor Tagouri, Playboy and the Porn Industry," Muslimah Media Watch, May 8, 2018, http://www.muslimahmediawatch .org/2018/05/08/noor-tagouri-playboy-and-the-porn-industry/.

25. Hannah Allam, "A Muslim Woman in Playboy: What Could Go Wrong?," *Charlotte Observer*, September 27, 2016, https://www.charlotteobserver.com /living/article104353276.html.

26. Hina Tai, "Noor Tagouri Is Not the Controversy, Muslim Women Representation Is," HuffPost, March 10, 2017, https://www.huffpost.com/entry /noor-tagouri-is-not-the-controversy-muslim-women-representation_b_57ed513 9e4b07f20daa104bb.

27. Allam, "Muslim Woman in Playboy."

28. Sara Salem, "Feminist Critique and Islamic Feminism: The Question of Intersectionality," *Postcolonialist* 1, no. 1 (2013): 1–8.

29. Ibid.

30. Rafia Zakaria, *Against White Feminism: Notes on Disruption* (New York: W. W. Norton, 2021), 209.

31. Salem, "Feminist Critique and Islamic Feminism."

32. Valentine M. Moghadam, "Islamic Feminism and Its Discontents: Toward a Resolution of the Debate," *Signs: Journal of Women in Culture and Society* 27, no. 4 (2002): 1135–71.

33. Margot Badran, "Re/placing Islamic Feminism," *Critique Internationale* 1 (2010): 25–44.

34. On her personal website, http://www.monaeltahawy.com, Eltahaway shares a short biography, as well as links to her prodigious output as a journalist and writer. Eltahaway has written about Egyptian politics, Islamic feminism, and even the experience of being a fan of Egyptian soccer star Mo Salah.

35. Mona Eltahaway, "#MosqueMeToo: What Happened When I Was Sexually Assaulted during the Hajj," *Washington Post*, February 15, 2018, https:// www.washingtonpost.com/news/global-opinions/wp/2018/02/15/mosquemetoo -what-happened-when-i-was-sexually-assaulted-during-the-hajj/?arc404=true.

36. Mona Eltahaway, *Headscarves and Hymens: Why the Middle East Needs a Sexual Revolution* (New York: Farrar, Straus and Giroux, 2016).

37. Kecia Ali, "Across Generations: The Making of the 'Lady Imam,'" *Journal of Feminist Studies in Religion* 35, no. 1 (2019): 67–79.

38. amina wadud, "Islam beyond Patriarchy through Gender Inclusive Qur'anic Analysis," in *Wanted: Equality and Justice in the Muslim Family*, ed. Zainah Anwar (Malaysia: Musawah, 2009), 95–112, 103.

39. *Aljazeera*, "Woman Leads Controversial Prayer," March 19, 2005, https:// www.aljazeera.com/news/2005/3/19/woman-leads-controversial-us -prayer.

40. Kecia Ali and amina wadud, "The Making of the 'Lady Imam': An Interview with Amina Wadud," *Journal of Feminist Studies of Religion* 35, no. 1 (2019): 77.

41. Rafia Zakaria, "The Myth of Women's 'Empowerment,'" *New York Times*, October 5, 2017, https://www.nytimes.com/2017/10/05/opinion/the-myth-of -womens-empowerment.html.

42. Kate Cronin-Furman, Nimmi Gowrinathan, and Rafia Zakaria, "Emissaries of Empowerment," Colin Powell School for Civic and Global Leadership, City College of New York, September 2017, https://www.ccny.cuny .edu/colinpowellschool/emissaries-empowerment.

43. Lorna Stevens and Pauline Maclaren, "Exploring the 'Shopping Imaginary': The Dreamworld of Women's Magazines," *Journal of Consumer Behavior* 4, no. 4 (2005): 282–92.

44. Julia Twigg, "Fashion, the Media, and Age: How Women's Magazines Use Fashion to Negotiate Identities," *European Journal of Cultural Studies* 21, no. 3 (2018): 334–48.

45. Amy Beth Aronson, "Domesticity and Women's Collective Agency: Contribution and Collaboration in America's First Successful Women's Magazine," *American Periodicals* 11 (2001): 1–23.

46. Brita Ytre-Arne, "Women's Magazines and Their Readers: The Relationship between Textual Features and Practices of Reading," *European Journal of Cultural Studies* 14, no. 2 (2011): 213–28.

47. Merja Mahrt, "The Attractiveness of Magazines as 'Open' and 'Closed' Texts: Values of Women's Magazines and Their Readers," *Mass Communication & Society* 15, no. 6 (2012): 852–74.

48. Jennifer A. Schlenker, Sandra L. Caron, and William A. Halteman, "A Feminist Analysis of Seventeen Magazine: A Content Analysis from 1945 to 1995," *Sex Roles* 38, no. ½ (1998): 135–49.

49. Meenakshi Gigi Durham, "Myths of Race and Beauty in Teen Magazines: A Semiological Analysis," Paper presented at International Communication Association Conference, San Francisco, 2007, 17.

50. Other magazines included in the preliminary search were *Vanity Fair*, *Vogue*, *Elle*, and *W*. A search of the archives of these four outlets using the terms *Muslim* or *Islam* returned fewer than five articles per outlet, and so these magazines were excluded from the analysis.

51. Betty de Hart, "Not without My Daughter: On Parental Abduction, Orientalism, and Maternal Melodrama," *European Journal of Women's Studies* 8, no. 1 (2001): 51–65.

52. Megan Goodwin, "'The Do That to Foreign Women': Domestic Terrorism and Contraceptive Nationalism in Not without My Daughter," *Muslim World* 106, no. 4 (2016): 761.

53. Asra Nomani, "My Big Fat Muslim Wedding," *Marie Claire*, July 9, 2009, https://www.marieclaire.com/sex-love/news/a3330/muslim-wedding/.

54. Jan Goodwin, "Pakistan: Only Women Can Rescue Women," *Marie Claire*, April 27, 2007, https://www.marieclaire.com/politics/news/a171/pakistan-female-rescue/.

55. Ibid.

56. Arjana, *Muslims in the Western Imagination*; Abu-Lughod, "Do Muslim Women Really Need Saving?"

57. Colleen Curry, "Anti-Muslim Hate Crimes Are on the Rise after Recent Terror Attacks," *Teen Vogue*, June 21, 2016, https://www.teenvogue.com/story/anti-islam-hate-crimes-increase-after-terror-attacks-trump.

58. Joshua Eaton, "Gay Republicans Throw WAKE UP Party at RNC 2016 That Perpetuates Islamophobia," *Teen Vogue*, July 21, 2016, https://www.teenvogue.com/story/gay-republicans-wake-up-party-islamophobia-rnc-2016.

59. Amani al-Khatahtbeh, "A Letter to My Future Muslim Daughter," *Cosmopolitan*, October 27, 2016, https://www.cosmopolitan.com/politics/a7557079/amani-al-khatahtbeh-muslim-girl-daughter-letter/.

60. Hishaam Siddiqi, "How to Talk about ISIS without Islamophobia," *Teen Vogue*, July 18, 2016, https://www.teenvogue.com/story/talking-about-islam-isis-terrorism-language.

61. Emma Sarran Webster, "2016 Rio Olympic Gold Medalist Dalilah Muhammad on Making History," *Teen Vogue*, October 7, 2016, https://www.teenvogue.com/story/2016-rio-olympic-gold-medalist-dalilah-muhammad-on-making-history.

62. *Marie Claire*, "Shopping in Dubai," August 3, 2007, https://www.marieclaire.com/fashion/news/a644/dubai-shop-blog/.

63. Ibid.

64. Amani al-Khatahtbeh, "Watch Muslim Girls Get REAL about Love, Faith, and Trump," *Teen Vogue*, May 9, 2016, https://www.teenvogue.com/story/muslim-girl-videos-islamophobia-america.

65. Evelyn Alsultany, "The Cultural Politics of Islam in U.S. Reality Television," *Communication, Culture & Critique* 9, no. 4 (2016): 60.

66. Noor Tagouri (@NTagouri), "I'm SO heartbroken and devastated. Like my heart actually hurts. I've been waiting to make this announcement for MONTHS. One of my DREAMS . . . ," Twitter, January 17, 2019, 5:26 a.m., https://twitter.com/NTagouri/status/1085893518478987265.

67. Noor Tagouri (@NTagouri), "Misrepresentation and misidentification is a constant problem if you are Muslim in America. And as much as I work to fight this, there are . . . ," Twitter, January 17, 2019, 5:36 a.m., https://twitter.com/NTagouri/status/1085893536724238336.

68. Rafia Zakaria, "What Vogue Did to Noor Tagouri Tells a Bigger Story," CNN, January 18, 2019, https://www.cnn.com/2019/01/18/opinions/noor-tagouri-vogue-misidentification-zakaria/index.html.

69. Kristen Warner, "In the Time of Plastic Representation," *Film Quarterly* 71, no. 12 (2017), https://filmquarterly.org/2017/12/04/in-the-time-of-plastic-representation/.

70. Ibid.

—⁓—

CONCLUSION

The Complications of Visibility

IN LATE 2021, MARVEL FANS got a glimpse of Kamala Khan's Ms. Marvel on the small screen when Disney+ released its "first look" reel for a number of its upcoming series. The short peek into the show featured images of Muslims praying in a mosque edited next to an image of Kamala dressed as Ms. Marvel looking at herself in a mirror. The choice to show Muslims at prayer juxtaposed against Kamala dressed as a hero foregrounds for viewers the importance of her Muslim heritage to this new Ms. Marvel's identity. Fans flocked to social media outlets sharing their excitement to see Kamala physically brought to life. Then, in March 2022, Disney+ released a full trailer for the program, showing Kamala struggling to find her place both in high school and among the pantheon of other Marvel heroes. For Canadian sports writer Shireen Ahmed, seeing Kamala in the trailer was a very big deal.

In a second tweet, Ahmed wrote, "I'm a 45 year-old Muslim woman from AfPak community. A mainstream superhero that looks like me is not something I could have dreamed of. But here we are. It is the 20th anniversary of 'Bend It Like Beckham' and that film was the last time I saw myself. So, yeah. This matters."[1]

The excitement that erupted with the trailer's release was an echo of the enthusiasm that exploded for the program right after Marvel made public its production and after it was announced that Muslim actress Iman Vellani would fill Kamala's boots on the small screen. Vellani shares both the Muslim Ms. Marvel's youth and her heritage as a child of Pakistani immigrants. Fan sites, blogs, and entertainment publications all celebrated the fact that the Muslim superhero was actually going to be played by a Muslim. However, production on the series tempered the excitement somewhat, as the program's release

Shireen Ahmed ✓
@_shireenahmed_

SCREAMS AND SOBS WITH JOY INTO MY HIJAB
I. Have. Waited. My. Whole. Life. For. This.
@MarvelStudios

youtube.com
Marvel Studios' Ms. Marvel | Official Trailer | Disney+
The future is in her hands. Ms. Marvel, an Original series from Marvel Studios, starts streaming June 8 on Disney+. ▶ ...

10:18 AM · Mar 15, 2022 · Twitter for Android

7 Retweets **2** Quote Tweets **82** Likes

Fig. 6.1 Canadian sportswriter Shireen Ahmed often writes about, and discusses on podcasts, the issues faced by Muslims and people of color in sports as well as in society more broadly. She was among the many Twitter users expressing their excitement upon the release of the *Ms. Marvel* TV show trailer in March 2022.

was delayed several times. One of the cocreators of *Ms. Marvel*, Sana Amanat, tweeted about the show's production that "The pressure and responsibility we all feel is intense. The love we have is immense."[2] Though Kamala Khan has appeared in video games and cartoons, the Disney+ program was her first live action representation. It was also the first time that a Muslim appeared before American TV audiences as a physical embodiment of good in the battle between good and evil. Critics who had early access to the program did raise some concerns over how Islam was treated in the first two episodes they were provided, while also suggesting that the representation of Kamala was a reason to celebrate.[3] When the program officially launched in June 2022, many Muslim viewers echoed Shireen Ahmed's excitement in finally seeing a representation of the Muslim experience that seemed to move beyond caricature and stereotype. However, that does not mean that critiques weren't leveled at the program, with some viewers concerned with how conservative Muslims are treated on the show while others took issue with the fact that viewers don't really see Kamala practicing her faith. According to Kristian Petersen, the debate over *Ms. Marvel* and shows like it highlights one of the complications of visibility: "The more complicated kernel buried under this mound of criticism is what it reveals about the circumstances surrounding Muslim representation in popular media. When a product comes together with seemingly all the right components—Muslims as writers, directors, producers and more—it will still fail to meet the internal expectations of the entire community it seeks to represent."[4]

Representation is a powerful thing. It can provide opportunities for connection and disconnection. It can help shape the borders of our imagined communities. Representation also provides an opportunity to engage with meaning. Meaning is something author Orhan Pamuk contemplates in his novel, *My Name Is Red*. The narrative bounces between people and objects, as each chapter considers, in its own way, what it means to exist, what it means to be in the world. One chapter, "I Am a Tree," is narrated not by an actual tree but by the illustration of one. As the tree describes the various stories it might have been used to illustrate—it has been severed from its text—it eventually states, "I don't want to be a tree; I want to be its meaning."[5] What are representations if not attempts to capture meaning? For a very long time, the representations of Muslims in American media have communicated meanings shaped by non-Muslim creators who often portrayed Islam as a foreign faith and Muslims as monolithic believers. But as discussed in this book, things are beginning to change as popular media spaces are filling with representations that communicate meanings produced by Muslims. Importantly, these meanings are produced by a diverse array of individuals, helping audiences understand that Muslims are not a monolith.

Even as popular media have begun showcasing diverse Muslim media producers, it can still be difficult to avoid the good Muslim / bad Muslim binary in Muslim representation, which can get in the way of seeing Muslims as whole and complicated human beings. This is an issue writer Viet Thanh Nguyen takes up in his discussion of how memory shapes our definitions of self and our definitions of other. In order to avoid binary understandings of those we think belong inside our communities and those we imagine existing outside our communities, Thanh Nguyen thinks we should move toward what he calls an "ethics of recognition" during intercultural encounters. This ethics, he suggests, would allow people to be seen in all their glory and in all their ghastliness, without forcing them into some kind of good versus bad framing: "Without such a recognition, we can make peace with old enemies only to continue wars with newer enemies not recognized as friends or even human. Identifying *with* [sic] the victim and the other in an act of empathy, has the unexpected, inhuman side effect of perpetuating the conditions for further victimization."[6]

In the case of Muslims, the lack of such an ethics of recognition has often led to particular Muslims being seen as "safe" in some way—often Sufi Muslims or Muslims who grew up in the West—while others continue being framed as a threat of some kind. In connection to media representations of Arabs and Muslims, Evelyn Alsultany has identified such binaries as "simplified complex representations" where media producers counterbalance a negative and Islamophobic representation of a Muslim character with a more positive one. Both Alsultany and Nguyen argue for something much more nuanced and complex when it comes to the representations of people from minority backgrounds— they argue for a framing in which the contradictory and uncomfortable messiness of human experience is foregrounded, not avoided, a framing that allows individuals to be complex human beings who are both awful and awesome. It could be argued that the Muslim Ms. Marvel steps toward this as one storyline featured in the first run of the comic features Kamala taking on a Muslim bad guy, a bad guy who uses their shared heritage to get close to Kamala but who does not use that heritage to fuel his villainous deeds. One could argue that this storyline steps toward Nguyen's idea of an ethics of recognition that ensures we recognize the humanity and inhumanity in ourselves as well as in others. "If we do not recognize our capacity to victimize," Nguyen writes, "then it would be difficult for us to prevent the victimization carried out on our behalf, or which we do ourselves."[7]

The inability, or unwillingness, to see Muslims as human beings helped lead to the shootings in Christchurch, New Zealand; the attacks on Muslim communities in China, Myanmar, and India; and the shooting of three Muslims in their home in Chapel Hill, North Carolina. The labeling of Muslims as somehow "inhuman" has led to both large-scale and small-scale violence targeted toward anyone who seems to adhere to the teachings of Islam. To be visibly Muslim in such an environment takes courage, an idea Council on American-Islamic Relations National Board chair Roula Allouch reinforced in a podcast about Muslims in Southwest Ohio: "In these days where people have such an increased level of hate and hatred towards Islam and Muslims, I like standing out as a Muslim. Even though I know that puts me as a target, and it puts in me in a situation where at times, I am, unfortunately, perhaps in danger and I shouldn't be, but as an American, as an attorney, and as a civil rights activist, I feel like it's even more necessary to practice my First Amendment right to wear hijab."[8]

Muslim communities in the United States often find themselves the subject of surveillance by both government and cultural forces. Imagined as criminal or terrorist threats, they have seen their mosques infiltrated by law enforcement, their names placed on no-fly lists, their right to build places of worship denied out of fear. They have to ask for their holidays to be recognized, for their children to not be fed pork at school, for their right to simply exist in America. The danger they sometimes face simply for being Muslim is real and oppressive. And yet so many individuals do not shy away from making their identities visible. For some, to be visible is a purposefully and overtly political act. For others, it is simply an attempt to live their lives as authentically as they can (though one might argue that, itself, is a political act).

Pierre Bourdieu noted that for members of minority groups debates about identity and belonging are often "struggles over the monopoly of the power to make people see and believe, to get them to know and recognize, to impose the legitimate definition of the divisions of the social world and, thereby, to *make and unmake groups*."[9] For American Muslims, the struggle for visibility is partly to ensure they are not erased from the American public sphere. It is a struggle to make an American identity that includes Muslim experiences. Edward Said wrote that "self-definition is one of the activities practiced by all cultures: it has a rhetoric, a set of occasions and authorities . . . and a familiarity all its own."[10] American Muslims want to participate in the process of American self-definition as they seek recognition that Muslims belong to and in the United States. It is a struggle to force the United States to live up to its lofty rhetoric of being a land that welcomes everyone. If that's truly to be the case, then everyone must be involved in the making of what it means to be American. This is one of the narrative threads in the second season of the Hulu show *Ramy*.

The sophomore season begins as the main character returns from a disastrous trip to visit family in Egypt, hoping to find some direction for his life. Upon his return, Ramy Youssef connects with a sheik, played by Mahershala Ali, in order to reconnect with Islam as he works to create a meaningful American Muslim life. The second season of the show also features storylines focused on Ramy's sister and mother, giving viewers insight into the lives of Muslim women who do not apologize for their faith. In the case of Ramy's mother, viewers even get to see a Muslim immigrant on her path to American citizenship. In the program Islam is a lived religion set against a New Jersey backdrop and Youssef, playing an avatar of himself, works to unmake an understanding of America that is hegemonically white and Christian and remake it to be more reflective of the country's multiracial, multiethnic, and multireligious reality. Youssef helps make visible an accessible American Muslim experience. However, even with the success of shows like *Ramy* and comic books like *Ms. Marvel*, the work toward inclusion is fraught and complicated.

Fig. 6.2 "Islam is like an orange," Mahershala Ali's character Sheikh Ali tells Ramy in an episode of the Hulu program. "There's an outer part and an inner part. If someone only got the rules and rituals, they might think Islam is tough and bitter like the outside of an orange. But there's an inside, a juicy flesh, the divine intimacy, the spiritual experience."

For Michel Foucault, the danger in becoming visible lies in the possibility of being trapped by the expectations of the viewers. Even if you are seeking to be your most authentic self, there is a feeling of some pressure to not be so much yourself that you run afoul of those who would deem you "normal" or "safe." Our performances of self in this environment are "individualized and constantly visible"[11] and, for Muslims, can often reinforce what Nabil Echchaibi calls the "double burden of representation."[12] Muslims often find themselves in a position to defend their faith from accusations of it somehow being violent or promoting terrorism or oppressing others and in that defense, Echchaibi suggests, lies a trap. It puts Muslims in a position of suggesting that perhaps some interpretations of Islam *are* problematic as they seek to convince us that not all Muslims are violent. Muslims are pushed to publicly recognize the "humanity and inhumanity" of their communities while the non-Muslims they are speaking to rarely are. We often hear people proclaim that "not all Muslims are violent" or "not all Muslims hate the West," but rarely do we hear echoed back "not all Americans believe Muslims are violent" or "not all Americans believe Muslims are dangerous." Becoming visible, in this instance, reinforces the representational cage that traps Muslims and Islam in a stereotyped understanding of what the two are. It's a trap that many American Muslim producers

CONCLUSION

and creators are all too aware of as they work to create media that both reflects their experiences and is accessible to a broad American audience. That certainly seems to be true of comedian Hasan Minhaj. During an interview promoting the third season of his Netflix show *Patriot Act*, Minhaj was asked how his background—he is the Muslim Indian American son of immigrants—has shaped his particular approach to comedy. "I'm an Indian American Muslim. I'm always reminded of that. And as a result, I've always had an insider-outsider relationship with America. I'm a citizen, and I grew up here and loved it as any American kid would. But at the same time, there have been moments when I've felt like, man . . . I'm an outsider regardless of what's on my birth certificate. I don't fit in at the party."[13]

Seemingly part of Minhaj's mission is to make space for himself and others like him to exist in the American imagination. To force a recognition of the experiences of American Muslims *as* American. What would it be like for Muslims like Minhaj to not be reminded of their outsider status? To not be seen as outsiders at all? At the close of a conference called Cyber Muslims, Nabil Echchaibi asked what it would mean for Muslims to not feel a "compulsion to represent," to not have to be constantly concerned about how they are being understood.[14]

It's an idea that Kamala Khan wrestles with in the second issue of the *Ms. Marvel* relaunch, after she has spent some time embodying Carol Danvers's version of Ms. Marvel. Reflecting on her experience, Kamala thinks to herself, "being someone else isn't liberating. It's exhausting."[15] After spending seemingly years wanting to feel more "normal," wanting to not have to worry about how her Muslim identity is being understood by non-Muslims, Kamala realizes that she should be enough, that her experience as an American Muslim is meaningful enough, heroic enough. In a just world, no one would be forced to fit into a mold in order to be understood and included; they would simply be accepted as they are. Muslims would be allowed, as Echchaibi suggested, to "just live." It's the hope of such a world Kamala begins to work toward in her role as Ms. Marvel. It's the expectation of such a world that seems to drive the work of Muslim comedians, actors, and reality show contestants. But, for now, it is seemingly more a hope than a reality.

The representations of Muslims explored in this book are not studies in fidelity or truth—they are not representations designed to suggest that one way of being Muslim is truer or more honest than another. They are representations designed to help the audience understand what it *means* to be Muslim in America, what it *means* to be an American Muslim. In the case of Marvel's Kamala Khan, being an American Muslim means finding a way to reconcile the

164 POP ISLAM

expectations of family, community, and self in a way that feels true to herself. In *Ms. Marvel*'s second series, Kamala struggles with the fact that she is now a known entity, people know she's out there, fighting for the common good. "Now I'm some kind of symbol," she says, "and I don't have any say in what it means."[16] What Kamala is struggling with is the fact that no matter what she does, she cannot control how people will respond to her; she has no control over what she *means* to other people. Kamala has been transformed in the minds of the public from superhero to the *meaning* of superhero. Eventually, she reconciles herself to the fact that all she can do is to continue to do good as best she can, to live her life as authentically as she can, and to hope that it is enough.

The Muslim representations appearing in prime-time TV dramas are often heroic in their own ways. *Lost*'s Sayyid constantly fights against the expectations of others that he will be violent, *American Crime*'s Aliyah fights against an unjust justice system that seems to presume her brother's guilt, and *The Night Of*'s Naz fights against a system that would transform him into the violent caricature it expects him to be—a battle he seemingly loses in the end. All of these representations work to help audiences understand what it *means* that Muslims are continually associated with violence, that they are continually framed as enemy others. Comedians, of course, can poke fun at such stereotypes. They can throw them back at the audience, expose the racist foundations on which they are built, and force the audience to laugh at the absurdities of such stereotypes and their own perpetuation of them. Together, the comedian and their audience can remake the boundaries marking us and others, even if for just a moment. All of this works to reshape the meaning of Muslim in the American imagination.

When it comes to representations of "real" Muslims, things get trickier. There is some expectation that not only is it a representation of the Muslim experience, not only is it meant to signify in some way what it means to be an American Muslim, but also these representations are imagined to somehow be true to life or authentic. They are expected to be *both* tree and meaning. For contestants on American reality TV shows, if what they produce is not judged authentic—and by authentic, the judges mean tied in some way to the contestants' ethnic or religious identity—then they are castigated for conforming in an attempt to get ahead. Of course, what this critique ignores are the histories that have forced members of marginalized or minority groups to attempt to assimilate, to attempt to erase those things that made them stand out, in order to survive in an American culture defined by a white, Protestant experience. One way to become nonthreatening, to be woven into the fabric of the culture,

CONCLUSION

is to produce things that can be consumed or to become consumable yourself. When Fatima Ali was criticized for her food not being authentic, when Ayana Ife was celebrated for foregrounding modesty in her clothing designs, when magazines featured Muslim women in Dubai who watch *Desperate Housewives* and shop for designer goods, it was all designed to help sell these Muslim women to a broad American audience. To make them, their stories, and what they produce something that could be bought or sold. What does it mean to be real when that realness is predicated on whether an audience or a panel of judges buys into your performance of your identity?

For the American Muslims who appear in popular media, and who are creating some of it, it can be difficult to escape the traps that broad visibility poses for them. It can be difficult to subvert conventions when those very same conventions structure the media in which you appear or that you create. American Muslim activist and writer Taz Ahmed highlighted this struggle when she tweeted, "We do SO much work as Muslim culture shifters, narrative tellers, advocates & activists. We recenter POVs, disrupt stereotypes, amplify margins. We insist to be seen, heard, not be forgotten."[17] Her tweet was one of despair, as she was seemingly feeling frustrated that even as Muslims gain more visibility in the United States, the suffering of Muslims in places such as India and China are still largely undercovered or ignored by American media. What use is visibility, she seems to suggest, if it can't affect change or serve to help others? What use is meaning if one is only partially recognized as a tree? Only partially recognized as human?

On December 16, 2019, Twitter was ablaze as the hashtag #kumail began trending. The hashtag was connected to comedian, actor, and writer Kumail Nanjiani. Nanjiani is among the most successful and visible American Muslim pop culture figures. He gained widespread notice after appearing in HBO's comedy *Silicon Valley* and then for writing and starring in *The Big Sick*, a film about how he met and fell in love with his wife. The trending #kumail hashtag in December 2019, however, had nothing to do with his intellectual output or his comedic performances. Instead, it was devoted to an active discussion of Kumail Nanjiani's body spurred by photos he'd posted to his Instagram account. The photo showed a shirtless Nanjiani standing with his hands on his hips, the veins of his upper arms bulging, and his arms and shoulders looking as though they'd been chiseled from marble. Nanjiani wrote in the caption of the photo, "I never thought I'd be one of those people who'd post a thirsty shirtless, but I've worked way too hard for way too long so here we are."[18]

Nanjiani was cast in the Marvel superhero film *The Eternals* and had spent the last year observing a very strict diet and very strenuous exercise regime in order to portray a timeless superhero. The photos were an unveiling of sorts of the body this year of work produced—one fans have come to expect of Marvel heroes. The *New York Post* wrote that Nanjiani's photos served as "a thirst trap of himself looking like the whole darn meal."[19] So impressed with the photos were some segments of the internet that Pornhub, a website that features a variety of pornography, used Nanjiani's photo as the entryway to its "Muscular Men" section of porn.[20] Twitter was filled with posts about the photos, most of which were hashtagged #kumail, expressing admiration of the actor's appearance. One Twitter user wrote, "Here I was worried about Rise of Skywalker spoilers, but all twitter wants to talk about are #Kumail and his washboard abs. I am very much okay with this."[21] Others joked that the photo got them "instantly pregnant" and Mashable India tweeted that "@TheBigSickMovie actor @kumailn's thirsty AF photos have left the internet parched. #KumailNanjiani #Kumail."[22] Many Twitter users pointed out that it was a "big moment" for Desis, or members of the Pakistani diaspora. It was also a big moment for Muslims. Not perhaps since Disney's *Aladdin* has a Muslim man so captured the public imagination for something unrelated to sports, villainy, or terrorism. Here was a brown Muslim man showing off his physical prowess, and people were celebrating it, not recoiling in fear from it. Nanjiani later called the whole experience "weird"—weird, but also perhaps transformative when it comes to Muslim representation.

Of course, an argument could be made that Nanjiani's framing as a "thirst trap" or sex symbol is not transformative at all. Edward Said, in *Culture and Imperialism*, wrote of the ways colonized places, colonized bodies, and colonized narratives were often used to elicit pleasure in the colonizer. The colonized had two choices in the situation: "serve or be destroyed."[23] Having shared photos of himself in social media, photos that he seemingly loses control of and that prove pleasurable to a number of viewers, has Nanjiani fallen into this service trap? Does this reinforce the idea of Muslims as somehow inhuman objects to be viewed or surveilled? Or by choosing to share the photos himself has Nanjiani avoided a dehumanizing objectification that would reduce him to a thing? Perhaps, it is a little of both.

While American Muslims are often trapped by histories of Islamophobia, racism, and imperialism, they do seem to have more choices available to them and to be more empowered to choose how they will be represented. Social media have proven to be particularly fruitful spaces to challenge stereotype. Gary Bunt has called digital spaces where Muslims gather "cyber Islamic environments"[24] as they are spaces where the diversity of Muslim belief and experience is communicated and is made visible. Young Muslims often turn to

Fig. 6.3 Kumail Nanjiani spent hours in the gym each day to get in shape for his part as Kingo in the Marvel film *Eternals*. As part of the media blitz leading up to the film's release, *Men's Health* produced a video feature in which Nanjani shows the viewer the workout that got him into superhero shape.

digital environments in order to connect to their faith while also exploring alternate ways of being Muslim.[25] They have also sometimes turned to new media technologies to explore new ways of being devout, new ways of engaging with the Qur'an, and new ways of engaging with one another.[26] In my own work on Muslim life online, I've found evidence that digital media can offer up a space for some Muslims to safely connect to others to talk about their faith and their lives as well as work to challenge the stereotypes Muslims face in their day-to-day lives.[27] The trouble with digital media spaces is that if you are not a user of a space or not connected to a particular set of users, you may not have access to this kind of content. There's also the issue that individuals have little control over how their posts in these spaces will be received. Muslims producing other kinds of media content face a similar issue in that they have no control over whether their work will be celebrated, reviled, objectified, or repurposed. Even so, such representations are perhaps a start toward something approaching fuller, more meaningful representation. Kumail Nanjiani's shirtless photos, Zaineb Johnson's sometimes crass jokes, and Ayana Ife's *Project Runway* success all help push back against historic stereotypes of who Muslims are and of what Muslims mean to America. They are perhaps imperfect, and are certainly not enough, but they are a start toward something beyond the simplified complex representations of the early twenty-first century.

This book is limited in scope, focusing on a handful of popular media produced since the turn of the millennium. There is an entire universe of material, from children's literature to Muslim punk rock, which this book does not examine, all of it ripe for scholarly exploration. The plethora of media is something to celebrate on its own—we live in a moment when wide-ranging and diverse media are featuring Muslims in some way. Twenty or thirty years ago, Muslims most often featured in media appeared in news stories about faraway wars or as the villains in Hollywood blockbusters—now Muslims appear in novels and comic books and video games, as both characters and creators. It feels as though we are living in a moment of transition from simplified complex representations to simply complex representations. However, hope and celebration must be tempered because, even as Muslim actors become Marvel superheroes and Muslim contestants win reality shows, Islamophobia and anti-Muslim sentiment continue to grow.

In February 2022, a New York City police officer was charged with a hate crime—accused of punching a man until he passed out while yelling anti-Muslim slurs at the victim.[28] The policeman was off duty at the time of the alleged incident, which took place after the officer blocked the victim's car on a busy New York street. The officer is alleged to have mentioned the terms *ISIS*, *terrorist*, and *al-Qaeda* during the assault. The hate crime took place about six months after the Council on American and Islamic Relations issued a report noting that it had continued to see spikes in anti-Muslim hate crimes in the United States in the first part of 2021, as well as evidence of anti-Muslim bullying in American schools and on social media.[29] Islamophobia and anti-Muslim sentiment predate September 11 and the war on terror, but since the early 2000s, anti-Muslim sentiment has steadily increased in the United States. Muslims have continued to be framed as enemy others, problems to be solved, or people to be modernized as politicians and media figures alike use rhetoric that dehumanizes Muslims. It is a rhetoric that anchors Islam to an imagined and unmodern past, one in which the religion developed, and continues to develop, isolated from the rest of the world. Muslims, in turn, are imagined as less modern and as less worthy of an ethics of recognition than their non-Muslim compatriots. It is hard to draw a straight line from media content to human behavior—we cannot say definitively that hate speech directly causes specific hate crimes. But when whole Muslim nations are banned from traveling to the United States, when some nations are framed as "shithole countries," when an entire religion is framed in public, political, and mediated discourse as a violent threat—then an environment has been created that can lead to acts of violence, an environment in which acts of violence can be seen as almost necessary in

CONCLUSION

fig. 6.4 The Council on American-Islamic Relations (CAIR) keeps track of anti-Muslim incidents in the United States. The 2021 report notes that those documented in the first half of that year "include hate crimes, harassment, school bullying, discrimination, hate speech, and anti-mosque incidents." Of particular concern was a marked increase in the bullying that Muslim students reported they experienced in American classrooms and the continued use of anti-Muslim hate speech by politicians in social media.

order to keep America safe. Media are not the lone creators of this environment, but they are certainly complicit in its perpetuation. They aid in the making and the unmaking of the various groups to which we imagine we belong.

We cannot divorce media from the histories, social contexts, or cultural frameworks in which they sit. The frames that appear in media and that help us organize the way we see the world come from that nexus of history and culture. If representations of Muslims are to improve in the United States, the way we, as a culture, understand the place of Muslims in America must change. That involves work; work recognizing the histories of misrepresentation, work recognizing our own perpetuation of those misrepresentations, and work recognizing the violence that perpetuation helps produce. It requires a political discourse that moves away from vitriol and caricature and moves toward one of reconciliation and understanding. It requires a recognition of all that makes us human. Media are nothing without the people producing, circulating, and consuming them. If media representations of Muslims are to be something more substantial than plastic, more complex than simple, more authentic than performative, then we must be willing to recognize and reward complicated and nuanced representations when we find them. The Muslim Ms. Marvel, Hasan Minhaj's late night show, and *Project Runway*'s Ayana Ife are all steps toward a fuller, richer, more complex understanding of American Muslims— but they cannot take us very far if we are not willing to create space for them and all who follow. What is the point of accessible representation if it does not, in the end, change something within us?

NOTES

1. Shireen Ahmed (@_shireenahmed_), "I'm a 45 year-old Muslim woman from AfPak community. A mainstream superhero that looks like me is not something I could have dreamed of. But here we are," Twitter, March 15, 2022, 3:23 p.m., https://twitter.com/_shireenahmed_/status/1503738562474356739.

2. sana amanat (@MiniB622), "Been working hard with an incredible team to bring this show to life. The pressure and responsibility we all feel is intense. The love we have is immense. Praying we can make you all proud," Twitter, November 13, 2021, 3:43 a.m., https://twitter.com/MiniB622/status /1459351121680424970?ref_src=twsrc%5Etfw.

3. Rotam Rusak, "Ms. Marvel's First Reactions Praise Iman Vellani's Joyous Kamala Khan," Nerdist, May 24, 2022, https://nerdist.com/article/ms-marvel -first-reactions-praise-iman-vellani-joyous-relatable-kamala-khan/.

4. Kristian Petersen, "'Ms. Marvel,' 'Ramy,' and 'Hala' Fuel Debate on Muslim Representation," *New Lines Magazine*, October 12, 2022, https:// newlinesmag.com/argument/ms-marvel-ramy-and-hala-fuel-debate-on -muslim-representation/.

5. Orhan Pamuk, *My Name Is Red* (New York: Alfred A. Knopf, 2001), 51.

6. Viet Thanh Nguyen, *Nothing Ever Dies: Vietnam and the Memory of War* (New York: New York University Press, 2016), 72.

7. Ibid.

8. Allouch's comments came in an episode of the Goethe Institut's "Big Pond Listening Series" podcast. The episode, "Being Muslim in the Midwest," featured the experiences of Muslims living in Oxford and Cincinnati, Ohio. You can listen to the episode on the series website: https://www.goethe.de/ins/us/en/kul/tec /tbp/mim.html.

CONCLUSION 171

9. Pierre Bourdieu, *Language and Symbolic Power* (Cambridge, MA: Polity, 1991).

10. Edward Said, *Culture and Imperialism* (New York: Alfred A. Knopf, 1993), 37.

11. Michel Foucault, *Discipline and Punish: The Birth of the Modern Prison*, 2nd ed. (New York: Vintage Books, 1995).

12. Nabil Echchaibi, "Unveiling Obsessions: Muslims and the Trap of Representation," in *On Islam: Muslims and the Media*, ed. Rosemary Pennington and Hilary Kahn (Bloomington: Indiana University Press, 2018), 57–70.

13. Noel Ransome, "*Patriot Act*'s Hasan Minhaj on the Value of Being an Outsider in America," Vice, June 24, 2019, https://www.vice.com/en_ca/article/mb8wa3/patriot-acts-hasan-minhaj-on-the-value-of-being-an-outsider-in-america.

14. Nabil Echchaibi, "Muslims between Transparency and Opacity," Presentation at Cyber Muslims Conference, Lehigh University, Bethlehem, PA, April 14–15, 2022.

15. G. Willow Wilson, *Ms. Marvel*, vol. 2, *Generation Why* (New York: Marvel, 2014–15).

16. G. Willow Wilson, *Ms. Marvel*, vol. 5, *Super Famous* (New York: Marvel, 2014–15).

17. Taz Ahmed (@TazzyStar), "We do SO much work as Muslim culture shifters, narrative tellers, advocates & activists. We recenter POVs, disrupt stereotypes, amplify margins. We insist to be seen, heard, not be forgotten," Twitter, December 18, 2019, 9:22 p.m., https://twitter.com/TazzyStar/status/1207395742060437504.

18. Kumail Nanjiani (@kumailn), "I never thought I'd be one of those people . . . ," Instagram, December 16, 2019, https://www.instagram.com/p/B6I7b2bnuJz/?hl=en.

19. Doree Lewak, "Fans Turning against Kumail Nanjiani over His Marvel 'Eternals' Body," *New York Post*, December 17, 2019, https://nypost.com/2019/12/17/fans-turning-against-kumail-nanjiani-over-his-marvel-eternals-body/.

20. Randall Colburn, "Our Sincere Congrats to Kumail Nanjiani, the New Face of Pornhub's 'Muscular Men' Section," AV Club, December 17, 2019, https://news.avclub.com/our-sincere-congrats-to-kumail-nanjiani-the-new-face-0-1840487505.

21. Tracey Walker (@esmeraldaqyo), "Here I was worried about Rise of Skywalker spoilers, but all twitter wants to talk about are #Kumail and his washboard abs. I am very much okay with this," Twitter, December 17, 2019, 8:38 a.m., https://twitter.com/esmeraldaqyo/status/1206841079095414785.

22. Mashable India (@MashableIndia), "@TheBigSickMovie actor @kumailn's thirsty AF photos have left the internet parched. #KumailNanjiani #Kumail," Twiter, December 17, 2019, 2:45 p.m., https://twitter.com/MashableIndia/status/1206933317024714757.

23. Said, *Culture and Imperialism*, 168.

24. Gary Bunt, *iMuslims: Rewiring the House of Islam* (Chapel Hill: University of North Carolina Press, 2009).

25. Peter Mandaville, "Reimaging Islam in Diaspora: The Politics of Mediated Community," *International Communication Gazette* 63, no. 2–3 (2001): 169–86.

26. The edited collection *Cyber Muslims: Mapping Islamic Digital Media in the Digital Age* by Rob Rozenhal (2022) would serve as a solid introduction to the ways Muslims in the twenty-first century navigate their lives and their faith in digital media spaces, with chapters touching on virtual visits to Mecca, the ways religions leaders navigate new technologies, and how Muslim women challenge stereotype in media.

27. I've written several things about Muslim use of digital media, including, "Social Media as Third Spaces? Exploring Muslim Identity and Connection in Tumblr," *International Communication Gazette* 80, no. 7, (2018): 620–36; "Making Space in Social Media: #MuslimWomensDay in Twitter," *Journal of Communication Inquiry* 42, no. 3 (2018): 199–217; and "Seeing a Global Islam? Eid al-Adha on Instagram," in *Cyber Muslims: Mapping Islamic Digital Media in the Internet Age*, ed. Rob Rozenhal (London: Bloomsbury, 2022), 176–88.

28. Chantal da Silva, "NYPD Officer Charged with Hate Crime in Alleged anti-Muslim Attack, Prosecutor Says," NBC News, February 2, 2022, https://www.nbcnews.com/news/us-news/nypd-officer-charged-hate-crime-alleged-anti-muslim-attack-prosecutor-rcna14514.

29. Huzaifa Shahbaz and Robert S. McCaw, "CAIR's Mid-Year Snapshot Summary Report of Anti-Muslim Bias Incidents," Council on American-Islamic Relations, July 2021, https://www.cair.com/wp-content/uploads/2021/07/Anti-Bias-Incident-Report-2021_online.pdf.

BIBLIOGRAPHY

Abad-Santos, Alex. "Spider-Woman Isn't Good for Women When She Looks Like This." *Vox*, August 20, 2014. https://www.vox.com/xpress/2014/8/20/6046577/marvel-spider-woman-cover-sexist.

Abdelaziz, Rowaida. "Malala Would Have to Remove Her Headscarf to Teach in Quebec: Education Minister." *HuffPost*, July 9, 2019. https://www.huffpost.com/entry/malala-quebec-education-headscarf_n_5d238397e4b04c4814183c83#:~:text=Education%20Minister%20Jean%2DFran%C3%A7ois%20Roberge,head%20covering%20she%20normally%20wears.

Abdo, Diya. "Uncovering the Harem in the Classroom." *Women's Studies Quarterly* 30, no. 1/2 (2002): 227–38.

Abu-Lughod, Lila. *Do Muslim Women Need Saving?* Cambridge, MA: Harvard University Press, 2013.

Abu-Lughod, Lila. "Do Muslim Women Really Need Saving? Anthropological Reflections on Cultural Relativism and Its Others." *American Anthropologist* 104, no. 3 (2002): 783–90.

Abu-Lughod, Lila. "Zones of Theory in the Anthropology of the Arab World." *Annual Review of Anthropology* 18, no. 1 (1989): 267–306.

Ahmed, Shireen (@_shireenahmed_). "I'm a 45 year-old Muslim woman from AfPak community. A mainstream superhero that looks like me is not something I could have dreamed of . . ." Twitter, March 15, 2022, 3:23 p.m. https://twitter.com/_shireenahmed_/status/1503738562474356739.

Ahmed, Taz (@TazzyStar). "We do SO much work as Muslim culture shifters, narrative tellers, advocates & activists. We recenter POVs, disrupt stereotypes, amplify margins. We insist to be seen, heard, not be forgotten . . ." Twitter, December 18, 2019, 9:22 p.m. https://twitter.com/TazzyStar/status/1207395742060437504.

BIBLIOGRAPHY

Akbari, Suzanne Conklin. *Idols in the East: European Representations of Islam and the Orient, 1100–1450*. Ithaca, NY: Cornell University Press, 2009.

Ali, Kecia. "Across Generations: The Making of the 'Lady Imam.'" *Journal of Feminist Studies in Religion* 35, no. 1 (2019): 67–79.

Ali, Kecia, and amina wadud. "The Making of the 'Lady Imam': An Interview with amina wadud." *Journal of Feminist Studies of Religion* 35, no. 1 (2019): 67–79.

Ali, Lorraine. "How HBO's *The Night Of* Has Humanized American Muslim Families." *Los Angeles Times*, August 28, 2016. https://www.latimes.com /entertainment/tv/la-ca-st-night-of-muslims-20160818-snap-story.html.

Aljazeera. "Woman Leads Controversial Prayer." March 19, 2005. https://www .aljazeera.com/news/2005/3/19/woman-leads-controversial-us-prayer.

al-Khatahtbeh, Amani. "A Letter to My Future Muslim Daughter." *Cosmopolitan*, October 27, 2016. https://www.cosmopolitan.com/politics/a7557079/amani -al-khatahtbeh-muslim-girl-daughter-letter/.

al-Khatahtbeh, Amani. "Watch Muslim Girls Get REAL about Love, Faith, and Trump." *Teen Vogue*, May 9, 2016. https://www.teenvogue.com/story/muslim -girl-videos-islamophobia-america.

Allam, Hannah. "A Muslim Woman in Playboy. What Could Go Wrong?" *Charlotte Observer*, September 27, 2016. https://www.charlotteobserver.com /living/article104353276.html.

Allam, Roula. "Getting to Know the Former 'America's Next Top Model' Contestant Sandra Shehab." About Her. Accessed July 20, 2023. https://www .abouther.com/node/17026/entertainment/celebrity/getting-know-former -%E2%80%98america%E2%80%99s-next-top-model%E2%80%99-contestant -sandra.

Allaudeen, Aqilah. "A Muslim Woman Comic Walks into a Bar: Changing Perceptions through Jokes." *Mother Jones*, September 19, 2019. https://www .csmonitor.com/The-Culture/2019/0918/A-Muslim-woman-comic-walks-into -a-bar-Changing-perceptions-through-jokes.

Alsultany, Evelyn. *Arabs and Muslims in the Media: Race and Representation after 9/11*. New York: New York University Press, 2012.

Alsultany, Evelyn. "The Cultural Politics of Islam in U.S. Reality Television." *Communication, Culture and Critique* 9, no. 4 (2016): 595–613.

amanat, sana (@MiniB622). "Been working hard with an incredible team to bring this show to life. The pressure and responsibility we all feel is intense. The love we have is immense. Praying we can make you all proud." Twitter, November 13, 2021, 3:43 a.m. https://twitter.com/MiniB622/status/1459351121680424970?ref _src=twsrc%5Etfw.

Amarsingam, Amarnath. "Laughter Is the Best Medicine: Muslim Comedians and Social Criticism in Post-9/11 America." *Journal of Muslim Minority Affairs* 30, no. 4 (2010): 463–77.

BIBLIOGRAPHY

Amaudo, Marco. *The Myth of the Superhero*. Baltimore: Johns Hopkins University Press, 2013.

American Crime. Season 1, episode 3. Directed by Gloria Muzio. Written by John Ridley. ABC, March 19, 2015.

American Crime. Season 1, episode 4. Directed by Joshua Marston. Written by Diana Son. ABC, March 26, 2015.

America's Next Top Model. "Beauty Is Social." Season 24, episode 8. Director Tony Kroll. *VH1*, February 27, 2018.

Amin, Samir. *Eurocentrism*. 2nd ed. New York: Monthly Review, 2010.

Anderson, Benedict. *Imagined Communities: Reflections on the Origins and Spread of Nationalism*. 1986. Rev. ed. New York: Verso, 2006.

Appadurai, Arjun. *Fear of Small Numbers: An Essay on the Geography of Anger*. Durham, NC: Duke University Press, 2006.

Arjana, Sophia Rose. *Buying Buddha, Selling Rumi: Orientalism and the Mystical Marketplace*. London: Oneworld, 2020.

Arjana, Sophia Rose. *Muslims in the Western Imagination*. Oxford: Oxford University Press, 2015.

Arjana, Sophia Rose. *Veiled Superheroes: Islam, Feminism, and Popular Culture*. Lanham, MD: Lexington Books, 2017.

Aronson, Amy Beth. "Domesticity and Women's Collective Agency: Contribution and Collaboration in America's First Successful Women's Magazine." *American Periodicals* 11 (2001): 1–23.

Austin, Allan D. *African American Muslims in Antebellum America: Transatlantic Stories and Spiritual Struggles*. London: Routledge, 1997.

Avaray-Natale, Edward. "An Analysis of Embodiment of Six Superheroes in DC Comics." *Social Thought and Research* 32 (2013): 71–106.

Azim-Ahmed, Abdul. "Faith in Comedy: Representations of British Identity in Muslim Comedy." *South Asian Popular Culture* 11, no. 1 (2013): 91–96.

Badran, Margot "Re/placing Islamic Feminism." *Critique Internationale* 1 (2010): 25–44.

Baram, Amatzia. "The Iraqi Armed Forces and Security Apparatus." *Conflict, Security & Development* 1, no. 2 (2006): 113–23.

Barkman, Adam. "Superman: From Anti-Christ to Christ-Type." In *Superman and Philosophy: What Would the Man of Steel Do?*, edited by Mark T. White, 111–20, Malden, MA: Wiley Blackwell, 2013.

Becker, Ron. *Gay TV and Straight America*. New Brunswick, NJ: Rutgers University Press, 2006.

Bell-Jordan, Katrina E. "Black, White, and a Survivor of the Real World: Constructions of Race on Reality TV." *Critical Studies in Media Communication* 25, no. 4 (2008): 353–72.

Bignell, Jonathon. 2014. "Realism and Reality Formats." In *A Companion to Reality TV*, edited by Laurie Oulette, 97–115. Malden, MA: Wiley Blackwell.

Bilefsky, Dan. "Muslim Winner of Baking Contest Defies Prejudice in Britain." *New York Times*, October 8, 2015. https://www.nytimes.com/2015/10/09/world /europe/muslim-winner-of-baking-contest-defies-prejudice-in-britain.html.

Blakeley, Ruth. "Dirty Hands, Clean Conscience? The CIA Inspector General's Investigation of 'Enhanced Interrogation Techniques' in the War on Terror and the Torture Debate." *Journal of Human Rights* 10, no. 4 (2011): 544–61.

Bones. "A Beautiful Day in the Neighborhood." Season 5, episode 4. Directed by Gordon Lonsdale. Written by Janet Lin. FOX, October 8, 2009.

Bones. "Patriot in Purgatory." Season 8, episode 6. Directed by Francoise Velle. Written by Stephan Nathan. FOX, November 12, 2009.

Bourdieu, Pierre. *Language and Symbolic Power.* Cambridge, MA: Polity, 1991.

Bourget, Carine. 2013. "Complicity with Orientalism in Third-World Women's Writing: Fatima Mernissi's Fictive Memoirs." *Research in African Literatures* 44, no. 3: 30–49.

Boylorn, Robin M. "As Seen on TV: An Autoethnographic Reflection on Race and Reality Television." *Critical Studies in Media Communication* 25, no. 4 (2008): 413–33.

Brar, Miranda. "The Nation and Its Burka Avenger, the 'Other,' and Its Malala Yusafzai: The Creation of a Female Muslim Archetype as the Site for Pakistani Nationalism." *Prandium: The Journal of Historical Studies* 3, no. 1 (2014): 1–8.

Bravo TV. "Top Chef: Fatima Ali." Accessed July 20, 2023. http://www.bravotv .com/people/fatima-ali.

Bricken, Rob. "Check Out Spider-Woman #1, Starring Spider-Woman's Ass." *io9*, August 20, 2014. https://io9.gizmodo.com/check-out-spider-woman-1 -starring-spider-womans-ass-1624535918.

Brinkerhoff, Jennifer. *Digital Diasporas: Identity and Transnational Engagement.* New York: Cambridge University Press, 2009.

Brod, Harry. *Superman Is Jewish? How Comic Book Superheroes Came to Serve Truth, Justice, and the Jewish-American Way.* New York: Free Press, 2012.

Bucar, Liz. *The Islamic Veil: A Beginner's Guide.* New York: Simon and Schuster, 2012.

Bunt, Gary. *iMuslims: Rewiring the House of Islam.* Chapel Hill: University of North Carolina Press, 2009.

Cañas, Sandra. "*The Little Mosque on the Prairie*: Examining (Multi) Cultural Space of Nation and Religion." *Cultural Dynamics* 20, no. 3 (2008): 195–211.

Cantor, Hallie. "The Roast: A History." Vulture, June 17, 2011. https://www .vulture.com/2011/06/the-roast-a-history.html.

Cavender, Gray. "In Search of Community on Reality TV." In *Understanding Reality Television*, edited by Su Holmes and Deboray Jermyn, 154–72. London: Routledge, 2004.

Chakravarty, Dipesh. *Provincializing Europe: Postcolonial Thought and Historical Difference*. New ed. Princeton, NJ: Princeton University Press, 2008.

Chan-Malik, Sylvia. *Being Muslim: A Cultural History of Women of Color in American Islam*. New York: New York University Press, 2018.

Chanlieu, Pierre. "Why the Death of Ms. Marvel Is a Major Insult to Fans." The Direct, May 29, 2023, https://thedirect.com/article/ms-marvel-death-fans.

Chappell, Bill. "'Muslim Rage' Explodes on Twitter, but in a Funny Way (Yes, Really)." The Two-Way, September 17, 2012, https://www.npr.org/sections/thetwo-way/2012/09/17/161315765/muslim-rage-explodes-on-twitter-but-in-a-funny-way-yes-really.

Choudhury, Samah. "What Makes Humor Muslim?" In *American Examples: New Conversations about Religion*. Vol. 1, edited by Michael J. Altman, 106–24. Tuscaloosa: University of Alabama Press, 2021.

Chwastiak, Michele. "Torture as Normal Work: The Bush Administration, the Central Intelligence Agency and 'Enhanced Interrogation Techniques.'" *Organization* 22, no. 4 (2015): 493–511.

Cocca, Carolyn. "The 'Broke Back Test': A Quantitative and Qualitative Analysis of Portrayals of Women in Mainstream Superhero Comics, 1993–2013." *Journal of Graphic Noves and Comics* 5, no. 4 (2014): 411–28.

Colburn, Randall. "Our Sincere Congrats to Kumail Nanjiani, the New Face of Pornhub's 'Muscular Men' Section." AV Club, December 17, 2019. https://news.avclub.com/our-sincere-congrats-to-kumail-nanjiani-the-new-face-o-1840487505.

Conan. "Jean-Claude Van Damme/Barkhad Abdi/Dina Hashem." Directed by Billy Bollotino. Written by Levi MacDougall. TBS, December 5, 2017.

Coover, Gail. "Television and Social Identity: Race Representation as 'White' Accommodation." *Journal of Broadcasting & Electronic Media* 45, no. 3 (2001): 413–31.

Couldry, Nick. "Reality TV or the Secret Theater of Neoliberalism." *Review of Education, Pedagogy, and Cultural Studies* 30, no. 1 (2008): 3–13.

Cronin-Furman, Kate, Nimmi Gowrinathan, and Rafia Zakaria. "Emissaries of Empowerment." Colin Powell School for Civic and Global Leadership, City College of New York, September 2017. https://www.ccny.cuny.edu/colinpowellschool/emissaries-empowerment.

Curiel, Jonathon. *Al' America: Travels through America's Arab and Islamic Roots*. New York: New Press, 2008.

Curiel, Jonathon. *Islam in America*. London: I.B. Tauris, 2015.

Curry, Colleen. "Anti-Muslim Hate Crimes Are on the Rise after Recent Terror Attacks." *Teen Vogue*, June 21, 2016. https://www.teenvogue.com/story/anti-islam-hate-crimes-increase-after-terror-attacks-trump.

Curtis, Edward. "The Black Muslim Scare of the Twentieth Century: The History of State Islamophobia and Its Post-9/11 Variations." In *Islamophobia in American: The Anatomy of Intolerance*, edited by Carl W. Ernst, 75–106. New York: Palgrave Macmillan, 2013.

Curtis, Edward E., and Danielle Brune Sigler, eds. *The New Black Gods: Arthur Huff Fauset and the Study of African American Religions*. Bloomington: Indiana University Press, 2009.

Darowksi, Joseph. *X-Men and the Mutant Metaphor: Race and Gender in the Comic Books*. Lanham, MD: Rowman & Littlefield, 2014.

da Silva, Chantal. "NYPD Officer Charged with Hate Crime in Alleged Anti-Muslim Attack, Prosecutor Says." NBC News, February 2, 2022. https://www.nbcnews.com/news/us-news/nypd-officer-charged-hate-crime-alleged-anti-muslim-attack-prosecutor-rcna14514.

Deery, June. "Reality TV as Advertainment." *Popular Communication* 2, no. 1 (2004): 1–20.

de Hart, Betty. "Not without My Daughter: On Parental Abduction, Orientalism, and Maternal Melodrama." *European Journal of Women's Studies* 8, no. 1 (2001): 51–65.

Diouf, Sylviane A. *Servants of Allah: African Muslims Enslaved in America*. New York: New York University Press, 2013.

DiTrolio, Megan. "How 'Project Runway' Contestant Ayana Ife Is Making Conservative the New Cool." *Marie Claire*, September 21, 2017. https://www.marieclaire.com/fashion/news/a29578/ayana-ife-modest-muslim-fashion-designer.

Dockterman, Elain. "Marvel Is Actually Going to Publish That Sexist Spider-Woman Cover." *TIME*, November 19, 2014. https://time.com/3594514/marvel-spider-woman-cover/.

Doherty, Thomas. "Art Spiegelman's *Maus*: Graphic Art and the Holocaust." *American Literature* 68, no. 1 (1996): 69–84.

Doty, Mark. "Ararat." In *Fire to Fire: New and Selected Poems*. New York: HarperCollins, 2009.

Durham, Meenakshi Gigi. "Myths of Race and Beauty in Teen Magazines: A Semiological Analysis." Paper presented at International Communication Association Conference, San Francisco, 2007.

Eaton, Joshua. "Gay Republicans Throw WAKE UP Party at RNC 2016 That Perpetuates Islamophobia." *Teen Vogue*, July 21, 2016. https://www.teenvogue.com/story/gay-republicans-wake-up-party-islamophobia-rnc-2016.

Echchaibi, Nabil. "Muslims between Transparency and Opacity." Presentation at Cyber Muslims Conference Held at Lehigh University, Bethlehem, PA, April 14–15, 2022.

BIBLIOGRAPHY

Echchaibi, Nabil. "Unveiling Obsessions: Muslims and the Trap of Representation." In *On Islam: Muslims and the Media*, edited by Rosemary Penrington and Hilary Kahn, 57–70. Bloomington: Indiana University Press, 2018.

Eco, Umberto. *Inventing the Enemy and Other Occasional Writings*. New York: Houghton Mifflin Harcourt, 2012.

Ehrlich, Howard J. *Hate Crimes and Ethnoviolence: The History, Current Affairs, and Future of Discrimination in America*. New York: Routledge, 2018.

Eligon, John. "The 'Some of My Best Friends Are Black' Defense." *New York Times*, February 16 2019. https://www.nytimes.com/2019/02/16/sunday-review/ralph-northam-blackface-friends.html.

Ellis, Philip, "Tan France Reveals He Almost Quit 'Queer Eye' during the First Season." *Men's Health*, July 13, 2019. https://www.menshealth.com/entertainment/a28384902/tan-france-almost-quit-queer-eye/.

Eltahaway, Mona. *Headscarves and Hymens: Why the Middle East Needs a Sexual Revolution*. New York: Farrar, Straus and Giroux, 2016.

Eltahaway, Mona. "#MosqueMeToo: What Happened When I Was Sexually Assaulted during the Hajj." *Washington Post*, February 15, 2018. https://www.washingtonpost.com/news/global-opinions/wp/2018/02/15/mosquemetoo-what-happened-when-i-was-sexually-assaulted-during-the-hajj/?arc404=true.

Engle, Gary. "What Makes Superman So Darned American?" In *Popular Culture: An Introductory Text*, edited by Jack Nachbar and Kevin Lause, 314–43. Bowling Green, OH: Popular Press, 1992.

Entman, Robert. "Modern Racism and the Images of Blacks in Local Television News." *Critical Studies in Mass Communication* 7, no. 4 (1990): 332–45.

Entman, Robert. "Representation and Reality in the Portrayal of Blacks on Network Television News." *Journalism Quarterly* 71, no. 3 (1994): 509–20.

Esposito, John. *What Everyone Needs to Know about Islam*. New York: Oxford University Press, 2002.

Farsad, Negin. "Negin Farsad: Comedian, Writer, Actor, Director." Accessed July 20, 2023. http://neginfarsad.com/.

Florida Family Foundation. "The Learning Channel Officially Cancels All-American Muslim. Emails to Advertisers Made the Difference." Accessed July 20, 2023. https://floridafamily.org/full_article.php?article_no=108.

Foucault, Michel. *Discipline and Punish: The Birth of the Modern Prison*. 2nd ed. New York: Vintage Books, 1995.

Freedman, Ariela. "'Sorting through My Grief and Putting It into Boxes': Comics and Pain." In *Knowledge and Pain*, edited by Ester Cohen, Leona Toker, Manuela Consonni, and Otoniel E. Dror, 381–99. Leiden: Brill, 2012.

Frevele, Jamie. "Farewell to Ms. Marvel: An Open Letter from G. Willow Wilson." Marvel.com, December 14, 2018, https://www.marvel.com/articles/comics/farewell-to-ms-marvel-an-open-letter-from-g-willow-wilson.

Friedman, Sam, and Giseline Kuipers. "The Divisive Power of Humour: Comedy, Taste and Symbolic Boundaries." *Cultural Sociology* 7, no. 2 (2013): 179–95.

Garretson Jeremiah J. "Does Change in Minority and Women's Representation on Television Matter? A 30-Year Study of Television Portrayals and Social Tolerance." *Politics, Groups, and Identities* 3, no. 4 (2015): 615–32.

Georgiou Myra. *Diaspora, Identity, and the Media: Diasporic Nationalities and Mediated Spatialities*. Cresskill, NJ: Hampton Press, 2006.

GhaneaBassiri, Kambiz. *A History of Islam in America*. Cambridge: Cambridge University Press, 2010.

Gibson, Avi. "Even Marvel Knows Its Handling of Kamala Khan's Death Was Disrespectful." Screen Rant, July, 18, 2023, https://screenrant.com/ms-marvel -kamala-khan-death-disrespectful-mutant-mcu/.

Gilber, Joanne. 1997. *Performing Marginality: Humor, Gender, and Cultural Critique*. Detroit, MI: Wayne State University Press.

Gloeckner, Phoebe. "Comic Books: A Medium Deserving Another Look." *Et Cetera* 46, no. 3 (1989): 246.

Goatface: A Comedy Special. "Does Baba Really Know Best?" Directed by Aristole Athiras. Written by Asif Ali, Fahim Anwar, Aristotle Athiras, and Hasan Minaj. Comedy Central, November 27, 2018.

Goodwin, Jan. "Pakistan: Only Women Can Rescue Women." *Marie Claire*, April 27, 2007. https://www.marieclaire.com/politics/news/a171/pakistan-female -rescue/.

Goodwin, Megan. "'They Do That to Foreign Women': Domestic Terrorism and Contraceptive Nationalism in *Not without My Daughter*." *Muslim World* 106, no. 4 (2016): 759–80.

Gottschalk, Peter. *American Heretics: Catholics, Jews, Muslims, and the History of Religious Intolerance*. New York: St. Martin's, 2013.

Gottschalk, Peter, and Gabriel Greenberg. *Islamophobia: Making Muslims the Enemy*. Lanham, MD: Rowman & Littlefield, 2008.

Gray, Herman. "Race, Media, and the Cultivation of Concern." *Communication and Critical/Cultural Studies* 10, no. 2–3 (2013): 253–58.

Green, Aaryn, and Annulla Linders. "The Impact of Comedy on Racial and Ethnic Discourse." *Sociological Inquiry* 86, no. 2 (2016): 241–69.

Green, Todd H. *Presumed Guilty: Why We Shouldn't Ask Muslims to Condemn Terrorism*. Minneapolis: Fortress Press, 2018.

Gross, Larry. *Up from Visibility Lesbians, Gay Men, and the Media in America*. New York: Columbia University Press, 2001.

Guardian. "Mipsters: Like Hipsters, but Muslim." April 10, 2016. https://www .theguardian.com/society/shortcuts/2016/apr/10/mipster-muslim -hipster-exploitative-marketing-term-growing-urban-trend.

BIBLIOGRAPHY

Hake, Rolf. "Counter-Stereotypical Images of Muslim Characters in the Television Serial 24: A Difference That Makes No Difference?" *Critical Studies in Television* 10, no. 1 (2015): 54–72.

Hall, Stuart. "Culture, Identity, and Diaspora." In *Identity, Community, Culture, & Difference*, edited by Jonathon Rutherford, 392–403. London: Lawrence & Wishart, 1990.

Hankins Rebecca, and Joyce Thornton. "The Influence of Muslims and Islam in Science Fiction, Fantasy, and Comics." In *Muslims and American Popular Culture*. Vol. 1, *Entertainment and Digital Culture*, edited by Iraj Omidvar and Anne Richards, 323–48. Santa Barbara, CA: Praeger, 2014.

Hasan Minhaj: Homecoming King. Comedy standup special. Directed by Christopher Storer. Written by Hasan Minaj. Netflix, May 23, 2017.

Hayes Kevin J. "How Thomas Jefferson Read the Qur'an." *Early American Literature* 39, no. 2 (2004): 247–61.

Heffernan, Teresa. *Veiled Figures: Women, Modernity and the Spectre of Orientalism.* Toronto: University of Toronto Press, 2016.

Henkle, Roger B. "The Social Dynamics of Comedy." *Sewanee Review* 90, no. 2 (1982): 200–16.

Hersey, Eleanor. "Word-Healers and Code-Talkers: Native Americans in *The X-Files.*" *Journal of Popular Film & Television* 26, no. 3 (1998): 103–19.

Hill, Anette. 2005. "Reality TV: Performance, Authenticity, and Television Audiences." In *A Companion to Television*, edited by Janet Wasko. Malden, MA: Wiley Blackwell, 449–76.

Hirji, Faiza. "Through the Looking Glass: Muslim Women on Television—An Analysis of 24, *Lost*, and *Little Mosque on the Prairie.*" *Global Media Journal, Canadian Edition* 4, no. 2 (2011): 33–47.

Hogan, Jon. "The Comic Book as Symbolic Environment: The Case of Iron Man." *ETC: A Review of General Semantics* 66, no. 2 (2009): 199–214.

Huntington, Samuel. "The Clash of Civilizations?" *Foreign Affairs* 72, no. 3 (1997): 22–49.

Hussain, Amir. *Muslims and the Making of America.* Waco, TX: Baylor University Press, 2016.

Hussain, Amir. "(Re)presenting Muslims on North American Television." *Contemporary Islam* 4, no. 1 (2010): 55–75.

Hutton, James H. "The Founding Fathers and Islam: Library Papers Show Early Tolerance for Faith." *Library Congress Information Bulletin* 61, no. 5 (2002). https://www loc.gov/loc/lcib/0205/tolerance.html.

Ismail, Ayman. "Muslims Should Praise Hijabi Journalism Noor Tagouri, Not Criticize Her " *Slate*, September 27, 2016. https://slate.com/human-interest /2016/09/playboy-photographed-muslim-american-woman-noor-tagouri-in -her-hijab.html.

Ismail, Nishaat. "I Fail to See Why I Should Celebrate a Hijab-Wearing Muslim Woman Appearing in Playboy for the First Time." *Independent*, September 26, 2016. https://www.independent.co.uk/voices/noor-tagouri-first-hijab-wearing-muslim-woman-playboy-magazine-hugh-hefner-bunniers-celebrate-first-time-a7330806.html.

Jhally, Sut, and Justin Lewis. *Enlightened Racism: The Cosby Show, Audiences, and the Myth of the American Dream*. New York: Routledge, 2019.

Johnson, Zainab. *Model Citizen*. Super Artists, B01CB5VKHI, 2016, digital download.

Kadhim, Abbas. *Reclaiming Iraq: The 1920 Revolution and the Founding of the Modern State*. Austin: University of Texas Press, 2012.

Kahera, Akel. "God's Dominion: Omar Ibn Said Use of Arabic Literacy as Opposition to Slavery." *South Carolina Review*, 2014.

Kahf, Mohja. *Western Representations of the Muslim Woman: From Termagant to Odalisque*. Austin: University of Texas Press, 1999.

Kassam, Shelina. "'Settling' the Multicultural Nation-State: *Little Mosque on the Prairie*, and the Figure of the 'Moderate Muslim.'" *Social Identities* 21, no. 6 (2015): 606–26.

Kastan, David Scott. "*All's Well That Ends Well* and the Limits of Comedy." *ELH* 52, no. 3 (1985): 575–89.

Kasunc, Anna, and Geoff Kaufman. "'At Least the Pizzas You Make Are Hot': Norms, Values, and Abrasive Humor on the Subreddit r/RoastMe." *Proceedings of the International AAAI Conference on Web and Social Media* 12, no. 1 (2018).

Kelner, Simon. "Nadiya Hussain Serves Up the Perfect Rebuttal to Theresa May's Xenophobic Rhetoric." *Independent*, October 8, 2015. https://www.independent.co.uk/voices/great-british-bake-off-nadiya-hussain-serves-up-the-perfect-rebuttal-to-theresa-mays-xenophobic-a6686601.html.

Kent, Miriam. "Unveiling Marvels: Ms. Marvel and the Reception of the New Muslim Superheroine." *Feminist Media Studies* 15, no. 3 (2015): 522–27.

Kepel, Gilles. *Allah in the West: Islamic Movements in America and Europe*. Stanford, CA: Stanford University Press, 1997.

Khabeer, Su'ad Abdul. *Muslim Cool: Race, Religion, and Hip Hop in the United States*. New York: New York University Press, 2016.

Khaleeli, Homa. "Bake Off Winner Nadiya Hussain: 'I Wasn't Thinking about Representing Muslims, I Was Thinking about My Bakes.'" *Guardian*, October 12, 2015. https://www.theguardian.com/tv-and-radio/2015/oct/12/bake-off-winner-nadiya-hussain-muslims-britain.

Khan, Aysha. "'The X-Files' Draws Backlash with Islamic Terrorism Plot." *Washington Post*, February 17, 2016. https://www.washingtonpost.com/national/religion/the-x-files-draws-backlash-with-islamic-terrorism-plot/2016/02/17/dc67733c-d5b3-11e5-a65b-587e721fb231_story.html.

Kraidy, Marwan. *Hybridity; Or, the Cultural Logic of Globalization*. Philadelphia: Temple University Press, 2005.

Kozloff, Sarah. "Superman as Saviour: Christian Allegory in the Superman Movies." *Journal of Popular Film and Television* 9, no. 2 (1981): 78–82.

Kozlovic, Anton K. "Superman as Christ-Figure: The American Pop Culture Movie Messiah." *Journal of Religion and Film* 6, no. 1 (2016): Article 5.

Kumar, Deepa. *Islamophobia and the Politics of Empire*. Chicago: Haymarket Books, 2012.

Lakshmi, Padma. "Padma Lakshmi Pens Emotional Tribute to Her 'Angel' Fatima Ali." *People*, January 29, 2019. https://people.com/food/padma-lakshmi-essay -fatima-ali-tribute/.

Lambe, Stacy. "How 'The Real World' Star Pedro Zamora Humanized AIDS (Flashback)." *E! Online*, June 21, 2018. https://www.etonline.com/how-the -real-world-star-pedro-zamora-humanized-aids-flashback-104687.

Lambropoulous, Vassilis. *The Rise of Eurocentrism: Anatomy of Interpretation*. Princeton, NJ: Princeton University Press, 1993.

Lange, Ariane. "What It's Like to Play a Muslim on Network TV." *BuzzFeed*, February 22, 2017. https://www.buzzfeed.com/arianelange/pej-vahdat -bones-arast30.

Late Night with Seth Myers. "Pete Davidson/Mary Lynn Rajskub/Zainab Johnson/ Ben Sesar." Written by Ben Warheit. NBC, September 27, 2018.

Lean, Nathan. *The Islamophobia Industry: How the Right Manufactures Fear of Muslims*. London: Pluto Press, 2012.

Lew, J. W. "The Deceptive Other: Mary Shelley's Critique of Orientalism in *Frankenstein*." *Studies in Romanticism* 30, no. 2 (1991): 255–83.

Lewak, Doree. "Fans Turning against Kumail Nanjiani over His Marvel 'Eternals' Body." *New York Post*, December 17, 2019. https://nypost.com/2019/12/17 /fans-turning-against-kumail-nanjiani-over-his-marvel-eternals-body/.

Lincoln, Charles Eric. *The Black Muslims in America*. Boston: Beacon Press, 1961.

Lipka, Carolyn. "'Top Chef' Colorado Recap: Episode 6—'Now That's a Schnitzel.'" *Food & Wine*, January 11, 2018. https://www.yahoo.com/news/apos -top-chef-apos-colorado-035942501.html.

Live from Here. "Negin Farsad." Filmed October 2018. YouTube video, 7:17. Posted October 2018. https://www.youtube.com/watch?v=bYYuKzE-2HI.

Loftus, Lauren. "All Eyes on Noor: Local Woman Wants to Be the First Hijabi Anchor on American TV." *Washington Post*, June 18, 2015. https://www .washingtonpost.com/news/arts-and-entertainment/wp/2015/06/18/all -eyes-on-noor-local-woman-wants-to-be-first-hijabi-anchor-on-american-tv/.

Lost. "The Candidate." Season 6, episode 14. Directed by Jack Bender. Written by Elizabeth Sarnoff. ABC, May 4, 2010.

Lost. "One of Them." Season 2, episode 14. Directed by Stephen Williams. Written by Jeffrey Lieber, J. J. Abrams, and Damon Lindlof. ABC, February 15, 2006.

Lost. "Pilot: Part Two." Season 1, episode 2. Directed by J. J. Abrams. Written by J. J. Abrams and Damon Lindelof. ABC, September 29, 2004.

Lund, Martin. *Re-constructing the Man of Steel: Superman 1938–1941, Jewish American History, and the Invention of Jewish-Comics Connection.* New York: Palgrave Macmillan, 2016.

Macdonald, Myra. "Muslim Women and the Veil: Problems of Image and Voice in Media Representations." *Feminist Media Studies* 6, no. 1 (2006): 7–23.

Mahmood, Saira. "Noor Tagouri, Playboy and the Porn Industry." Muslimah Media Watch, May 8, 2018. http://www.muslimahmediawatch.org/2018/05/08/noor-tagouri-playboy-and-the-porn-industry/.

Mahrt, Merja. "The Attractiveness of Magazines as 'Open' and 'Closed' Texts: Values of Women's Magazines and Their Readers." *Mass Communication & Society* 15, no. 6 (2012): 852–74.

Mamdani, Mahmood. *Good Muslim, Bad Muslim: America, the Cold War, and the Roots of Terror.* New York: Three Leaves Press, 2004.

Mandaville, Peter. "Reimaging Islam in Diaspora: The Politics of Mediated Community." *International Communication Gazette* 63, no. 2–3 (2001): 169–86.

Marie Claire. "Shopping in Dubai." August 3, 2007. https://www.marieclaire.com/fashion/news/a644/dubai-shop-blog/.

Marvel.com. "Kamala Khan Joins the X-Men in 'Ms. Marvel: New Mutant.'" July 18, 2023, https://www.marvel.com/articles/comics/ms-marvel-the-new-mutant-variant-covers-kamala-khan-joins-x-men.

Marzouki, Nadia. *Islam: An American Religion.* New York: Columbia University Press, 2017.

Mashable India (@MashableIndia). "@TheBigSickMovie actor @kumailn's thirsty AF photos have left the internet parched. #KumailNanjiani #Kumail." Twitter, December 17, 2019, 2:45 p.m. https://twitter.com/MashableIndia/status/1206933317024714757.

Mastnak, Tomaz. "Western Hostility toward Muslims: A History of the Present." In *Islamophobia/Islamophilia: Beyond the Politics of Enemy and Friend*, edited by Andrew Shryock, 29–52. Bloomington: Indiana University Press 2010.

Mastro, Dana. "A Social Identity Approach to Understanding the Impact of Television Messages." *Communication Monographs* 70, no. 2 (2003): 98–113.

Mastro, Dana, Andrea Figuero-Caballero, and Alexander Sink. "Primetime Television: Portrayals and Effects." In *The Routledge Companion to Media and Race*, edited by Christopher P. Campbell, 89–98. New York: Routledge, 2016.

Mastro, Dana, and Bradley S. Greenberg. "The Portrayal of Minorities in Prime Time Television." *Journal of Broadcasting & Electronic Media* 44, no. 4 (2000), 690–703.

McAlister, Melani. *Epic Encounters: Culture, Media & U.S. Interests in the Middle East since 1945.* Updated ed. Berkeley: University of California Press, 2005.

McCloud, Aminah Beverly. "African American Islam: A Reflection." *Religion Compass* 4, no. 9 (2010): 538–50.

McGrath, Karen. "Gender, Race, and Latina Identity: An Examination of Marvel Comics." *Atlantic Journal of Communication* 15, no. 4 (2007): 268–83.

McLean, Adrienne. "Media Effects, Marshall McLuhan, Television Culture, and 'Media Effects.'" *Film Quarterly* 51, no. 4 (1998): 2–11.

Meeker, Joseph W. "The Comedy of Survival." *North American Review* 257 (1972): 2.

Meer, Nabar. "Racialization and Religion: Race, Culture and Difference in the Study of Antisemitism and Islamophobia." *Ethnic and Racial Studies* 36, no. 3 (2013): 385–98.

Michael, Jaclyn. "American Muslims Stand Up and Speak Out: Trajectories of Humor in Muslim American Stand-Up Comedy." *Contemporary Islam* 7, no. 2 (2013): 129–53.

Mintz, Lawrence E. "Standup Comedy as Social and Cultural Mediation." *American Quarterly* 37, no. 1 (1985): 71–80.

Mirza, Heidi Safia. "'Dangerous Muslim Girls? Race, Gender and Islamophobia in British Schools." In *The Runnymede School Report: Race, Education and Inequality in Contemporary Britain,* edited by Claire Alexander, Debbie Weekes-Bernard, and Jason Arday, 40–43. London: Runnymede Trust, 2015.

Moghadam, Valentine M. "Islamic Feminism and Its Discontents: Toward a Resolution of the Debate." *Signs: Journal of Women in Culture and Society* 27, no. 4 (2002): 1135–71.

Monk-Turner, Elizabeth, Mary Heiserman, Crystle Johnson, Vanity Cotton, and Manny Jackson. "The Portrayal of Racial Minorities on Prime Time Television: A Replication of the Mastro and Greenberg Study a Decade Later." *Studies in Popular Culture* 32, no. 2 (2010): 101–14.

Morley, David, and Kevin Robins. *Spaces of Identity: Global Media, Electronic Landscapes and Cultural Boundaries.* New York: Routledge, 1995.

Muslim Girl. "Meet the First Headscarf-Clad Chef on Primetime Television." May 20, 2015. http://muslimgirl.com/12349/meet-first-headscarf-clad -chef-primetime/.

The Muslims Are Coming! Directed by Negin Farsad and Dean Obeidallah. Vaguely Qualified Productions, New York, 2013.

Nanjiani, Kumail. "I never thought I'd be one of those people . . ." Instagram, December 16, 2019. https://www.instagram.com/p/B6I7b2bnu_z/?hl=en.

Navarro, Laura. "Islamophobia and Sexism: Muslim Women and the Western Mass Media." *Human Architecture: Journal of Sociology of Self-Knowledge* 8, no. 2 (2010): 95–11.

Nguyen, Viet Thanh. *Nothing Ever Dies: Vietnam and the Memory of War.* New York: New York University Press, 2016.

Niazi, Amil. "'The Big Sick' Is Great, and It's Also Stereotypical toward Brown Women." Vice News, July 7, 2017. https://www.vice.com/en_us/article/zmvmp3/the-big-sick-is-great-and-its-also-stereotypical-toward-brown-women.

The Night Of. "Samson and Delilah." Episode 6. Directed by Steven Zaillian. Written by Steven Zaillian and Richard Price. HBO, August 14, 2016.

Nilsen, Sarah, and Sarah E. Turner. "Introduction." In *The Colorblind Screen: Television in Post-Racial America,* edited by Sarah Nilsen and Sarah E. Turner, 1–14. New York: New York University Press, 2014.

Nomani, Asra. "My Big Fat Muslim Wedding." *Marie Claire,* July 9, 2009. https://www.marieclaire.com/sex-love/news/a3330/muslim-wedding/.

Ogan, Christine. *Communication and Identity in the Diaspora: Turkish Migrants in Amsterdam and Their Use of Media.* Lanham, MD: Lexington Books, 2001.

Orbe, Mark P. "Representations of Race in Reality TV: Watch and Discuss." *Critical Studies in Media Communication* 25, no. 4 (2008): 345–52.

Orgad, Shani. *Media Representation and the Global Imagination.* Cambridge: Polity, 2012.

Pamuk, Orhan. *My Name Is Red.* New York: Alfred A. Knopf, 2001.

Parks and Recreation. "Born and Raised." Season 4, episode 3. Directed by Dean Holland. Written by Aisha Muharrar. NBC, October 6, 2011.

Parks and Recreation. "Pawnee Rangers." Season 4, episode 4. Directed by Charles McDougall. Written by Alan Yang. NBC, October 13, 2011.

Parks and Recreation. "The Stakeout." Season 2, episode 2. Directed by Seth Gordon. Written by Rachel Axler. NBC, September 24, 2009.

Paul, J. Gavin. "Ashes in the Gutter: 9/11 and the Serialization of Memory in DC Comics' Human Target." *American Periodicals* 17, no. 2 (2007): 208–27.

Pennington, Rosemary. "Dissolving the Other: Orientalism, Consumption and Katy Perry's Insatiable Dark Horse." *Journal of Communication Inquiry* 40, no. 2 (2016): 111–27.

Pennington, Rosemary. "Making Space in Social Media: #MuslimWomensDay in Twitter." *Journal of Communication Inquiry* 42, no. 3 (2019): 199–217.

Pennington, Rosemary. "Seeing a Global Islam? Eid al-Adha on Instagram." In *Cyber Muslims: Mapping Islamic Digital Media in the Internet Age,* edited by Rob Rozenhal, 176–88. London: Bloomsbury, 2022.

Pennington, Rosemary. "Social Media as Third Spaces? Exploring Muslim Identity and Connection in Tumblr." *International Communication Gazette* 8, no. 70 (2018): 620–36.

Pérez, Raúl. "Learning to Make Racism Funny in the 'Color-Blind' Era: Stand-Up Comedy Students, Performance Strategies, and the (Re)production of Racist Jokes in Public." *Discourse and Society* 24, no. 4 (2013): 478–503.

Petersen, Kristian. "'Ms. Marvel,' 'Ramy,' and 'Hala' Ruel Debate on Muslim Representation." *New Lines Magazine*, October 12, 2022. https://newlinesmag.com/argument/ms-marvel-ramy-and-hala-fuel-debate-on-muslim-representation/.

Peterson, Lucas. "Masterchef's Amanda Saab Is the First Woman in a Hijab on an American Cooking Show." Eater, May 21, 2015. https://www.eater.com/2015/5/21/8640161/masterchefs-amanda-saab-is-the-first-woman-in-a-hijab-on-an-american.

Piela, Anna. *Islam and Popular Culture*. New York: Routledge, 2017.

Project Runway. "Driving Miss Unconventional." Season 16, episode 10. Directed by Rich Kim. Lifetime, October 19, 2016.

Project Runway. "Finale Part 2." Season 16, episode 14. Directed by Ryan Bunnell. Lifetime, November 16, 2017.

Pumphrey, Nicholas. "Avenger, Mutant, or Allah: A Short Evolution of the Depiction of Muslims in Marvel Comics." *Muslim World* 1 (2016): 781–94.

Quantico. Season 1, episode 11. Directed by Thor Freudenthal. Written by Joshua Safran. ABC, December 13, 2015.

Queer Eye. "Saving Sasquatch." Season 1, episode 2. Netflix, February 7, 2018.

Rana, Junaid. "The Story of Islamophobia." *Souls* 9, no. 2 (2007): 148–61.

Ransome, Noel. "*Patriot Act*'s Hasan Minaj on the Value of Being an Outsider in America." Vice, June 24, 2019. https://www.vice.com/en_ca/article/mb8wa3/patriot-acts-hasan-minhaj-on-the-value-of-being-an-outsider-in-america.

Reyns-Chikuma, Chris. "Lund, Martin. Re-constructing the Man of Steel, Superman 1938–1941, Jewish American History, and the Invention of the Jewish–Comics Connection." *Belphégor: Littérature populaire et culture médiatique* 15, no. 2 (2017). https://doi.org/10.4000/belphegor.947.

Rife, Katie. "Marvel Cancels Milo Manara Covers after Spider-Woman Butt Controversy." AV Club, September 23, 2014. https://news.avclub.com/marvel-cancels-milo-manara-covers-after-spider-woman-bu-1798272365.

Rizavi, Zehra. "Noor Tagouri Responds—But Is *Playboy* the Medium for Muslim Women's Empowerment?" *Altmuslim*, September 30, 2016. https://www.patheos.com/blogs/altmuslim/2016/09/noor-tagouri-responds-but-is-playboy-the-medium-for-muslim-womens-empowerment/.

Royal, Derek Parker. "Coloring America: Multi-ethnic Engagements with Graphic Narrative." *MELUS* 32, no. 3 (2007): 7–22.

Rozenhal, Robert. *Cyber Muslims: Mapping Islamic Digital Media in the Digital Age*. London: Bloomsbury, 2022.

Rusak, Rotam. "Ms. Marvel's First Reactions Praise Iman Vellani's Joyous Kamala Khan." Nerdist, May 24, 2022. https://nerdist.com/article/ms-marvel-first-reactions-praise-iman-vellani-joyous-relatable-kamala-khan/.

Saab, Amanda. "MasterChef: Breakfast and TV Dinners." *Amanda's Plate*, June 25, 2015. http://amandasplate.com/masterchef-breakfast-and-tv-dinner/.

Saeed, Sana. "Somewhere in America, Muslim Women Are 'Cool.'" *Islamic Monthly*, December 2, 2013. http://theislamicmonthly.com/somewhere-in-america-muslim-women-are-cool/.

Saha, Anamik. "*Citizen Smith* More Than *Citizen Kane*? Genres-in-Progress and the Cultural Politics of Difference." *South Asian Popular Culture* 11, no. 1 (2013): 97–102.

Said, Edward. *Covering Islam. How the Media and the Experts Determine How We See the Rest of the World*. New York: Vintage Books, 1997.

Said, Edward. *Culture and Imperialism*. New York: Alfred A. Knopf 1993.

Said, Edward. *Orientalism*. New York: Vintage Books, 1979.

Said, Edward. "Orientalism Reconsidered." *Race & Class* 27, no. 2 (1985): 1–15.

Salem, Sara. "Feminist Critique and Islamic Feminism: The Question of Intersectionality." *Postcolonialist* 1, no. 1 (2013): 1–8.

Saturday Night Live. "Aziz Ansari/Big Sean." Season 42, episode 12. Directed by Don Roy King. Written by Chris Kelly, Sarah Schneider, Bryan Tucker, and Kent Sublette. NBC, January 21, 2017.

Saturday Night Live. "Kumail Nanjiani/P!nk." Directed by Don Roy King. Written by Bryan Tucker and Kent Sublette. NBC, October 14, 2017.

Schlenker, Jennifer A., Sandra L. Caron, and William A. Halteman. "A Feminist Analysis of Seventeen Magazine: A Content Analysis from 1945 to 1995." *Sex Roles* 38, no. 1/2 (1998): 135–49.

Schulman, Norma. "The House That Black Built: Television Stand-Up Comedy as Minor Discourse." *Journal of Popular Film and Television* 22, no. 3 (1994): 108–15.

Scott, Anna Beatrice. "Superpower vs. Supernatural: Black Superheroes and the Quest for a Mutant Reality." *Journal of Visual Culture* 5, no. 3 (2006): 295–314.

Selod, Saher. "Citizenship Denied: Racialization of Muslim American Men and Women Post-9/11." *Critical Sociology* 41, no. 1 (2015): 77–95.

Semati, Mehdi. "Islamophobia, Culture and Race in the Age of Empire." *Cultural Studies* 24, no. 2 (2010): 256–75.

Shahbaz, Huzaifa, and Robert S. McCaw. "CAIR's Mid-Year Snapshot Summary Report of Anti-Muslim Bias Incidents." Council on American-Islamic Relations, July 2021. https://www.cair.com/wp-content/uploads/2021/07/Anti-Bias-Incident-Report-2021_online.pdf.

Shaheen, Jack. "Arab Images in Comic Books." *Journal of Popular Culture* 28, no. 1 (1994): 123–33.

Shaheen, Jack. *Reel Bad Arabs: How Hollywood Vilifies a People*. 3rd ed. Northampton, MA: Olive Branch Press, 2015.

Shehab, Sandra (@sandrashehab). Instagram profile. https://www.instagram.com/sandrashehab/feed/?hl=en.

Shryock, Andrew. "Attack of the Islamophobes: Religious War (and Peace) in Arab/Muslim Detroit." In *Islamophobia in American: The Anatomy of Intolerance*, edited by Carl W. Ernst, 145–74. New York: Palgrave Macmillan, 2013.

BIBLIOGRAPHY

Siddiqi, Hishaam. "How to Talk about ISIS without Islamophobia." *Teen Vogue*, July 18, 2016. https://www.teenvogue.com/story/talking-about-islam-isis-terrorism-language.

Signorielli, Nancy. "Minorities Representation in Prime Time: 2000 to 2008." *Communication Research Reports* 26, no. 4 (2009): 323–36.

Silicon Valley. "Articles of Incorporation." Season 1, episode 3. Directed by Tricia Brock. Written by Matteo Borghese and Rob Turbovsky. HBO, April 20, 2014.

Sills, Liz. "Hashtag Comedy: From Muslim Rage to #MuslimRage." *Re-Orient* 2, no. 1 (2017): 160–74.

Sjober, Laura, and Caron E. Gentry. "Reduced to Bad Sex: Narratives of Violent Women from the Bible to the War on Terror." *International Relations* 22, no. 1 (2013): 5–23.

Sorkin, Amy Davidson. "The Attack on 'All American Muslim.'" *New Yorker*, December 13, 2011. https://www.newyorker.com/news/daily-comment/the-attack-on-all-american-muslim.

Spiegelman, Art. "Golden Age of Superheroes Were Shaped by the Rise of Fascism." *Guardian*, August 17, 2019. https://www.theguardian.com/books/2019/aug/17/art-spiegelman-golden-age-superheroes-were-shaped-by-the-rise-of-fascism.

Stabile, Carol A., and Deepa Kumar. "Unveiling Imperialism: Media, Gender and the War on Afghanistan." *Media, Culture & Society* 27, no. 5 (2005): 765–82.

The Stand NYC. "RoastMasters @NYCF 11.10.17 Championship Match: Eli Sairs (C) vs. Dina Hashem." Filmed November 2017. YouTube video, 34:46. Posted November 2017. https://www.youtube.com/watch?v=BrjBljSDWug.

Staub Micheal E. "The Shoah Goes On and On: Remembrance and Representation in Art Spiegelman's Maus." *Melus* 20, no. 3 (1995): 33–46.

Stevens, Lorna, and Pauline Maclaren. "Exploring the 'Shopping Imaginary': The Dreamworld of Women's Magazines." *Journal of Consumer Behavior* 4, no. 4 (2005): 282–92.

Stewart, Ashleigh. "'Shameful Hypocrisy': Canadian Education Minister Called Out after Posting Picture with Malala Yousafzai." *National AE*, July 7, 2019. https://www.thenational.ae/arts-culture/shameful-hypocrisy-canadian-education-minister-called-out-after-posting-picture-with-malala-yousafzai-1.883403.

Streitmatter, Roger. *From Perverts to Fab Five: The Media's Changing Depiction of Gay Men and Lesbians.* New York: Routledge, 2009.

Tagouri, Noor. (@NTagouri) "I'm SO heartbroken and devastated. Like my heart actually hurts. I've been waiting to make this announcement for MONTHS. One of my DREAMS . . ." Twitter, January 17, 2019, 5:26 a.m., https://twitter.com/NTagouri/status/1085893518478987265.

Tagouri, Noor. (@NTagouri), "Misrepresentation and misidentification is a constant problem if you are Muslim in America. And as much as I work to fight this, there are . . ." Twitter, January 17, 2019, 5:36 a.m., https://twitter.com /NTagouri/status/1085893536724238336.

Tai, Hina. "Noor Tagouri Is Not the Controversy, Muslim Women Representation Is." HuffPost, March 10, 2017. https://www.huffpost.com/entry/noor-tagouri-is -not-the-controversy-muslim-women-representation_b_57ed5139e4b07f20daa 104bb.

Tamborini, Ron, Dana E. Mastro, Rebecca M. Chory-Assad, and Ren He Huang. "The Color of Crime and the Court: A Content Analysis of Minority Representation of Television." *Journalism and Mass Communication Quarterly* 77, no. 3 (2000): 639–53.

Tasker, Yvonne. "Television Crime Drama and Homeland Security: From Law & Order to 'Terror TV.'" *Cinema Journal* 4, no.4 (2012): 44–65.

Top Chef. "Bronco Brouhaha." Season 15, episode 9. Directed by Ariel Boles. Bravo, February 1, 2018.

Top Chef. "Now That's a Lot of Schnitzel." Season 15, episode 6. Directed by Ariel Boles. Bravo, January 11, 2018.

Trafton, Scott. *Egypt Land: Race and Nineteenth-Century American Egyptomania.* Durham, NC: Duke University Press, 2004.

Trushell, John. "American Dreams of Mutants: The X-Men-'Pulp' Fiction, Science Fiction, and Superheroes." *Journal of Popular Culture* 38, no. 1 (2004): 149–68.

Tukachinsky, Riva, Dana Mastro, and Moran Yarchi. "Documenting Portrayals of Race/Ethnicity on Primetime Television over a 20-Year Span and Their Association with National-Level Racial/Ethnic Attitudes." *Journal of Social Issues* 71 (2015): 17–38.

Turner, Richard Brent. *Islam in the African-American Experience.* Bloomington: Indiana University Press, 2003.

Twigg, Julia. "Fashion, the Media, and Age: How Women's Magazines Use Fashion to Negotiate Identities." *European Journal of Cultural Studies* 21, no. 3 (2018): 334–48.

Uddin, Asma T. *When Islam Is Not a Religion: Inside America's Fight for Religious Freedom.* New York: Pegasus Books, 2019.

Ulaby, Neda. "In 2015, TV Broke Ground by Showing Relatable Women in Hijab." NPR, January 1, 2016. https://www.npr.org/2016/01/01/461490153/in-2015 -tv-broke-ground-by-showing-relatable-women-in-hijab.

van Nieuwkerk, Karin, Mark Levin, and Martin Stokes. "Introduction." In *Islam and Popular Culture*, edited by Karin van Nieurwkerk, Mark Levine, and Martin Stokes, 1–20. Austin: University of Texas Press, 2016.

Veloso, Francisco, and John Bateman. "The Multimodal Construction of Acceptability: Marvel's Civil War and the PATRIOT Act." *Critical Discourse Studies* 10, no. 4 (2013): 427–43.

BIBLIOGRAPHY

wadud, aminda. "Islam beyond Patriarchy through Gender Inclusive Qur'anic Analysis." In *Wanted: Equality and Justice in the Muslim Family*, edited by Zainah Anwar, 95–112. Malaysia: Musawah, 2009.

Walker, Tracey (@esmeraldoaqyo). "Here I was worried about Rise of Skywalker spoilers, but all twitter wants to talk about are #Kumail and his washboard abs. I am very much okay with this." Twitter, December 17, 2019, 8:38 a.m. https://twitter.com/esmeraldaqyo/status/1206841079095414785.

Walther, Karine V. *Sacred Interests: The United States and the Islamic World, 1821–1921.* Chapel Hill: University of North Carolina Press, 2015.

Wang, Grace. "A Shot at Half-Exposure: Asian Americans in Reality TV Shows." *Television & New Media* 11, no. 5 (2010): 404–27.

Warner, Kristen. "In the Time of Plastic Representation." *Film Quarterly* 71, no. 2 (2017): 32–37.

Webster, Emma Sarran. "2016 Rio Olympic Gold Medalist Dalilah Muhammad on Making History." *Teen Vogue*, October 7, 2016. https://www.teenvogue.com/story/2016-rio-olympic-gold-medalist-dalilah-muhammad-on-making-history.

Wheeler, Andrew. "Oh Captain My Captain: How Carol Danvers Became Marvel's Biggest Female Hero." Comics Alliance, November 10, 2014. http://comicsalliance.com/captain-marvel-carol-danvers-marvel-biggest-female-hero/.

Wheeler, Kayla. "On Centering Black Muslim Women in Critical Race Theory." Maydan, February 5, 2020. https://themaydan.com/2020/02/on-centering-black-muslim-women-in-critical-race-theory/.

Whitbrook, James. "Kamala Khan's Creator Is Stepping Away from Ms. Marvel." *io9*, December 14, 2018. https://io9.gizmodo.com/kamala-khans-creator-is-stepping-away-from-ms-marvel-1831104153.

Wilson, G. Willow. *Ms. Marvel*, no. 001. New York: Marvel, 2014.

Wilson, G. Willow. *Ms. Marvel*, no. 002. New York: Marvel, 2014.

Wilson, G. Willow. *Ms. Marvel*, no. 005. New York: Marvel, 2014.

Wilson, G. Willow. *Ms. Marvel*, no. 006. New York: Marvel, 2014.

Wilson, G. Willow. *Ms. Marvel*, no. 016. New York: Marvel, 2014.

Wilson, G. Willow. *Ms. Marvel*, no. 018. New York: Marvel, 2014.

Wilson, G. Willow. *Ms. Marvel*, no. 019. New York: Marvel, 2014.

Wilson, G. Willow. *Ms. Marvel*. Vol. 2: *Generation Why*. New York: Marvel, 2014–15.

Wilson, G. Willow. *Ms. Marvel*. Vol. 5: *Super Famous*. New York: Marvel, 2014–15.

Wong, James. "Here's Looking at You: Reality TV, Big Brother, and Foucault." *Canadian Journal of Communication* 26 (2001): 33–45.

Wurzburger, Andrea. "Drew Elliott Sits Down with Contestant Who Was Made for Instagram, but Not the Top Model Competition." VH1, February 28, 2018. http://www.vh1.com/news/350767/americas-next-top-model-exit-interview-sandra-shehab/.

Yaqin, Amina. "Inside the Harem, Outside the Nation." *Interventions: The International Journal of Postcolonial Studies* 12, no. 2 (2010): 226–38.

Yegenoglu, Meyda. *Colonial Fantasies: Toward a Feminist Reading of Orientalism.* Cambridge: Cambridge University Press, 1998.

Yehl, Joshua. "Ms. Marvel #1 Review." IGN, February 5, 2014. https://www.ign.com/articles/2014/02/05/ms-marvel-1-review-2.

Ytre-Arne, Brita. "Women's Magazines and Their Readers: The Relationship between Textual Features and Practices of Reading." *European Journal of Cultural Studies* 14, no. 2 (2011): 213–28.

Yuen, Nancy Wang, and Cassidy J. Ray. "Post 9/11 but Not Post-Racial." *Contexts* 8, no. 2 (2009): 68–70.

Zakaria, Rafia. *Against White Feminism: Notes on Disruption.* New York: W. W. Norton, 2021.

Zakaria, Rafia. *Veil.* New York: Bloomsbury, 2017.

Zakaria, Rafia. "The Myth of Women's 'Empowerment.'" *New York Times,* October 5, 2017. https://www.nytimes.com/2017/10/05/opinion/the-myth-of-womens-empowerment.html.

Zakaria, Rafia. "Prisoners of Paradigm." In *On Islam: Muslims and the Media,* edited by Rosemary Pennington and Hilary Kahn, 51–56. Bloomington: Indiana University Press, 2018.

Zakaria, Rafia. "What Vogue Did to Noor Tagouri Tells a Bigger Story." CNN, January 18, 2019. https://www.cnn.com/2019/01/18/opinions/noor-tagouri-vogue-misidentification-zakaria/index.html.

Zeiny, Esmaeil, and Noraini Md Yusof. "The Said and the Not-Said: New Grammar of Visual Imperialism." *GEMA Online Journal of Language Studies* 16, no. 1 (2016): 125–41.

INDEX

Accessibility, 1–3, 18, 20, 21, 30, 73, 80, 83, 87, 92, 97, 99, 107, 119, 121, 161, 163, 170
Affective insurgencies, 69
African American Muslims, 8, 12, 14, 67, 96; see also Black Muslims
Ali, Fatima, 113–114, 165
All American Muslim, 108–110
Alsultany, Evelyn, 15, 19, 41, 60, 67, 120–121, 147, 160
American Crime, 2, 20, 67–68, 72–73
An American Family, 106–107, 108
American flag, 90, 145
Ansari, Aziz, 79–80, 82, 86, 92, 97, 99
Antisemitism, 31, 95, 96
Arjana, Sophia Rose, 3, 20, 35, 40, 133, 143
Assimilation, 4, 140
Austin, Allen, 8, 10
Authenticity, 19, 21, 37, 58, 69, 98, 106–108, 113, 115, 117, 162, 164–165, 170

Belonging, 1, 18, 21, 32, 58, 161
Binaries, 19–20, 37, 47, 117, 122, 159
Black Muslims, 12–15, 67–69, 89, 97, 115; see also African American Muslims
Black nationalism, 13–14
Bones, 64–65, 71, 72, 73
Bourdieu, Pierre, 18, 161

Captain Marvel, 27–28, 40, 42, 44, 45, 46, 47
Chan-Malik, Sylvia, 14, 68, 70, 97

Christianity, 3–4, 6, 10, 12, 14, 95, 109, 118, 134, 161
Comic books, 2, 17, 22, 28–30, 32–33, 40, 44, 45, 161, 168
Consumption, 15–16, 119, 121, 129, 139, 146–148
Crusades, 4
Curtis, Ed, 8, 13

Danvers, Carol, 27–28, 39, 45, 47, 163

Echchaibi, Nabil, 19, 36, 162, 163
Eco, Umberto, 5, 18
Egypt, 7, 16, 161
Eltaway, Mona, 136–139
Empowerment, 129, 135–136, 139
Eurocentrism, 6

Farsad, Negin, 94–96, 97
Feminism, 42, 135–137, 139, 140
Foucault, Michel, 18–19, 58, 98, 108, 121, 129, 149, 162
France, Tan, 122–123

Great British Bake Off, 21, 104–105

Hall, Stuart, 5
Harem, 130–131
Hashem, Dina, 93–94, 96

INDEX

Headscarf, 43, 71–72, 119, 123, 134–135, 144, 145, 150, 151; see also Hijab

Hijab, 43, 44, 64, 67, 70, 71, 105, 111, 113, 116, 117, 128, 135, 144, 145, 147, 160; see also Headscarf

Hussain, Nadiya, 104–105

Hybridity, 4

Identity, 4, 8, 11, 12, 13, 14, 18, 19, 20, 21, 27, 31, 36, 37, 39, 44, 45, 46, 47, 48, 56, 62, 64, 65, 71, 79, 80, 82, 85, 87, 88, 91, 92, 94, 96, 97, 99, 105, 107, 112, 114, 117, 118, 123, 146, 149, 157, 161, 163, 164–165

Ife, Ayana, 115–117, 165, 167, 170

Imagined communities, 159

Immigration, 1, 12, 39, 47, 59, 79, 89, 90–91, 111, 114, 123, 157, 163

Islamophobia, 2, 6, 11, 21, 63, 66, 68, 84, 91, 95–96, 97, 98, 99–100, 110, 134, 142, 144–145, 149, 166, 168

Johnson, Zanaib, 96–97

Khabeer, Su'ad Abdul, 15, 89, 116

Kumar, Deepa, 6, 15, 133

Little Mosque on the Prairie, 82

Lost, 20, 53–57, 62, 66, 72, 73, 164

Middle East, 7, 11, 16, 55, 59, 61, 93, 133, 134

Minaj, Hasan, 21, 22, 88–92, 97, 99, 163, 170

Mipsterz, 116–117, 119

Monstrosity, 3, 4, 17, 20, 56–57, 71, 133

Moorish Science Temple, 12–14

Mosque, 37, 67, 69, 82, 99, 144, 157, 160

MosqueMeToo, 137, 138

Muhammad, Dalilah, 145

Muhammad, Elijah, 68

Muhammad, Ibithaj, 145

Muhammad, Prophet, 3, 54, 61

Muhammad, Wallace Fard, 14

Muslim cool, 15, 89, 116

Muslim men, 14, 20, 41, 55, 59, 61, 66–67, 73, 99, 122, 124, 131, 134, 142, 143, 149

Muslim rage, 84–85

Muslim women, 14, 20, 21, 59, 67, 68–72, 73, 88, 92, 97, 113, 116–117, 119, 128–129

Nanjiani, Kumail, 87–88, 92, 97, 99, 165–167

Nation of Islam, 12, 67–70

Nguyen, Viet Thanh, 159–160

The Night Of, 20, 62–64, 72, 164

North Africa, 6, 8, 15, 62

Not Without My Daughter, 142

Orientalism, 16–17, 34, 56–57, 73, 89, 120, 131, 133, 135, 138, 139, 141–142, 143, 147, 148, 151; art, 7, 10, 17, 130–138, 141, 142, 143, 144, 145, 146, 147–148, 149, 150, 151, 161, 165

Othello, 4–5

Othering, 30, 85, 149, 150

Ottomans, 4, 6

Panopticon, 18, 121

Quantico, 20, 70–73

Qur'an, 8, 10, 94–95, 136, 137, 167

Racism, 12, 14, 19, 40, 58, 63, 68–69, 82, 91, 95, 96, 99, 142, 166

Ramy, 1, 17, 92, 99, 161

Ramy, Youssef, 1, 92, 161

The Real World, 106–107, 112, 117, 122

Representation, 2–4, 6, 11, 17, 18, 19, 20, 21, 29, 33, 36–37, 44, 46–47, 56–58, 59, 62, 63–64, 66, 67, 68, 80, 83, 107, 117, 119, 120, 128, 129–130, 131, 132, 133, 135, 140, 149, 150, 158–160, 162, 164, 166, 167, 170; double burden of, 19, 36, 163; plastic, 46, 47, 56, 63–64, 150, 170

Saab, Amanda, 111–114, 116

Safe harbor, 14, 68, 69, 94

Said, Edward, 11, 56, 70, 131, 161, 166

Said, Omar ibn, 8

Saturday Night Live, 79–80, 82, 98

Science fiction, 17

September 11th, 11, 28, 29, 59, 60, 66, 84, 90, 168

Shahs of Sunset, 15, 120–121

Shehab, Sandra, 117–119

Slavery, 8–10, 82

Social media, 21, 43, 48, 84–85, 114, 117, 120, 128, 137, 138, 141, 145, 147, 148, 149, 157, 166, 168

INDEX

Stereotype, 3, 8, 18, 19, 20–21, 32, 34, 41, 43, 55, 56, 58, 60, 61–62, 65–66, 73, 80, 81, 82, 83–85, 88, 95, 96, 98, 104, 107, 108, 110, 112–113, 117, 122–123, 128, 135, 140, 142, 145–148, 150–151, 158, 162, 164, 165, 166, 167

Superheroes, 17, 27–48, 157, 164, 165, 166, 168

Superman, 31–32, 45

Surveillance, 13, 18, 28, 71, 121, 149, 160, 166

Tagouri, Noor, 128–129, 134–135, 136, 145, 149–151

Trump, Donald, 2, 79, 99, 141, 142, 144, 148

Turner, Richard Brent, 12

24 (TV series), 15, 20, 59–60, 71, 134

Visibility, 2–3, 5, 7, 8, 12, 15, 18–19, 20, 21, 28, 43, 44, 47, 57, 58, 59, 63, 64, 66, 84, 87, 89, 92, 97–98, 99, 106, 111, 122, 124, 129, 135, 137, 141, 144, 145, 147–150, 159, 160, 161–162, 165, 166

Wadud, amina, 137

War on terror, 1, 60, 132, 134, 168

X-Men, 27, 30–31, 33, 38, 48

Xenophobia, 97, 142

Zakaria, Rafia, 70, 136, 139, 150, 151

ROSEMARY PENNINGTON is Associate Professor of Journalism in Miami University's Department of Media, Journalism, and Film. She is coeditor of two IU Press books, *On Islam: Muslims and the Media* and *The Media World of ISIS*.

For Indiana University Press

Brian Carroll, Rights Manager
Anna Garnai, Editorial Assistant
Sophia Hebert, Assistant Acquisitions Editor
Samantha Heffner, Marketing and Publicity Manager
Brenna Hosman, Production Coordinator
Katie Huggins, Production Manager
Darja Malcolm-Clarke, Project Manager/Editor
Bethany Mowry, Acquisitions Editor
Dan Pyle, Online Publishing Manager
Jennifer Witzke, Senior Artist and Book Designer